*Private Black Colleges
at the Crossroads*

CONTRIBUTIONS IN AFRO-AMERICAN
AND AFRICAN STUDIES

1. The Oratory of Negro Leaders: 1900-1968
   Marcus H. Boulware
2. Black Labor in America
   Milton Cantor, Editor
3. The Black Teacher and the Dramatic Arts: A Dialogue, Bibliography, and Anthology
   William R. Reardon, Thomas D. Pawley, Editors
4. Refugees South of the Sahara: An African Dilemma
   Hugh C. Brooks, Yassin El-Ayouty, Editors
5. Bittersweet Encounter: The Afro-American and the American Jew
   Robert G. Weisbord, Arthur Stein
6. The Black Infantry in the West, 1869-1891
   Arlen L. Fowler
7. The Decline and Abolition of Negro Slavery in Venezuela, 1820-1854
   John V. Lombardi
8. A Bio-Bibliography of Countée P. Cullen, 1903-1946
   Margaret Perry
9. The Abbé Grégoire, 1787-1831: The Odyssey of an Egalitarian
   Ruth F. Necheles
10. The Political Philosophy of Martin Luther King, Jr.
    Hanes Walton, Jr.
11. The American Slave: A Composite Autobiography
    George P. Rawick, Editor
12. Nigeria, Dilemma of Nationhood: An African Analysis of the Biafran Conflict
    Joseph Okpaku, Editor
13. Private Black Colleges at the Crossroads
    Daniel C. Thompson
14. Ebony Kinship: Africa, Africans, and the Afro-American
    Robert G. Weisbord

PRIVATE BLACK COLLEGES AT THE CROSSROADS

Daniel C. Thompson

CONTRIBUTIONS IN AFRO-AMERICAN
AND AFRICAN STUDIES

Number 13

GREENWOOD PRESS, INC.

WESTPORT, CONNECTICUT ● LONDON, ENGLAND

Library of Congress Cataloging in Publication Data

Thompson, Daniel Calbert.
    Private Black colleges at the crossroads.

    (Contributions in Afro-American and African studies,
no. 13)
        Bibliography: p.
        1. Negro universities and colleges—United States.
I. Title. II. Series.
LC 2781.T46   378.73   72-841
ISBN 0-8371-6410-9

LIBRARY OF CONGRESS CATALOG CARD NUMBER: 72-841

ISBN: 0-8371-6410-9

FIRST PUBLISHED IN 1973

GREENWOOD PRESS, INC., PUBLISHING DIVISION

51 RIVERSIDE AVENUE, WESTPORT, CONNECTICUT 06880

MANUFACTURED IN THE UNITED STATES OF AMERICA

To Danelle and Wilma

Contents

Acknowledgments

My research in the sociology of higher education formally began 20 years ago when I was enrolled in a seminar on the professions at Columbia University, under the direction of Professor Robert K. Merton. That research resulted in my Ph.D. dissertation entitled "Teachers In Negro Colleges." I would again like to express my lasting indebtedness to Professor Merton for sharing some of his valuable insights into the sociology of the professions and for his wise guidance during the early years of my research endeavors.

The research for this study began in September 1968. Since that time at least 2,342 students, 400 teachers and 300 knowledgeable persons directly or indirectly related to private Black colleges have generously contributed their time, knowledge and opinions to this attempt to understand and interpret the role of these colleges as they enter their second century of service to the nation and to the advancement of Black people. For the privilege of codifying, analyzing and interpreting the information they supplied, I am deeply grateful.

I extend special recognition to Dr. Myron F. Wicke, General Secretary, Division of Higher Education, The United Methodist Church, who conceived the idea of making this study and who has cooperated fully with me throughout the years of research and writings, and to Dr. James W. Armsey of the Ford Foundation who recommended financing the project.

I wish to express my obligations to President Emeritus A. W. Dent of Dillard University who committed the facilities of Dillard as the study headquarters and to President Broadus N. Butler of Dillard for his personal interest and the continuing cooperation of the University.

I respectfully acknowledge the invaluable assistance and cooperation so generously extended by the presidents of all the sample colleges. Without them the research could not have succeeded.

I am particularly indebted to members of the *Commission on Special College Study*, a group formed to assist in this study who gave unstintingly of their time, influence and wisdom. I only hope that I have been able to understand and interpret a few of the ideas and insights they have articulated so well.

Members of the Commission

Dr. W. Astor Kirk, Chairman
Dr. Richard N. Bender
Dr. E. Craig Brandenburg
President A. F. Christ-Janer
Bishop Eugene M. Frank
Bishop Charles F. Golden
Bishop Fred P. Corson
President V. W. Henderson

President John T. King
Mr. DeWitt LeFevre
Dr. Willa B. Player
Dr. Julius S. Scott
Bishop James S. Thomas
Chancellor W. P. Tolley
Dr. Myron F. Wicke
Dr. Daniel W. Wynn

Finally, I am grateful to those who have worked with me very closely on this project: Mrs. Margaret G. Dabney who served as Research Associate and was responsible for the field work phase of the study, and whose ideas and interpretations are

Acknowledgments

reflected throughout the book; Miss Barbara M. Guillory, Associate Professor of Sociology at Dillard who served as my Research Assistant and contributed immeasurably to every phase of this project; Miss Sonia C. Merrin who perceptively performed the laborious tasks of painstakingly producing numerous reports and manuscripts and who typed the final copy of this book; and to the Center for Advanced Study in the Behavioral Sciences which provided excellent facilities and expert assistance while I prepared the final changes in the manuscript.

*Private Black Colleges
at the Crossroads*

1.

Introduction

The movement to provide higher education for Black Americans began during the intensely racist-ridden decade after the Civil War. Before that time, the most successful attempts were Lincoln University, established by the Presbyterians in Chester County, Pennsylvania, in 1857, and Wilberforce University, established at Tawawa Springs, near Zenia, Ohio, in 1856, by the Methodist Episcopal Church. These special colleges provided the only reliable opportunity for Black youth to acquire some level of higher education. The only *raison d'être* for the founding of these colleges was that Blacks were completely excluded by laws in the South, and virtually excluded by *de facto* segregation outside the South, from other institutions of higher learning. At that time the education of Black youth, even on an elementary level, was largely ignored or, at most, given half-hearted support by both the public and private sectors throughout the United States. For instance, prior to the Civil War there were only 28

3

known Black college graduates in the United States. White power figures in the South, supported by strong anti-Black sentiments, refused to make any serious effort to provide anything like equal educational opportunities for Black youth. Some even opposed the churches' efforts to provide schools and colleges for them.[1]

Today, after a century of constant struggle to provide higher education for Black youth, private Black colleges have come upon a critical crossroads in their development. For fifteen years or more they have been caught up in a far-reaching, in-depth social revolution and, like all school systems and colleges in this nation, they have been forced to pause and take a long, hard, critical look at themselves. All around them other institutional structures have changed. This nation's role in the world of nations has changed. Wars and rumors of war, technology and its fantastic developments have caused people to change. And Black people have changed. Black youth expect more from their schools and colleges than their parents expected. They expect that their educational institutions will prepare them to live and serve in the larger society as well as in the Black society. Graduates of private Black colleges, then, demand to be prepared to compete as equals with other college graduates, regardless of what colleges their competitors might represent.

This study is an attempt to understand the role of private Black colleges in terms of the radically changing American society and the rising expectations of Black youth. While focus is upon certain basic, perennial problems which undermine the full effectiveness, and in some cases threaten the survival of private Black colleges *per se*, I am fully aware that many private white colleges throughout the United States are grappling with most of the same problems: poverty, geographic and academic isolation, inadequate plants and facilities, antiquated curricula, student unrest, imbalanced or mediocre faculties, backward or unimaginative administrations, confused purposes and identities. Many are seriously disadvantaged in competition with the more prestigious colleges for top students, competent teachers, and funds. Some of them, too, are facing precarious survival. For instance, in 1965 "there were 401 white colleges in the country too feeble in academic performance to be rated by any one of the

4

six regional accrediting agencies, which places them below the weakest of the (71) accredited Negro colleges."[2]

I am also mindful that public Black colleges are in imminent danger of losing their identity and, in some cases, are being systematically dismantled: "Merger with larger state universities, integration (becoming predominantly white *vis-à-vis* students and administration), new competition from nearby white public colleges or outright abolishment are among the causes of the (public) black colleges' threatened demise."[3]

Notwithstanding, the main contention of this study is that private Black colleges should be given special consideration for at least two primary reasons:

1. Historically, private Black colleges have been dedicated to racial uplift. This central unique mission identifies them with the struggles and aspirations of the Black masses, rather than with the interests and welfare of the more affluent classes, as is likely to be the case with prestigious white colleges.

2. Private Black colleges are the only institutions of higher education controlled by Black people. They are, therefore, the most responsive to the needs and demands of the Black community. With their demise Blacks, as a distinct racial group, would lose their most effective vehicle for the training of indigenous leaders and professionals, and for economic and social mobility.

Whether poor white colleges eventually succeed or perish will depend upon the merit of their academic programs and the resources they can secure as individual institutions. The demise of one will hardly influence the welfare of others, because in the minds of those who support them each must justify its own existence. Unfortunately, this is not true of Black colleges. According to persuasive historical evidence, there is a persistent tendency for philanthropists, foundations, the federal government and the academic world at large to classify Black colleges under some common rubric and deal with them as if they were a single unit, and to ignore certain individual differences. They are too often stereotyped in the same manner Blacks are stereotyped. Therefore, the most serious weaknesses and problems known to be associated with one or a few Black colleges are likely to be generalized as those inherent in Black colleges on the whole. We can expect, then, that major decisions to support or withhold support from certain individual Black colleges will soon become what might be described as a national policy involving all Black colleges.

Essentially, this study seeks to address itself to a series of hard, compelling questions regarding these colleges. Among them are four key questions:

* To what extent are private Black colleges fulfilling their traditional goals?
* What is likely to be the most desirable or needed role of these colleges in our desegregating social order?
* To what extent are the churches, the federal government, and the various funding agencies assuming responsibility for the financial support and guidance of these colleges?
* Are they in fact worth saving?

In order to gather substantial facts regarding the present status and potential of private Black colleges, the following research operations were carried out:

An examination of pertinent literature. From the very beginning, the research has included a continuous, systematic review of insightful descriptions and interpretations of higher education in American society generally, and the higher education of Black Americans specifically. Official documents and records published by a cross section of the colleges have also been carefully reviewed.

The selection of a representative sample of colleges to be studied extensively. While a wide range of pertinent information about Black colleges generally has been systematically reviewed and evaluated, ten senior colleges, representing just about all major characteristics common to church-related or private Black colleges, constitute the *Sample* or *"Experimental"* group of colleges. These representative colleges were the ones in which all working hypotheses were tested, and were the sources of the basic data underlying the key interpretations, conclusions, and recommendations in this report. The sample colleges will not be identified because much of the essential data that the officials of these colleges supplied for this study were regarded as highly confidential.

The construction and administration of questionnaires. Two lengthy questionnaires were constructed for this study—one for teachers and another for students. Essentially, these questionnaires were designed to elicit a wide range of information about students and teachers.

In 1970-1971 there were almost 8,000 students in the sample colleges. Of these, 2,342, or about 30 percent, completed the questionnaire used in the study, and 400 of the 614 full-time teachers in the sample colleges completed the questionnaire prepared for them. This means that over 65 percent of the teachers involved responded to the questions.

The construction and administration of interview schedules. Special thought and design were given to a series of questions that could best be answered by selected trustees, "friends" of the colleges, college presidents, academic deans, personnel deans, deans of chapel or religion, registrars, admissions officers, placement officers, alumni officers, development officers, business managers, division chairmen and/or department heads, AAUP leaders and student leaders. In all, more than 300 personal interviews were conducted with individuals closely associated with the sample colleges, including more than 100 top administrators.

Codification and analysis of information. Data gathered by the questionnaires were computerized so that they could be presented in tabular form or as proportions or percentages. Information received from interviews was carefully documented and is discreetly quoted throughout this book. In most instances, the sample colleges are regarded as a single unit. A given college is designated only when it is in some respects different from other colleges, or if it has made some unique contribution to our understanding of particular issues or problems.

While no attempt has been made to present a systematic analysis of higher education generally, or public Black colleges in particular, every effort has been made to interpret the role of private Black colleges in the total context of higher education in American society.

NOTES

1. See Henry A. Bullock, *A History of Negro Education In The South* (Cambridge, Massachusetts: Harvard University Press, 1967), pp. 38-52 and 74-88. See also W.E.B. Du Bois and A. G. Gill, *The College-Bred Negro American* (Atlanta: Atlanta University Press, 1900), Publication No. 5, p. 45.

2. Benjamin E. Mays, "The American Negro College," *Harvard Educational Review*, Vol. 37, No. 3, p. 456.

3. For an excellent discussion of this, see *Ebony Magazine*, Vol. 27, No. 12, October 1972, pp. 92-101.

2.

Private Black Colleges In Perspective

In the tense, traumatic aftermath of emancipation and the Civil War, there were 4 million confused and leaderless Black freedmen. Since the formal education of slaves was generally forbidden by law, whatever education slaves had received was informal and superficial. The sporadic, informal education some few received was provided by benevolent societies, humanitarian whites (usually children of slave owners), literate slaves, who often risked punishment in order to teach fellow slaves, an occasional slave owner who sought to increase the economic value of his slaves and free Blacks who were allowed to teach certain house slaves how to read and write.

There is no way of knowing exactly what proportion of the freedmen was literate. However, according to the most reliable estimates available, only about 2 or 3 percent of them were able to read and write. It is also estimated that only about 5 percent of the total Black population of 4,441,830 (including the 400,000 or more "free people of color") were literate in 1860.[1]

9

During the critical decade following the Emancipation Proclamation of January 1, 1863, it became clear to all concerned observers—the president of the United States, leading congressmen, some top military officers, several church bodies, foundation representatives, and Black leaders themselves—that the education of the freedmen was absolutely essential if they were to hold onto their debated, tenuous freedom, or even survive in the highly charged anti-federal, anti-Black atmosphere which prevailed throughout the South. They agreed that there was an urgent need to establish schools directly relevant to the condition and problems of the new Black citizens. They desperately needed to develop, as quickly as possible, a cadre of Black teachers, ministers, physicians, businessmen and leaders who would be devoted to racial uplift, and capable of ministering to the many needs of the illiterate, disorganized, still-oppressed and frightened ex-slave population. It was this that prompted General O. O. Howard, head of the powerful humanitarian Freedmen's Bureau which established over 4,000 Black schools, and for whom Howard University was named, to insist publicly that "Education underlies every hope of success for freedmen." The Freedmen's Bureau, which was set up by an Act of Congress in 1865 and administered by the War Department, gave protection and assistance to several church bodies—led by the American Missionary Association—which established schools for Blacks throughout the South. Some of the schools they started developed into the first institutions of higher education available to Black youth in the South.

The daring and much-debated experiment in the education of the new Black citizens was surprisingly successful from the start. Despite strong opposition from whites in all walks of life and dire poverty on the part of Blacks, large numbers of parents manifested a determined willingness to send their children to these schools. Looking back upon the enthusiasm of Blacks for formal schooling, Professor Henry A. Bullock believes that freedmen placed unusually strong faith in education and were highly motivated to improve themselves because—

10

The seeds of their faith in formal education had long been planted. Ever since their earliest contact with the printed page, southern Negroes had maintained an almost blind confidence in schooling. In many instances their earliest interracial experiences had been the result of an involvement with the wealthiest and most cultured element of the white South. By the time of their emancipation, almost all of them had come to believe that those qualities of white people which they admired so much and tried so hard to emulate had resulted from formal education and that they, too, could acquire them if they once got the necessary schooling.[2]

Whatever their primary sources of motivation, one historical fact is unequivocal: from the very beginning, Black Americans have tended to place unusual faith in the efficacy of formal education, and, despite many unique handicaps, they have tended to take full advantage of the opportunities available to them.

Those who pioneered in attending the Black missionary colleges were apparently imbued with the desire to help their fellowmen, and graduates of private Black colleges have been outstanding in their dedication to racial uplift. While only about 3 to 5 percent of the adult Black population was literate in 1860, by 1900 the rate of literacy had increased to about 55 percent; by 1920 it was nearly 77 percent, and today only about 5 percent of the adult Black population can be classified as illiterate. Therefore, during their first century, Black colleges, with little or no cooperation from white colleges, trained Black teachers who were able to reverse the rate of literacy among Black Americans—from 5 percent literate to only 5 percent illiterate. While the average educational level of Blacks is still below that of whites, the gap between them has been constantly narrowed so that by 1970 the median educational level for white adults was 12.1 years of schooling, for Black adults 9.3 years.[3]

From a very uncertain beginning a century ago, and despite many difficult and unique obstacles including chronic poverty, private Black colleges have somehow managed to make a distinct, basic and lasting contribution to the survival and progress of Black Americans and to the enrichment and strength of this nation. A convincing indication of their significant contribution is the fact that—

> Among their 385,000 alumni are substantative numbers of this country's black government officials, Army officers, professors, doctors, lawyers, and members of other professions . . . They have prepared most of the teachers employed for the education of many generations of Negro children in the South.[4]

It is ironic that today, after a century of varied and rich contributions to the cause of individual dignity and freedom, private Black colleges are experiencing a serious crisis which threatens their very survival as they come upon a decisive crossroads in their history. Basic to a constructive response to this crisis is an understanding of the nature and force of the Black student revolt of the 1960s.

STUDENT REVOLT

Until a decade ago, Black college students, like the institutions established for them, had not been taken seriously as an integral part of the academic life of American society. This had been true whether the context was athletic, social or purely academic. For the most part, students in Black colleges—even in the highest ranking of these schools—had been ignored or accorded only peripheral or secondary recognition as participants in higher education in this country. Seldom, if ever, were their achievements and earned credentials given full recognition or even regarded as legitimate by honor societies, universities, fellowship awarding foundations, professional associations, potential employers, mass media, or the general public. Only three Black colleges, for example, have Phi Beta Kappa chapters. Regardless of how noble their aspirations or worthy their accomplishments, Black students, especially those in Black colleges, had found it extremely difficult to transcend the stigma of damaging stereotypes the vast majority of whites still associated with the Black race on the whole. Despite the fact that they had made every possible effort to prove themselves, Black college students continued to be a disesteemed minority in the world of higher education just as Blacks, as a racial minority, had been disesteemed in American society.

It is quite obvious that the overall status of Black Americans and especially of Black students, changed very significantly during the 1960s. It might be instructive, therefore, to pause for a moment to take a brief look at a major cause for this change.

It is, of course, difficult to pinpoint a single incident that set into motion any of the great social movements or revolutions in history. It would be particularly difficult to single out any such incident that began the civil rights movement in this country. The causes of major social changes are always complex: the central ideology undergirding a viable social movement or genuine social revolution, as well as its inherent goals and characteristic strategies, will be found deeply rooted in the intellectual, moral, and spiritual ethos of the society in question.

It is entirely possible, however, to discover and identify certain incipient manifestations of the present Black student revolt. The new revolutionary phase of the civil rights movement, which is reflected in the aggressive, defiant stance of today's college students—especially Black college students can be traced back to its first relevant manifestation on February 1, 1960. It was at that time that the tone, specific goals, and basic strategies of the new Black thrust for equal citizenship and dignity began to emerge. The incident involved four Black students, enrolled at the Black A & T College in Greensboro, North Carolina, who staged a meaningful confrontation with the "establishment." The act was simple, its implications revolutionary: they entered a "five and ten cents store", sat down at a lunch counter reserved for "whites only" and requested service. They were of course refused. This incident proved to be the catalyst that was destined to set in motion a chain reaction of numerous carefully planned incidents designed to unmask the stark details of inherent racism in American society.

The Greensboro incident very quickly escalated into a full-blown racial revolution that polarized this nation in a way it had not experienced since the Civil War and Reconstruction years. Directly or indirectly, it affected every institution in American society to some important degree. The unfolding of this vital, sustained racial revolution throughout the 1960s revealed the logistic genius of the Black students who pioneered in the strategy of direct confrontation with the most vicious forms of established, institutionalized racism. Beginning with segregated lunch counters, Black students deliberately selected one ancient bastion of racism after another in widely scattered communities throughout the South. Eventually Black student-inspired, often Black student-led, cadres relentlessly zeroed in on at least six crucial targets where racism had been most damaging to Black Americans: the use of public facilities, education, voting, housing, worship and employment.

The racial revolution of the 1960s, like all social revolutions in history, presented only two clearly distinguishable sides: the "right" and the "wrong." The narrow, generally indiscernible zone between the pro and the anti-civil rights forces was really quite uncomfortable, and occasionally dangerous. Almost all social issues were interpreted as essentially racial, and those who tried to remain neutral or open-minded in regard to these issues were certain to incur the wrath of one side or the other.[5] This was a particularly critical decade for Black leaders and institutions. Those who did not participate wholeheartedly in the movement were accused of supporting the "white establishment" and called "Uncle Toms" or "Super Toms."

Ironically, the institution most harrassed by the racial revolution has been the Black college. This is true despite the fact that these colleges, *per se*, constitute the most identifiable fountainhead of the racial revolution now in progress. During the hundred years of their existence they have been the primary cause (in some states the only dependable cause) for the rising educational level of Black Americans. More than any other institution in American society, they have been committed to the teachings of democratic principles and evaluations. By precepts and examples, their students have been taught that all men are equal and have inherent worth and dignity. The Greensboro incident reminds us again of a prediction made by Gunnar Myrdal almost thirty years ago. He said: *The long-range effect of the rising level of education in the Negro people goes in the direction of nourishing and strengthening the Negro Protest.*[6]

Though all too frequently overlooked by their critics, Black colleges have trained the great majority of this nation's Black leader-ship. Some of this century's most creative leadership, regardless of race or nationality, has emerged from behind the creaking walls of Black colleges—some of which were/are unaccredited. Black college professors and graduates of Black colleges have always dominated the leadership of the civil rights movement. By and large, they have headed Black civil rights organizations, defined the central issues, enunciated the primary goals, and master-minded the strategies for Black progress. This is one of the main criticisms made by the new Black militants (who, incidently, are also mostly Black college graduates). They complain that the civil rights movement has always been a "Black Bourgeoisie" instrument—too far removed from the problems of the Black ghetto.

Though the Greensboro incident and the numerous similar Black student confrontations that followed were specifically intended to literally break down legally established patterns of racial segregation, unwittingly their action immediately reverberated to put their own colleges in an embarrassing position. The historical stance of Black colleges made this identity crisis inevitable. Throughout their history, Black colleges—which are mostly located in rigidly segregated communities—have played a dual role: on the one hand, they have endeavored to prepare Black leadership to serve as a catalyst of racial protest and change. But on the other, they have worked out patterns of accommodation within the segregated communities in which they are located. The most common pattern of accommodation has been withdrawal. Before the Black student revolt, Black colleges were socially, academically, and politically isolated from the white community and maintained only occasional, indirect contacts with the problems and issues of the Black community.

Until the 1960s Black colleges—in the words of a Black private college president—were regarded as "good niggers" in

15

their respective communities. They scrupulously refrained from taking any active part in the disruption or embarrassment of the local white social system. Consequently, when their students began to march, stage all manner of sit-ins, and publicly denounce local and regional patterns of racial segregation, many white citizens were shocked and enraged. The white power structure instantly demanded that these colleges should reaffirm control over their students by severely disciplining those who had been recalcitrant in regard to local racial patterns. And so it was that Black colleges began immediately to see the end of their long-established neutrality in their local communities, and eventually in the Black community at large. While the white power structure insisted that these colleges should function as instruments to support patterns of segregation, Black students and their sympathizers were demanding that the colleges should support their students, who were risking their very lives to destroy racial segregation.

The incipient racial revolution begun by Black students became more evident when Black colleges, which had always symbolized the highest level of conformity to law and order, could no longer effectively control their students, and when Black students who had been indoctrinated to represent the quintessential middle class Americans seemed determined to fill up the local jails. By the end of summer 1960, over 70,000 students had taken an active part in disruptive civil rights demonstrations.

In at least one respect, the Black students' revolt against established patterns of segregation has been unlike any other revolution in history: its grand strategy was designed to achieve goals and effectuate values that are already acknowledged to be inherent in a political democracy and which are firmly established in our national culture. Their mass demonstrations, like their smaller, more personal demonstrations against segregation, were always well-organized and disciplined. Their dignity, decorum, reasoned impatience with sham and injustice, and their willingness to suffer for what they believed to be right articulated this nation's most cherished political and religious values. At the same time, their behavior was a radical departure from old, widely-propagandized Black stereotypes. Americans in all walks of

16

life, including some militant Black leaders, and just about all Black college presidents, were amazed and shocked by the audacious direct action protest on the part of Black students. Some whites insisted that the students were Communists, or certainly inspired and used by Communists. Some blamed mysterious "trouble-making outsiders;" some of the more prejudiced interpreted their behavior as another clear manifestation of the alleged "inherent criminal nature" of Blacks; while some of the more academically-oriented theorized that it was some form of mass hysteria or maybe even just some sort of strange spring fever that would simply disappear in due course. Even some of the more thoughtful social experts and analysts at first interpreted the students' behavior as irrational, childish, foolhardy or purely exhibitory.

There were, of course, other observers, more sympathetic with the student activists, who took them very seriously. The most responsive were the civil rights activists who were already dedicated followers of Dr. Martin Luther King, Jr. Consequently, by April, 1960—just two months after the explosive Greensboro incident—the Southern Christian Leadership Conference had sponsored the establishment of the Student Nonviolent Coordinating Committee.

> The original purpose of SNCC was to coordinate the abundance of restless energy of college students who were anxious to aid the Black poor in the rural South. SCLC, like the other more established civil rights organizations, was primarily identified with the Black middle class and gave sanction and support to middle class values and ways, SNCC was identified with the Black working class. And where the public pronouncements, mass meetings, demonstrations, and even mode of dress and speech of other civil rights participants usually conformed to "middle class" patterns, the personal behavior, dress and methods of action of SNCC gave sanction to the way of life of the Black working class.[7]

17

Immediately members of SNCC, in conjunction with SCLC, became the real shock troops in the racial war. Students became the heroes of the civil rights movement. White northern students, aroused by the clear appeal and heroism of Black students, joined the movement in large numbers. During the summer of 1960, the then very militant SNCC forces literally decended upon the strong, entrenched bastions of segregation throughout the South.

By this time the greatly expanded memberships of white racist groups became highly organized into a powerful white backlash. They resorted to various forms of Black control: Southern legislatures passed scores of Black codes that were clearly unconstitutional; every local or state candidate for political office was called upon to pledge forever his opposition to civil rights, and all forms of mob violence and terror faced the SNCC workers as they moved against segregation in the small towns and rural areas of the South. However, the most significant resistance the civil rights activists faced was from the police. It was the vicious action of the police, not the unbound bloody action of the mobs, that reflected the true nature of the racial revolution. This revolution was not centrally concerned with changing the system of Black intimidations, violence, and lynchings which are expected of white hate groups, such as the Ku Klux Klan, the White Citizens Council, etc. Some of those groups were denounced even by other segregationists in the top power structures of the South. Instead, the Black student revolt took as its main targets those areas of segregation which were supported and protected by the legal structure of the South. The police, then, represented the real battle line. The local white power structures literally turned the police loose to "do their duty" insofar as civil rights demonstrations were concerned.

Evidently the police, by and large, had no compunction about doing their duty. They characteristically handled the students as if they were hardened, dangerous criminals, despite the well-known fact that those who took part in these demonstrations had been thoroughly schooled in non-violence, even non-resistance. In one community after the other, the police were accused of using excessive force when dealing with peaceful civil rights demonstrators. Mass arrests were the order of the day. By

18

the end of the first semester of demonstrations in 1960, over 3,600 students had been arrested.

As soon as student arrests were made the colleges represented were automatically involved. This was unavoidable because it had been commonly assumed that a violation of any existing law was *ipso facto* a violation of basic college regulations, and the violator was subject to college discipline. This assumption placed some Black colleges in an extremely awkward, untenable position: they were expected to discipline their civil rights activist students even before the courts had time to determine their guilt or innocence. This is exactly what happened in several instances. During the first semester of demonstrations at least 141 Black students were dismissed by their colleges, and hundreds of others had received somewhat milder punishment.[8]

Insofar as the Black revolutionists were concerned, the disciplinary action by Black colleges dramatically underscored these colleges' pro-status quo, anti-revolutionary stance. They began to accuse the colleges of being alienated from the Black masses. They pointed out that when the crucial moment came to choose sides in the fight against racial segregation and discrimination, Black colleges, in effect, chose the side of the white establishment. More and more throughout the 1960s, Black colleges were regarded as ultimately "white colleges," used by the white establishment to control Black society. Even some long-standing, staunch friends of Black colleges began to raise some embarrassing questions about the disciplining of students who protested against deeply entrenched, damaging patterns of racial segregation and blatant discrimination in public places. The presidents, who have always symbolized the official authority in Black colleges, were naturally singled out to receive the brunt of the blistering criticism aimed at these colleges for their conservative, even "anti-civil rights," stance. Black non-student activists and spokesmen for established civil rights organizations, plus many powerful white individuals, joined Black students in their unrelenting attacks on Black college presidents.

Within a few months after the initial direct confrontations by students, most Black colleges (and several white colleges) felt it necessary to declare their official stand on the issue of student demonstrations. Surprised and shocked by severe criticism from all quarters of the civil rights movement, Black college presidents began to re-examine the traditional proposition that a violation of existing laws is *ipso facto* a violation of college regulations. As a rule, they gave a new, more liberal interpretation to that age-old principle. While some colleges continued to try in vain to dissuade their students from participating in demonstrations and would not permit SNCC, CORE and other such militant groups to meet on their campuses, they now generally refrained from disciplining students who engaged in off-campus demonstrations. A few Black college presidents actually gave limited support to the student revolution. That is, they personally expressed sympathy with the goals of the revolution but tended to question and doubt the tactics employed. Some of them even arranged to post bail for students who were arrested and interceded for them in the courts. The administrators in Black colleges finally came to the point where they raised little or no strong objections when some teachers, with their full knowledge, excused students from classes when they were engaged in demonstrations. There were also instances where college students were in jail for some considerable period of time and faculties voted to give them full academic credits for courses in which they were enrolled, despite the fact that they had incurred more than the maximum number of excused absences and had missed key examinations. For the most part, however, Black colleges did not easily give up their traditional community neutrality and their role as defenders of law and order. When they did make concessions it was under tremendous pressure which, in most cases, the white community understood, because some white institutions in the community, particularly business establishments, also had to make some drastic changes in their historic racial policies.

President A. W. Dent of Dillard expressed what later proved to be more or less the official stance of most Black colleges. In response to constant pressure from students and several teachers who supported them, he appeared before students and faculty on three formal occasions to interpret the college's policy on the matter of civil rights demonstrations: March 7, 1960 (just a month after the Greensboro incident), September 19, 1960, and September 23, 1963. The following are excerpts from his prepared remarks:

> It has been brought to my attention that some students are considering the feasibility of a public demonstration as a means of expressing their sentiments with regard to certain issues involving racial segregation.
>
> On behalf of the University, I think that I should make two points clear:
>
> First, that any such contemplated action involves only the individuals who may decide to participate; and
>
> Second, that the University in no instance assumes responsibility for actions not sponsored by it.
>
> In connection with the first point, let me say that students are free, of course, to express themselves, so long as the law and good taste are observed. However, all students may not agree on means, even if there be unanimous agreement on ends. Therefore, it should be clearly understood that individuals represent only themselves in any action of this sort.

The compromise position regarding the student revolution expressed by this president, and actually assumed by most other Black college presidents, was still unsatisfactory to civil rights activists, including their own students. Therefore, ever since the early days of the student revolution, most Black colleges have been in a virtual state of war with their students. A few of the colleges have been paralyzed for some important periods of time; some have experienced repeated disruptions, and almost all of them still carry on while maintaining a sort of uneasy truce between students and administration. There is hardly any chance or desire that they will ever revert to the old status quo.

NOTES

1. See Gunnar Myrdal, *An American Dilemma* (New York: Harper and Brothers, 1944), p. 887; Tilden J. and Wilbert J. LeMelle, *The Black College* (New York: Frederick A. Praeger, 1969), p. 33; John Hope Franklin, *From Slavery To Freedom* (New York: Vintage Books, 1969), pp. 202-203; and Henry A. Bullock, *A History of Negro Education In The South* (Cambridge, Massachusetts: Harvard Press, 1967), pp. 9-11.

2. Bullock, *History of Negro Education*, p. 169.

3. U.S. Department of Commerce, Bureau of the Census, *The Social and Economic Status of Negroes in the United States, 1970* (Washington, D.C.: Government Printing Office, July 1971), Report No. 394, p. 79.

4. The Carnegie Commission on Higher Education, *From Isolation to Mainstream* (New York: McGraw-Hill, 1971), p. 14.

5. Daniel C. Thompson, *The Negro Leadership Class* (Englewood Cliffs, N.J.: Prentice Hall, 1963), p. 58.

6. Myrdal, *An American Dilemma*, p. 881.

7. Daniel C. Thompson, "The Civil Rights Movement" in Patricia W. Romero, *In Black America: 1968 The Year of Awakening* (Washington, D.C.: United Publishing Corporation, 1969), pp. 68-69.

8. See *The Student Protest Movement: A Recapitulation* (Atlanta: The Southern Regional Council, September 29, 1961), pp. 1-23.

3.

Socio-Physical Setting

When the first Black colleges were founded, fully 90 percent of the 4 million Black Americans lived in the South. Between 85 and 90 percent of the Blacks in the South lived in rural communities. Consequently, it was indeed logical to locate some of these colleges in small towns surrounded by populous Black farming communities. These were precisely the communities where large slave plantations had existed and where Blacks were legally forbidden to learn to read and write: these were communities, then, where the vast majority of the Black population was illiterate, or at least presumed to be so.

The records show that Black colleges attempted from the very beginning to become relevant to the needs of their predominantly rural constituency. Though the founders of these institutions hopefully called them colleges and even universities, these institutions realistically geared their entrance requirements, academic expectations, and standards for graduation to the socio-academic background and needs of Black youth with ambition and promise who had been systematically denied, by laws and traditions, the opportunity of receiving anything like a proper high school education. Thus, in the beginning these institutions were little more than elementary schools according to national, or even regional, educational standards.

With very, very inadequate financial support, often strong opposition from the local white population, and little concrete evidence that they could succeed, Black church-related colleges assumed the primary responsibility for reducing illiteracy among Blacks and for training desperately needed preachers, teachers, homemakers, and other professionals and leaders. This was, to be sure, a tall order, but absolutely essential if Blacks in the South were to hold on to the conditional, precarious freedom they had been granted after the bloody Civil War. And so, despite all manner of handicaps, Black private colleges ably set about performing the miracle of transforming a Black rural, illiterate, powerless, persecuted, former slave people into a predominantly urban, highly literate, proud people who are now demanding equal citizenship, respect, and the social power to control their own destinies.

Fundamentally, it is necessary for this study to point out that since the beginning of the churches' experiment in the education of Black people, this nation has changed from a predominantly agrarian to a predominantly urban, industrial society. Today about 70 percent of the white population, compared to about 25 percent at the close of the Civil War, live in urban areas. The urbanization of Blacks has taken place even more rapidly and dramatically. Not only do approximately 75 percent of the Black people now reside in cities, but about half (48 percent) of them live in large cities outside the South. During the last fifty years or so, this nation has witnessed the shift of its population centers from rural to urban places. Even more significant is the fact that the culture of American society has begun to articulate mostly urban, rather than rural, social patterns, values, ideologies, moods, problems, challenges, and social power.

The blunt conclusion is clear and inescapable: *Black private colleges located at present in largely rural communities have been left stranded.* Most of the people they were founded to serve have migrated to large cities. This is particularly true of Black youth.

24

By a process which we might call selective migration, just about all of the ambitious Black youth who are born in rural communities begin to seek their fortune in large urban places as soon as they are old enough to enter college or to legally qualify for employment. The few who remain to attend these rural-oriented colleges are restless and impatient. They are demanding that these colleges provide them with the social, cultural and academic experiences necessary to assure an equal chance of success in the larger urban, industrial, international society. In order to do this all colleges will need the sustained, firm support of many basic, varied urban institutions. While some of the colleges are favorably located to receive this kind of support, others are not so fortunate. Let us look, then, at the three ideal-type communities in which Black private colleges are located:

Culturally Poor Communities. At least a third of the private Black colleges are located in culturally poor communities. Supporting institutions and the varied social and cultural experiences necessary for the best academic development simply do not exist. For the most part, students are shut off from the day by day activities, experiences, attitudes and involvements characteristic of urban American society. These experiences include the normal hustle and bustle of city life, rich and varied recreational and cultural options, supportive library resources, opportunities for academic research and field work in the larger community, and the availability of part-time or summer jobs in the world of business and industry.

On another level, and perhaps even more significant, culturally poor communities are stiflingly homogeneous. The nonstudent population, as well as the students themselves, are so similar in their backgrounds, attitudes and outlook that they do not provide one another with the rich interaction and dynamics needed for the best social and academic development. American society is far more complex and challenging than these rural-like communities suggest that it is. It would be quite difficult to prepare students for urban competition and creative urban leadership in colleges located in rural, more or less homogeneous, communities.

Also, the problem of faculty recruitment and retention is intensified for colleges in culturally poor communities. Younger faculty, regardless of salary offers, would be reluctant to become established in such communities. Even individual teachers who expressed a willingness to settle in such communities and devote themselves to the work of the colleges, pointed out that they had family members who were not satisfied to live in such relatively isolated places. More or less isolated colleges also do not offer enough opportunity for the social and professional development of their teachers. They are outside the mainstream of the academic life of this society. Teachers complain that they do not have sufficient opportunities to interact with others in their particular disciplines and they feel alienated from the main channels of thought in the non-academic world. There is, then, a real likelihood that teachers who are partially isolated professionally and culturally may eventually experience a sort of intellectual atrophy. Many teachers expressed this fear.

Culturally Adequate Communities. About half of the private Black colleges are located in communities that may be classified as having an adequate number of supportive or potentially supportive institutions and programs and a relatively large Black population. About 20 percent of these may be classified as border line communities: despite the fact that the small cities seem to have an ample number of relatively strong institutions and some potentially enriching civic and cultural programs, the colleges have little or no meaningful interaction with them. For the most part, the colleges are ignored by the business and cultural aspects of the larger communities in which they are located.

Perhaps 30 percent of the colleges in this group are in thriving small cities. Although most of these cities could hardly be considered as being at the crossroads of culture, their civic, business, and cultural institutions are relatively varied and sufficiently progressive to provide adequate support to the academic development students and faculty need as creative participants in our urban, industrial society. Some of these colleges have already established limited yet meaningful interaction with some major institutions in their communities. If these relationships are extended and refined, they could very definitely enhance the academic goals and professional development of students and teachers.

Culturally Rich Communities. Fully 20 percent of the private

Black colleges are located in culturally rich metropolitan centers—cities with large Black populations and strong, progressive Black institutions. They are also at the crossroads of activity and culture in the larger communities in which they are located. Perhaps nowhere in the country can students and faculty find richer academic laboratories than in these cities: there are several other institutions of higher education; varied types of graded schools, some representing the very highest level of academic excellence; highly developed research laboratories in medical schools, business, and industry; a variety of cultural and recreational facilities; and several highly developed forms of news media. What is even more significant is that these cities have a concentration of top professionals, businessmen, and technicians who may be called upon to enrich instruction in these colleges.

Unfortunately, these colleges, like the others just described, have not so far made the best use of the facilities, institutions, and talents in their communities. Furthermore, they have not developed the quality of interactional programs with their Black communities which could be cultivated. They, like the other colleges, have remained, to a large extent, "academic islands" in their communities.

If these well-located colleges would vigorously explore the possibilities and potentials existing in their cities, they could make a unique and larger contribution to higher education in this country, and to the development of Black Americans.

Wherever private Black colleges are located, they have one pervasive characteristic which prevents them from having maximum interaction with their socio-cultural environment: they are poor. As a group they have been always poor. Their poverty is much more extensive and serious than simply a shortage of current educational and general funds, as is the case with most private colleges, including some of the nation's most affluent and prestigious, today. Rather, the poverty characteristic of the sample colleges is a chronic condition resulting from decades of accumulated deprivations. Just about every aspect of these colleges attests to the deleterious effects of always having to "make do" with terribly inadequate financial support.

In other contexts I will contend that the primary reason these colleges have generally weak faculties, far below average student bodies, and inadequate, often sterile, academic programs is the fact that they have not been able to pay the costs of improvement. Most have never had enough money to pay the level of salaries required to attract anywhere near a significant number of truly top flight teachers, to mount effective national student recruitment efforts, or to initiate and develop significant, innovative, badly needed academic programs. In all instances, they have had to compromise worthy goals because inadequate funds made it necessary to scale down the quantity and quality of efforts needed to achieve them.

PHYSICAL PLANT

The most objective, and certainly one of the most reliable, indicators of the economic status of a college is the nature and condition of its physical plant and equipment, and the availability of supplies needed to execute the college's programs. With this in mind we took a close look at the types and condition of the buildings on each of the campuses visited and endeavored to evaluate the libraries, classrooms, laboratories, office space, recreation centers, dormitories, and dining rooms. In addition to our own observations, we asked all administrators, a cross section of teachers, and a representative number of students to appraise these facilities in their particular colleges. Of special interest are the appraisals of teachers who are immediately concerned with the use of these facilities.

All facilities were rated on a three point scale: *Adequate, Barely adequate* and *Inadequate*. There are two primary levels of adequacy recognized in these ratings: one, the physical plant in a given college may or may not be adequate to serve its *existing programs*. And two, even when such physical facilities on a particular campus are adequate to serve the existing, restricted programs, they may or may not be adequate to serve badly needed or *anticipated programs*.

The data to be presented forthwith are generally limited to the first level of adequacy. For the most part, we will be concerned with the primary, quantitative data furnished by the 400 teachers in the sample. The qualitative data or evaluations furnished by the 100 college administrators, a cross section of students, and various written reports are summarized and regarded as supporting information. Of special importance in this connection are evaluations and ratings of facilities by college personnel who were directly responsible for programs associated with certain key aspects of the physical plant, equipment, and resources on their campuses. Therefore, the data to be presented below do not necessarily mean that a given facility on any one campus falls completely into a particular category. For some of a college's personnel, a certain facility may be quite adequate for their particular needs. For others this same facility may be quite inadequate for the programs for which they are responsible. In nearly all instances the ratings given by teachers and suggested by students were validated by top administrators and the research team's personal observations.

Ratings by Teachers
  The Library

Adequate	36.7%
Barely adequate	42.4%
Inadequate	14.2%
No response	6.7%

The key datum that stands out in the evaluations above is that the great majority of teachers rate the libraries in their colleges as barely adequate to inadequate for the courses they teach, the programs for which they are responsible, and for their own intellectual edification. The ratings they gave were strongly supported by the 100 or so top administrators interviewed in the sample colleges, which included the presidents, deans, registrars, development officers, department chairmen, directors of special programs, and, especially, librarians. All tended to concur that their library (and other facilities to be mentioned subsequently) was adequate for some present needs, but barely adequate or totally inadequate to meet other current needs, to say nothing about expected future needs.

The evaluations of the library and its resources by teachers in the same college reflects at least three major points:

1. In each of the colleges there is usually an imbalance among the different major academic disciplines, so that one or two disciplines receive greater overall support than others. This often means that the favored discipline(s) will be able to recruit the best qualified teachers, make use of the better physical facilities, and, in this instance, acquire a more academically sound and extensive range of library resources. The favored discipline may be the social sciences, the natural sciences, the fine arts or, more often, education. Therefore, teachers in the favored disciplines might in fact find the library adequate for their particular needs, while teachers in other areas may find the library and its resources very much inadequate.

2. Some teachers in these colleges require their students to do little or no reading outside of an assigned text for each course. Librarians in each of the colleges complained about such teachers. One librarian made this statement:

> There are teachers on this campus who simply never visit this library. They have no idea about our resources or problems. I should add—students in certain teachers' classes and those who major in two popular fields in this college seldom or never use the library. Some don't even know how to use this facility.

Teachers who make little use of the library themselves, and those who do not require their students to use it, may adjudge its resources to be adequate for their needs when in fact it might be quite inadequate according to normal academic expectations.

3. Some teachers and deans evaluate library resources in terms of faculty as well as student needs. A given library might be adequate for the courses offered in the college but fall far short in providing teachers—especially those with a research bent—with the nature and extent of needed resources. Teachers who used their own needs as the main criterion of evaluating their library resources usually rated them as very inadequate.

Of special importance are the ratings by the librarians themselves. They usually cited five crucial areas which best indicate the strengths or weaknesses of the library: professional staff, the number of volumes and how they are balanced in terms of disciplines taught in the college, space, amount and condition of equipment, and the budget.

Each of the librarians interviewed reported serious inadequacies in at least two of the areas cited; most cited inadequacies in all five areas. Among the several examples that might be presented, three may be sufficient to illustrate the essential nature and range of inadequacies that exist in this very crucial aspect of the college—or its very heart—the library:

First, all of the librarians reported a critical shortage of professional personnel. In some instances, no librarian qualified as a head librarian and the position was filled by an acting head librarian. One head librarian complained that he had only two professional assistants and that one of them was academically unprepared and professionally incompetent. In several instances, librarians said that they had to depend almost entirely upon students to carry on the work of the library.

Second, with few exceptions, the libraries in the sample colleges are woefully inadequate in terms of the number of volumes needed to measure up to national norms. Most of them will need to double the number of volumes on hand in order to bring their acquisitions up to minimum standards.

Even those libraries with an adequate number of volumes do not measure up to national norms in terms of special collections, modern equipment, and/or sufficient space for independent study and research.

Third, even where there are new and beautiful library buildings, librarians report that they are too small and/or lack certain basic physical facilities. Usually they too have either a shortage of required acquisitions, lack balance in terms of different academic disciplines or do not have adequately developed special collections such as Black Studies, etc.

At least one basic conclusion is inevitable: all of the libraries in the colleges studied need large enabling grants to bring them up to acceptable national standards. If libraries in these colleges are to be adequate in terms of their student needs, they will have to gear themselves to render special, innovative services.

Classrooms

Adequate	50%
Barely adequate	36%
Inadequate	14%

The ratings above underscore two facts:

Some colleges have a greater shortage of classrooms than others. For instance, at one extreme a particular college has such a critical shortage of classrooms that it is necessary to schedule classes tightly throughout the day until 9:00 o'clock at night. At the other extreme is a college where there is an ample number of classrooms, even when classes are loosely scheduled.

While classrooms in a given college may be sufficient for the normal programs of some academic divisions or major areas, they may be quite inadequate for teachers in other areas. Teachers in the fine arts, physical education, and the natural sciences (with a few notable exceptions) most frequently complained about the shortage of classrooms. Even when adequate space was available, some teachers said that most of the classrooms they used were drab and unattractive.

Laboratories

Adequate	36%
Barely adequate	35%
Inadequate	29%

In some instances, teachers who said that laboratory facilities in their colleges were adequate quickly pointed out that all but a few students tended to shy away from the natural sciences, where laboratory experiences are an inherent aspect of the courses. Thus science teachers generally agreed that if anything near a fair proportion of the students in their colleges majored in the natural sciences, laboratories would be hopelessly overcrowded, with a great shortage of essential technology and supplies. Consequently, slightly more than a third of the teachers rated the laboratories as adequate. About the same proportion rated them as barely adequate. That is, they have learned to "make do" with facilities that normally fall below standard. Almost a third of the teachers rated the laboratories in their colleges as quite inadequate, even for their limited programs.

In addition to the fact that all but a very few of the colleges fall far below acceptable norms as far as science laboratories are concerned, all of them lack special badly needed non-natural science laboratories. Despite the fact that all of the academic administrators and teachers expressed a critical need for language, speech, and reading laboratories, only two or three of the ten sample colleges have well equipped laboratories in these academic areas. The great irony is this: while all of these colleges need the best equipped and staffed non-science laboratories possible, and none of them meet that standard, those colleges where the largest proportion of students need such facilities are precisely the ones where such facilities are generally the most inadequate or even non-existent.

Office Space

Adequate	42%
Barely adequate	32%
Inadequate	26%

While 42 percent of the teachers rated their office space as adequate, one of the most frequent teacher complaints was that their offices were either too small, overcrowded, or poorly equipped. Some colleges characteristically assign two or more teachers to each non-administrative office. Not only does this interfere with the amount of privacy a teacher needs for his/her own intellectual development and work, but it seriously interferes with the program of student counseling which all of the administrators and teachers insist is essential for the vast majority of their students.

One college president cited "cramped and unattractive office space" as a major cause for low faculty morale in his college.

Supporting Equipment and Services

Adequate	30%
Barely adequate	47%
Inadequate	23%

Several different items may be considered under this heading. However, we were primarily concerned with the extent to which teaching and learning were compromised by a shortage or lack of essential supplies and services. The vast majority of teachers and administrators cited the following common set of inadequacies: a critical shortage of efficient secretarial and clerical help; office supplies; business machines for student use; audio-visual equipment and supplies; properly stocked book stores; and all such special supplies as needed in music, speech, drama, recreation and so forth. A physical education teacher made a statement which is apropos to most teachers in these colleges: "There are never enough supplies, equipment and personnel to carry out the kind of program we plan during a given year. My hardest job is deciding on what phases of the program must be continued and what activities to cancel. There is a constant struggle to make ends meet."

In summary, all of the Black private colleges studied needed to expand and renovate some major portion of their physical plant. This was emphasized by a large majority of teachers and verified by each of the presidents. While some college plants, of course, are much more developed than others, on the whole they all fall far below any recognized standard of adequacy. In some instances, major construction is already underway or in the planning stages. Nevertheless, according to the most reliable information, even if all of the construction now planned is actually completed, the physical plants in these particular colleges will still be quite inadequate to support the kinds of programs that are badly needed. All of these colleges are presently struggling to bring their physical facilities up to a minimum standard with regard to their present programs. But even if this were done they would still be inadequate for new, badly needed innovative programs. Thus, according to summary estimates made by top administrators in the sample colleges, it would take approximately $25 million to improve the ten physical plants to the point where they would be adequate to support the kinds of programs which are already projected. Consequently, it would take about $100 million to bring the fifty-three private Black colleges' plants up to minimum standards. As it stands now, some of the colleges have more than doubled the size of their educational plants in the last ten years; however, according to audited reports about 56 percent of new construction is mortgaged. The expansion, therefore, has been made possible by borrowing funds from the federal government. If enrollment declines, the colleges with heavy loans would be in even more serious financial trouble than they are today.

4.

The Students: Social Background

All but three of the 53 private or non-public Black colleges are small. Even the three largest—Bishop, Hampton and Tuskegee—average only about 2,500-2,700 students each; half of these colleges average less than 700 students. The maximum number of students registered in all of the ten sample colleges during 1969-1970 was not quite 8,000 (7,996); an average of about 800 students per college. Consequently, the question of optimum size is of central importance in an evaluation of the present viability and future potential of the colleges in this study.

On the one hand, there are some highly respected educators and powerful and knowledgeable laymen who feel that there are several very definite advantages offered students in small colleges. They believe that students in small colleges will ordinarily have the best opportunities to develop positive self-identities, establish meaningful personal relationships with teachers, and acquire the skills and attitudes necessary to become socially conscious leaders. As a rule, presidents of Black colleges support this point of view. This is, in fact, a major theme in their recruitment of students and faculty. It is also their most convincing argument in what one president calls a "defense" of these colleges and basic in their campaign for funds. Some of these presidents like to picture their colleges as "families." This term is meant to describe the college as having an informal, personal academic atmosphere that allegedly prevails among students, teachers, and a sort of fatherly administration.

There are also a goodly number of students and teachers in our sample who espouse the family concept of the small Black college. Some argue that the small colleges with which they are connected are more conducive to study and learning than are the larger more cosmopolitan colleges. This, they feel, is particularly true for students who are products of inadequate high schools and from socio-economically disadvantaged families and communities. These are precisely the points made by most of the presidents and underscored by one who concluded:

> The kind of students we get here, and those who will select this college for at least another decade, must have the personal, dedicated attention which they can only expect to get in a small college. Here teachers understand the peculiar problems and appreciate the potentials of each individual student. Most of the students who select this college would be lost and frustrated in a large, impersonal university.

There are those, on the other hand, who see very definite disadvantages to the small college. These people are apparently as knowledgeable about, and sympathetic to the higher education of Black youth as are those who advocate small schools. Actually, a few of the presidents of Black colleges, several established faculty members, and a large number of students are convinced that there are many disadvantages inherent in smallness. They generally concur that it is extremely difficult for the very small college to project an image of viability that is necessary to attract the kinds of students, teachers, and support it must have. A top student leader was asked: "Suppose you were just now graduating from high school; knowing what you know now about this college, would you still enroll here?" The student replied, "no." He explained that he was encouraged to attend the college by one of his high school teachers who was "living in the past." He added:

> My teacher still talks about the college as if it had not changed since he graduated several years ago. At that time it had a good program in sports, exciting social life and some of the best Black professors. We don't have anything like that now. I am staying on to graduate this year because this school has been good to me, but this is an awfully dull campus.

Some of the best informed educators and supporters of Black colleges are beginning to feel that a truly viable college today must have at least 1,500-2,000 students.[1] They tend to agree that it would take that number of students to justify the very high cost of modern academic buildings, very costly academic technology (calculators, audio-visual equipment, special laboratories, etc.), and rapidly rising salaries of teachers, administrators and other personnel. One trustee of a private Black college confided:

> We have discussed this problem (optimum enrollment) with some experts on college financing. Most of them tell us that good private colleges of less than 1500 students are economically unsound. They must charge such high tuition that only youngsters from affluent families could be expected to attend. The good small colleges always have a number of rich alumni who see to it that they are well-supported so that their children may get an exclusive, class-oriented education.

In addition to the argument that small colleges (less than 1,500 students) are economically unsound ventures in our urban, industrial society there is another, purely academic demurrer. The proponents of this point of view call attention to the fact that a senior liberal arts college is expected to provide several subject-matter areas in which students may major, plus a number of special courses students may elect in order to broaden their general knowledge outside of their major fields. Small colleges, especially those which are impoverished, are very likely to have some one-man departments and a very limited number of elective courses. This situation, by definition, is an inherent contradiction to the concept of liberal education. It is hardly conducive to the development of a rich, challenging, exciting academic atmosphere.

Again, the student who described his college life as "dull" may be suggesting an important social dimension of collegiate viability as it is related to the problem of optimum size. In fact, many students and teachers commented at length on what they regarded as the lack of vitality on their campuses. A dean of students observed that "students don't enjoy life on this campus . . . This may be due to a kind of monotonous routine we have fallen into and haven't been able to shake." A student leader complained "life on this campus is pretty flat. We seldom get a glimpse of the outside world." What the spokesman meant was spelled out by other student leaders present. They pointed out that a large student body can invite expensive artists and speakers such as Flip Wilson, The Supremes, James Brown, Julian Bond and Lerone Bennett and pay them out of their budget or have enough students to pay them from charged admission. They pointed out that their own budget was very small or nonexistent and there were certainly not enough students on campus to pay expensive personages out of gate receipts. These students concluded that: "The only top people we ever get at this college are those selected and invited by the administration. Most of them we don't want. That's the reason we don't bother to come out and hear them. They would probably think that we are uncivilized anyway." Further, some students called attention to the fact that there are not enough of them to afford having well-known, accomplished bands to play for their dances. One student complained: "The worse thing about our dances is the lousy music."

What the students said about visiting personalities and entertainment is *apropos* to all intercollegiate activities and extra-curricular programs. All of these function to enrich, extend, and enliven academic life on the campus. They are quite indicative of the college's power to attract socially oriented students. But, small colleges operating on tight budgets simply cannot afford such expensive extra-curricular programs or the kind of varied, enriched curricula students desire and need in order to develop their potentials to the fullest during their college years. The fact that some of the colleges may be described as dull could be a major reason why they are virtually stunted in their growth. Their image is simply not as attractive as the image of other colleges with whom they must compete.

Though the actual number of students enrolled in the sample colleges usually fluctuates somewhat from year to year, only two or three of them at present manifest a significant, sustained pattern of growth. For instance, during the 1960s enrollment in higher education in this nation more than doubled, from about 3 million college students to 6.8 million or more by 1968. The proportional increase in Blacks enrolled in colleges was even greater. In 1960 there were approximately 100,000-125,000 Black students in all colleges.[2] Today, there are about 434,000. In 1960 approximately three-fourths, or about 75,000, of the Black students were enrolled in Black colleges. In the fall of 1968 only 36 percent, or 156,000, were enrolled in Black colleges, with the other 278,000, or 64 percent, scattered among some 2,000 or so traditionally white colleges. It is quite astonishing that between 1960-1968 enrollment in Black colleges increased by 108 percent![3] Most of this increase was in public Black colleges, where the increase in enrollment was about 233 percent between 1956-1971. During the same period, enrollment in the 10 sample colleges only increased from about 6,000 to somewhat less than 8,000, or by just 33 percent. This is an average annual increase of approximately 200 students in all of these colleges. *Therefore, the average annual increase for the sample colleges was just 20 students each.* The truth is, most private Black colleges are literally fighting for their academic lives in the sense that their enrollments are relatively static. As will be discussed later, there is some fear that most of these colleges manage to maintain a more or less stable enrollment only by lowering customary admissions requirements.

There are, of course, several reasons why the enrollment in these colleges is increasing at such a slow rate and perhaps at the expense of higher academic standards. I shall cite just five:

1. *Competition with private white colleges.* Until a decade or two ago—actually until the 1954 United States Supreme Court Decision outlawing segregated public education—Black colleges had a virtual monopoly in the recruitment of Black high school graduates in the South. Soon they found themselves in the position of having to compete increasingly with traditionally white colleges, North and South. This competition is particularly keen when it comes to Black high school students with the greatest academic and athletic promise. Ironically, one of the most reliable and persistent allies white colleges have for their Black student recruitment programs are the generally well-organized Black student groups on their campuses. These groups are seldom modest in demands upon their college administrations when it comes to the rights of Black students. These demands may differ somewhat from one campus to the other, yet all of the Black groups make at least one demand in common: a so-called non-negotiable demand for a larger enrollment of Black students and for generous scholarships. As a result, some white colleges, even those in segregated southern communities, are offering scholarships to Black students which private Black colleges can hardly match. Consequently, admissions officers in the sample colleges report that they are getting fewer and fewer of the highest ranking, talented Black high school graduates. This is a major reason why most private Black colleges seem to be relatively stunted in their growth and maintain flexible academic standards.

2. *Competition with public Black colleges.* Simultaneously with the federal courts' firm demand for desegregation, southern legislators began to appropriate increasingly large sums of money to support public Black colleges. This marked a significant turning point in the development of Black higher education and ironically constituted the greatest challenge to private Black colleges. In the past the image of the public Black college was considerably less attractive than that of the private Black college; the latter boasted of having, on the average, superior physical plants, students and faculties. With heavier appropriations, during the 1960s some Black state colleges assumed an image of vitality and academic respectability that had been formerly associated with only a few of

the best private Black colleges. They certainly have achieved an aura of permanence which is not associated with some of the private Black colleges.

During the 1960s private Black colleges had their traditional range of student recruitment narrowed considerably because Black state colleges attracted a larger and larger number of Black high school graduates who would have formerly enrolled in them. This is especially true of Black students with special talents in athletics and music and those who are seeking what would amount to terminal degrees to immediately qualify them for teaching, nursing and so forth. Therefore, enrollment in public Black colleges has increased more than two-and-a-third times since 1956. At present, the 32 public Black colleges enroll more than 110,000 students, or about three-fifths (60%) of all students in Black colleges.[4]

3. *The desegregation of white state colleges.* Federal court decisions and guidelines for special programs have forced traditionally white public colleges to admit Black students. For the first few years these colleges only admitted a token number of Black students, but during the last five years or so a steadily increasing number of Black students have been enrolling in them.

According to reliable reports, Black students today do not encounter nearly as much hostility on white college campuses as they did a few years ago.[5] The official policies and practices insofar as Black students are concerned have certainly changed significantly. Even some of the formerly all white state colleges in the South are beginning to make special efforts to relate meaningfully to Black students. They are making available special laboratories in mathematics and communications designed to assist all students with certain academic deficiencies, employing Black counselors, and instituting courses in Black Studies with able Black professors. A few are actively recruiting Black high school graduates for their varsity teams. Despite widespread separatism, which has been described as "The New Black Apartheid . . . under the guise of black studies—for blacks, black dorms, and separate admission criteria for black students, demanded by black students . . . ,[6] present trends give every reason to believe that during the 1970s Black high school graduates in larger and larger numbers will be choosing formerly all white state colleges over private Black colleges.

Competition with formerly all white public colleges will become increasingly keen where state-supported city colleges are being developed. Unlike the parent state universities which emphasize vocational education, city colleges tend to emphasize the liberal arts, which has been the hallmark of the private Black college. Already, at least three of the sample colleges are beginning to experience direct competition with state-supported city colleges for local Black high school graduates.

4. *The rising costs of education.* A college education today is of course, much more expensive than it was a decade ago. It is especially expensive in private colleges. The cost of attending any one of the sample colleges is at least twice as much as it was in 1960, a fact which alarms the administrators. One president lamented: "In order to meet the increasing costs of operating my college we must continue to raise tuition and board. We are literally pricing ourselves out of existence." Despite scholarships, student aid, and other types of student funds available from the federal government, all of the presidents agree that the necessity to continually raise tuition is putting them at a great disadvantage in the recruitment of the type of students they have normally attracted. This is particularly true regarding students of high potential from lower middle class families. There is ample evidence that these are the Black students that are most often attracted to white state colleges in the South. They, their parents, and their counselors seem to feel that since private education is so expensive, their next preference would be white state colleges.

5. *The negative image of Black colleges.* Reinforcing all of the salient factors mentioned above which militate against the healthy growth and development of Black colleges, is the negative image of Black higher education *per se*. This image has been especially tarnished during the last decade or two. In the past, Black colleges were largely ignored in the world of higher education and philanthropy. Since student protests literally thrust them into the midst of academic controversy, Black colleges have been the ob-

ject of a virtual avalanche of devastating criticism. The Jencks and Riesman characterization of Black colleges as an "Academic Disaster Area" which is an "ill-financed, ill-staffed caricature of white higher education" was by no means a new evaluation.[7] They only gave a succinct, dramatic formulation of some deeply-rooted, ancient stereotypes of the Black experience wherever and in whatever form it may exist.

The widely shared negative attitudes expressed by these influential authors have functioned to give popular validity to damaging stereotypes of all Black institutions. They form a part of what results in a vicious cycle. The image of inherent inferiority of Black education evidently prevents some prominent educators, representatives of powerful philanthropic foundations, legislators and leading churchmen from extending the recognition and financial support these colleges must have in order to become or remain first-rate. Some key decision-makers withhold support from these colleges because of their alleged weaknesses. In other words, they tend to demand that these colleges prove themselves without getting needed help. Professor Merton refers to this type of cyclical response as a "self-fulfilling prophecy."[8]

Perhaps the most ironic example of the assumption that Black schools are *ipso facto* inferior is the monumental United States Supreme Court's 1954 Decision outlawing segregated public education. That decision and several other subsequent federal court decisions and rulings legally underscored the principle that the all-Black experience is inferior. Chief Justice Warren read the unanimous decision of the Supreme Court which held that: "Separate educational facilities are inherently unequal." The Supreme Court's Decision itself reflected conclusions that had been made previously by systematic social science research. Such allegedly validating scientific research has continued ever since the 1954 decision.

An excellent example of such research is the much-publicized "Coleman Report,"[9] whose main thesis is that Black schools are inherently inferior to white schools. Coleman even emphasized this thesis by statistically "proving" that the larger the proportion of white students enrolled in a given school the higher will be the learning rate and the level of achievement of Black students. Conversely, the larger the proportion of Black students the lower the rate and level of learning.

The "validating" social science research and federal court decisions aimed at removing segregation in education articulate what might be termed cultural or environmental explanations for the inferiority of Black schools. These have been interpreted as meaning that any racially segregated institution is inferior. The layman's conclusion is obviously that all Black institutions are inferior, with the popular interpretation that Black students will gain from association with white students. The idea of mutual gain has been underplayed.

It is only logical then that ambitious high school graduates in search of a good college would be led to extrapolate the findings of social science research and the unanimous opinion of the U.S. Supreme Court in their judgement of the academic merits of Black colleges. An increasing number of high school graduates apparently agree that according to so-called reliable evidence Black colleges are not first-rate. It is not surprising, then, that an impressive number of the most promising, talented Black high school graduates are beginning to enroll in formerly all-white or desegregated colleges in preference to the most prestigious, but still generally segregated, Black colleges. This trend makes it doubly important for us to take a close look at the major characteristics of students who are still attracted to the Black private colleges.

SOCIAL CHARACTERISTICS OF THE STUDENTS

All but two of the private colleges are located in the South. The history, traditions and ethos of the communities in which they are located differ in some specific respects, yet they have at least one characteristic in common: all of these communities have a history of slavery and have been subsequently organized around the doctrine of white supremacy. This historical fact has, until this day, constantly influenced the structure, programs, image and composition of the student bodies of these colleges.

Geographic Distribution. All of the colleges make a point of publicizing the geographic areas from which their students come. Evidently, the basic reason for this is to establish the image of being national colleges. This desire is underscored in the information about the colleges used by recruiters. For example, these colleges have their recruiters point out that they have students from, say, "twenty states and five different foreign countries," often without specifying the actual number. A close look, however, will reveal that the student bodies in private Black colleges in the deep South are quite homogeneous insofar as their origins are concerned. Fully 95 percent of the students enrolled in these colleges were born and reared in the South. The actual percentages range all the way from 88 percent in one to 97 percent in another. The number of foreign students in these colleges is not significant, ranging from one to ten.

Approximately 70 percent of the students in each of the sample colleges are natives of the states in which the colleges are located. As a rule, their students are recruited from the various small towns within a radius of a hundred miles or so. Consequently, none of these colleges could be classified as national colleges. Neither do they classify as city colleges in the sense that a large majority of their students come from the cities in which they are located. At one time, a few of the colleges like Clark and Dillard, located in large cities, generally drew half or more of their students from their respective cities. Now they draw only 40-45 percent of students from their local communities. Even urban colleges like Clark and Dillard are becoming more and more like their counterparts in small cities in that they are recruiting an increasing proportion of their students from small high schools throughout the states in which they are located.

It is indeed surprising that these colleges have recruited so few students from the large Black ghettos outside the South. After all, there is a relatively large proportion of Black parents in the North who were born in the South. Many of them are alumni of Black colleges. It would seem then that recruiters from these colleges would have greater success in encouraging them to enroll their children in private Black colleges in the South.

Another point: during the past decade a great deal of emphasis has been placed upon the need for Black youth to identify with the history and culture of Black peoples. A number of so-called Black ghetto or community schools have been established primarily to teach the Black experience. They are usually unaccredited. I expected that this new desire for Black identity would have resulted in a much more significant enrollment of students from outside the South in long-established Black colleges than it actually has. It seems that the very reverse is occurring. That is, though the enrollment of Black students from outside the South has never been great, admissions officers in the sample colleges report that it even declined somewhat during the 1960s.

Basic, therefore, to an understanding and a fruitful evaluation of the colleges in this study is the realization that the vast majority of their students are recruited from communities where blatant discrimination in public schools has always been a notoriously established fact. Most of these communities, even now, do not even pretend that Black public schools are anywhere near equal to white public schools. This, in fact, is the rationale that white politicians and many educators in the South generally give for their continued resistance to school desegregation. They are particularly incensed about the probability that white children may have to attend the once-designated Black schools. Yet these are precisely the Black schools from which Black colleges have had to recruit just about all of their students. According to the most reliable information (particularly standardized tests), only a few of these Black high school graduates get the well-balanced academic and social experiences necessary to prepare them for first-rate colleges. Even so, the possibility of enhancing the academic level of these colleges by recruiting a larger number of qualified students from outside the South has not been fully exploited.

Interviews with students revealed that most of them would like to have more fellow students from outside the South. They concurred that the academic and social life of their colleges would be a great deal more viable if the campuses were more cosmopolitan. A few of the more sophisticated recruits from large cities disdainfully described their colleges as "country colleges." Some of the college presidents, however, seem to differ with their students about the desirability of a cosmopolitan college. One president frankly admitted: "We don't attempt to get students from northern cities because we find too many of them are trouble-makers. Practically all of them characteristically complain about one thing or another. Some of them call attention to themselves by stirring up student unrest." This president volunteered to add: "One of the reasons why Woodrow Wilson Fellows were of such little service to us was that they wanted to make our college over. Nothing here pleased them."

Other college presidents did not share this point of view. They expressed a desire to have more students from large northern cities and said that the only reason they do not have recruiting programs outside the South is because they do not have the funds to support them. However, there is some evidence that underlying the reluctance of these colleges to recruit students from outside the South is the fear that they would be unable to sell their segregated colleges in such areas. Some doubt that northern students will want to come South in large enough numbers to justify expensive recruitment programs. One dean expressed another dimension of his college's timid recruitment practices. In acknowledging that his college does not even have a recruiting program for Black students who are attending predominantly white high schools in the South, he said, "Most of them, like those in the North who attend integrated high schools, do so because they are preparing to go to predominantly white colleges. We would be wasting our time trying to get them to come here." This means in effect that the more integrated southern high schools become, the narrower will be the range of student recruitment unless the present policies and practices of these colleges are revised.

Male-Female. Private co-educational Black colleges have traditionally had student bodies that were 60 to 70 percent female. This resulted from a complex of sociological forces—the strong feminist attitude of the Black matriarchy, discrimination in employment, lack of a sufficient number of stable male symbols of success, all too well known to go into at this time. The important point is that these colleges never intended to be predominantly female and have always made sustained attempts to achieve a more sexually balanced student body. Sometimes they deliberately violated entrance requirement policies in order to increase the number of male students. That is, the cut-off point on standardized tests and high school grades is usually somewhat lower for male high school graduates than for females. Further, these colleges usually give preference to male students when it comes to the awarding of scholarships and other forms of student aid.

In attempting to square their practices of giving preference to potential male students over against female students, officials in these colleges gave the following rationales which I shall summarize:

(1) The imbalance of the sexes on campus results in a somewhat distorted social life among the students. They reasoned that in a community where *de facto* segregation and strong traditions supporting it remain deeply ingrained, the Black college campus proves to be a sort of cultural oasis for some youth. Here they can attend social, recreational, and intellectual affairs where the most refined middle class standards of behavior prevail. Since the average age of these students is about 19, they are in the midst of what seems to be the most romantic courtship period. Thus, campus affairs planned to meet co-educational needs, and actually attended mostly by females, tend to lose their appeal to both male and female students. This is particularly true of purely social affairs, dances, and so forth, but is also true to some extent of all campus activities. For instance, some students even acknowledged that they go to the library frequently in order to meet friends of the opposite sex. All female students interviewed expressed a desire to have more male peers.

(2) The imbalance of the sexes in Black colleges tends to jeopardize the race's struggle for equality in American society. One fact may illustrate this. Despite the more or less persistent feminist movement, most of the desirable jobs with high prestige and substantial salaries in the United States are still generally regarded as men's jobs. The vast majority of them (called merit employment by some) are monopolized by whites. If there is to be a significant democratization in the distribution of merit jobs, Black men in considerably larger numbers must be trained to compete successfully for them. "Therefore, the degree to which Negro men fail to measure up to high levels of technical and

academic standards will be the degree to which Negroes as a race will fail to achieve the full citizenship for which they are striving so hard."[10]

(3) The demands of the nuclear age in which we live make it necessary for our schools to train a large number of technical and professional people. The demand for such persons is so great that a dangerous shortage usually exists in practically every occupational area of American life where extensive education is a prerequisite. Government on all levels, as well as private enterprise, has expressed the need to recruit talent from all segments of American society. Much effort is being made to extend this search for talent to Black males. Far too few Black men qualify for top jobs now open to them for the first time. It is in this area that Black colleges can make a distinct contribution to the Black revolution.

In spite of these colleges' determined attempts to achieve a more male-oriented balance in their student bodies, they have accomplished little. Only one or two of the coeducational colleges actually showed any significant progress in achieving an even balance of the sexes during the 1960s. Nevertheless it is interesting and very significant that while the private Black colleges are still predominantly female, the proportion of all Black male college students and graduates has constantly increased. Thus, in 1960 only 3.9 percent of the Black males between 25 and 34 years of age had graduated from college, compared with 4.6 percent of Black females. In 1969 the proportion of Black male college graduates in that age group had almost doubled to 7.6 percent, which is significantly higher than the 5.6 percent for Black females.[11] In other words, today there are more Black males in college than Black females, if we include those enrolled in non-Black colleges.

The fact that at long last the number of Black male college students exceeds Black female college students has far-reaching sociological implications. Basically, it reflects the rapid increase in the size of the Black middle class. Clearly the "Black Bourgeoisie" in 1970 is a different "Black Bourgeoisie" than when Frazier published his controversial treatise.[12] It has increased from about 5 percent to approximately 25 percent, and now includes a much wider variety of professionals and executives in both the public and private sectors of American life. The Black Bourgeois model is more varied and its values more flexible and complex than during the 1950s. It represents a wider range of occupations and styles of life.

This change is reflected in the mood, aspirations and outlook of ambitious Black youth in that they are aspiring to a wider range of middle class occupations. As opportunities for Black college graduates open up in the larger society, Black male youth particularly are enrolling in desegregated colleges where they expect that their preparation for such positions will be better. This is another reason why colleges in the sample are losing out in competition with white colleges for the more ambitious Black high school students.

Not only do many Black youth seek out desegregated white colleges, but these colleges have mounted an effective, sustained effort to attract them. Since, as a rule, white colleges have more money and better trained recruiters, they are succeeding in siphoning off the "cream of the crop." As is well known, they generally prefer male to female students. Also, some educators are convinced that foundations and agencies awarding college scholarships tend to prefer males. All of this adds up to the conclusion that during the 1960s Black male high school graduates had more incentives and greater opportunities to enroll in college than they ever had before. Today they are responding in much larger numbers than anticipated. This turn of events explodes, of course, some long-standing stereotypes of Black males as lazy, apathetic, undisciplined etc. While this might be true of some, it is certainly not supported generally insofar as their differential academic achievements are concerned.

Another reason why the enrollment in the sample colleges still reflects a feminine imbalance is that most of these colleges have seriously curtailed their intercollegiate sports—especially football. At the same time, public Black colleges have been giving great emphasis to intercollegiate sports, and; their all-Black teams are, for the first time receiving wide publicity and recognition. For example, Grambling College in Louisiana emerged as one of the most significant colleges, without regard to race, for the training of football players. During the 1960s it trained more players to be accepted in the big leagues than any other college. In addition to successful football teams, some public Black colleges have also developed equally successful big bands. Not only do strong sports programs add vitality and excitement to these campuses but, *apropos* to our interest, they function to attract Black male high school graduates. Likewise, one strong attraction on the part of certain public white colleges in the South is their massive athletic programs. These colleges are beginning to recruit Black athletes in significant numbers as they enter truly national competition. This will also be an increasing challenge to the recruitment potential of Black colleges.

Finally, until quite recently Black women on the whole were better educated than Black men. Since 1960, young Black males have flocked to college in much larger numbers than their sisters, yet the sex ratio in the sample colleges has changed very little. We know that there are many complex reasons why a student selects a given college. Nevertheless, if private Black colleges are to better reflect the more positive Black male image that has definitely emerged in American society, they must develop attractive masculine curricula, and institute effective programs for recruiting Black male students who have the will and ability to qualify for exacting careers.

Racial Composition. There are very few white students in private Black colleges. Though the actual number varies from none in some to ten or so in a few, the total number in all of these colleges is only about one percent. In 1968, when there were 11,846 freshmen enrolled in the 34 United Negro College Fund institutions, only 33 were non-Black. This is somewhat surprising because during the 1960s civil rights leaders, Black and white, placed great emphasis upon the desirability of integration and the evils of racial segregation. During that decade these leaders were also successful in having the overall principle of integration endorsed by federal courts, government on all levels, all major religious denominations and most national organizations. It is likely that more time, effort, and money were spent to establish desegregation as a national policy than on any other domestic issue of the 1960s.

Emphasis, however, was placed upon Blacks integrating white

institutions at the expense of the prestige of Black institutions. Little or no effort was made by Black institutions to actively participate in the process of desegregation. This is unfortunate because private Black colleges have been predisposed by history and circumstances to set the pace and style of desegregation and integration in higher education. Their avowed commitment and inherent mission identify them with the disinherited masses rather than with the privileged classes with whom the more prestigious white colleges have always identified. For almost a century these colleges served as a sort of oasis in the segregated, anti-democratic southern communities where they were located. There were times, for example, when these colleges provided the only public places where a desegregated meeting could be held or where outspoken white liberals and noted Black leaders could find a platform. Since this is so, a central question naturally arises: why are private Black colleges still practicing what amounts to *de facto* racial segregation in the recruitment of their students?

The answer to this question is many-sided and complex. Underlying all of the plausible reasons for their almost total Black student bodies is the fact that these colleges have inherited the negative stereotypes perennially associated with Black people and the symbol of inferiority associated with blackness in American culture. That is, in much of American literature and legend black is a symbol of badness or that which is undesirable, and, as mentioned before, black stereotypes were given credence during the 1960s by over-zealous civil rights leaders who oversold the virtues of white educational institutions at the expense of Black institutions on the same academic level. The usual form of the civil rights argument for desegregation was to show how inferior Black schools and colleges were compared with similar white educational institutions. Unwittingly, these arguments functioned to reinforce the negative image of Black institutions—even blackness *per se*—which has long been perpetuated by white supremists. It is understandable, then, why some white high school graduates who may have otherwise chosen Black colleges have been frightened away from them.

Interviews with white students in the sample colleges revealed still another critical reason why Black colleges attract so few white students. They indicated that more white students would enroll in the Black colleges if there were not such great social pressure preventing them from doing so. This pressure comes from parents, from relatives, and from others who constitute the students' social world. Almost all of the white students interviewed regard themselves as rebels. Most pointed out that their attendance at a Black college was a violation of family tradition, community mores, and/or social class etiquette. This was summarized in an impassioned statement by a white female student. She said in part:

> I never get through explaining why I chose this college. It seems that everywhere I go—the church, beauty parlor, shopping, visiting, or what—people question me about this college and why I came here. They refuse to accept the fact that it is a good college and I like here better than I'd perhaps like any other college. They want to believe that there must be some deep psychological or social reasons which I cannot or will not reveal. Even my parents seem to feel that I am some kind of freak or deviant.

According to this and similar statements made by white students it seems that even now a strong, threatening taboo prevails against white students attending Black colleges, and, despite the widespread belief that this generation of youth is freer and more liberated from ancient, moribund mores than their predecessors, very few white students violate this taboo.

At this point another basic reason why there are so few white students in private Black colleges should be considered: none of these colleges has a systematic program aimed at recruiting white students. So far, they have no instrument to offset the well-organized, well-financed programs most white colleges have mounted to recruit Black students. This situation surfaces an old, entrenched pattern of racial discrimination—that Black business enterprises, social organizations, and other institutions have always had to compete with comparable white structures for Black constituents, while white enterprises and institutions have been protected from Black competition by a network of traditions, mores and taboos. This, naturally, puts the Black institutions at a great disadvantage. Even when Black college recruiters visit desegregated high schools, they seldom or never have ample opportunities to recruit white students. Sometimes school counselors in charge simply assume that they are interested in Black students only, or the Black recruiters don't ask to see white students, or the counselors actually refuse to make white students available. Consequently, whatever misconceptions white high school students might have of Black colleges tend to remain undisturbed and unchallenged because Black recruiters get few if any opportunities to dispel the prevailing stereotypes. The result: so far very few white students have chosen Black colleges.

The number of foreign students in Black colleges is negligible. Just as there are several complex reasons why there are only a few native white students in these colleges, there are also a number of reasons for the even smaller number of foreign students. Yet one basic reason stands out: Black colleges have no organized program to recruit foreign students, and have had little or no success in securing special scholarships for them. This is true even with regard to African students. There were only five African students in the ten sample colleges in 1970-1971, in spite of the fact that the sponsoring church bodies, through their missions, have manifested a long, sustained interest in African peoples. Besides, Black Americans have come rapidly to cherish their African heritage and identity. One would expect, then, that the Black church-related college would be a natural, rewarding focus through which churches would extend their mission to African peoples (particularly those recently achieving their independence) and for Black Americans to enter into a mutually rewarding effort to blend and enrich the Black experience. Yet, so far this is not so.

Administrative officers in the sample colleges often expressed a desire to have more foreign students, especially Africans. They would like for their colleges to have a more cosmopolitan image and to extend their services. They tend to agree, however, with the dean who reasoned: "We don't even have enough money to organize a strong recruitment program throughout this state. Recruiting foreign students and providing them with the scholarships they would need is out of the question." Therefore, despite the expressed desire to have more foreign students enrolled, the sample colleges have not been able to recruit them.

The "Identity Crisis". During recent years much has been said and written about the "identity crisis" characteristic of Black youth. Nothing underscores this very significant phenomenon more pointedly than their confusion about the term they prefer to designate their race. This confusion was manifested in both the questionnaires completed by students in the sample colleges and in certain nouns they used in interviews. For example, only about a third (33%) of the students in the sample colleges still prefer to be thought of as "Negro." Less than one percent (0.6%) think of themselves as "Colored," while 20 percent prefer the term "Afro-American," and the largest proportion, fully 47 percent, prefer to be called "Black." During interviews students who evidently said on their questionnaires that they preferred the term Negro or Afro-American characteristically used the term Black. The interviewers could not decide whether the students' frequent use of the term Black was deliberate, in conformity with their peer groups, simple habit, or personal preference. In any case, it is safe to say that Black college students today generally prefer to think of themselves and their race as Black.

In order to fully understand and appreciate this generation of Black youth's zealous concern with racial labeling, it is necessary to remember that ours has always been a racist society. In essence, racism means that an individual's general welfare is influenced more by his racial identity than it is by his character, education, professional competency, or national origin. Accordingly, every key area of American society is dominated by the white race. This race is in reality a combination of several ethnic branches of the Caucasian race. These ethnic branches differ in some important ways (religious beliefs, political persuasions, economic ideologies, social philosophies and cultural backgrounds) yet by and large they are bound together by at least one strong common thread— the belief that the white race is distinct from and perhaps superior to non-white races.

In the mythical hierarchy of races in this country Black people have traditionally been the most disesteemed. Greatly out-numbered (almost 10 to 1), most living in or close to poverty, politically weak or virtually powerless, Black Americans have had to struggle constantly against great odds in order to survive and to achieve some measure of respect, recognition and dignity. White Americans have regularly employed derogatory racial epithets as a most cruel, and psychologically damaging weapon to slur and insult Blacks. These epithets also function to emphasize avowed white superiority. Therefore, whites coined such demeaning terms as "Darky," "Nigger," "Nigra," "Sambo," "Aunt Jemima," and so forth. All of these terms were intended to express their contempt for Black folk, a contempt frequently expressed even by some of the most enlightened white politicians, writers, and scholars. For decades many white writers refused even to capitalize the noun "Negro," and when they used the noun "Black" it was done to convey excessive contempt and to emphasize the very opposite of "white"—physically, socially, and mentally.

In direct, predictable response to insulting epithets whites coined and pinned onto the Black race, Blacks themselves countered with their insistence upon being referred to in a more respectful manner. At one time or another some of the more thoughtful, militant members of the race have demanded to be referred to as "Negro," "Colored," "Afro-American" and now "Black." However, until quite recently the term Negro has been the most universally accepted. This is, in fact, the noun that appears in just about all legal documents, census reports, agency records and formal writings where members of the race are designated. It is the term most used to identify institutions, programs, activities and pursuits in the Black community. Even the most militant Black spokesmen and scholars are still likely to use the term Negro interchangeably with other more popular designates such as Afro-American and Black. (Incidentally, the term Afro-American is seldom used except in writing). Consequently, students in the sample who prefer to be thought of as Black are deliberately at odds with "the establishment," where the term Negro is firmly fixed in literary, legal and oral traditions.

Only a few students indicated that they preferred to be

thought of as "Colored;" none used the noun in conversation. Though this term was never generally popular, from time to time it has been regarded as the most respected racial designation. Until a decade or so ago it was the deliberate choice of white liberals who wanted to express their respect for the race, and of influential Black leaders who demanded such respect. Some of the most respected and influential organizations and activities in the Black community were labeled "Colored." The best example of this is the largest, historically most effective civil rights organization—The National Association for the Advancement of Colored People. This organization is so entrenched in the thinking and behavior of American society that it retains the designation "Colored" despite numerous attempts on the part of "Young Turks" to change it to "Black."

We were not altogether successful in finding out why Black students so emphatically reject the term "Colored," and even regard it as a joke or an insult. Perhaps the most plausible reason that emerged is that the term "Colored" was most generally associated with the old race relations organizations (including the NAACP) composed of Black and white middle class leaders, and is a term once preferred by erstwhile white liberals. Black students seem intent upon destroying this old alliance and the old symbols of accommodation which this term suggested.

We made repeated attempts to relate certain racial labels to distinct sub-groups, attitudes and ideological stances among the students. This effort was not fruitful: freshmen were as likely to prefer "Black" as seniors. Sorority and fraternity members were as likely to choose a particular racial identity as those who were non-members, and there was no significant difference in the choice of racial labeling preferred by men and women. Throughout the student body, a definite Black ethos was clearly emerging.

There was a resurgence of Black pride during 1968. Civil rights organizations sponsored many different kinds of projects intended to develop this.

Perhaps the most effective manifestation of such pride

was the fact that Black youth throughout the nation demanded that schools and colleges they attended set up courses in Black history and culture . . . Actually, so much emphasis was placed upon 'Black' as beautiful and honorable that some feared that Black Americans were borrowing pages from the dishonorable lexicons of white supremacy. Some Black leaders felt called upon to warn against substituting the theory of Black supremacy for the discredited theory of white supremacy . . . The concept 'Black' was transformed from a badge of inferiority and disesteem to one of beauty and honor.[13]

Socio-Economic Background. The socio-economic background of the students in private Black colleges is somewhat more varied than their geographic origins and race. Actually, these students represent almost all of the major social and economic categories in the Black communities from which they come. It should be remembered, however, that the vast majority of them do come from lower socio-economic class homes. Upon analysis we find that the great majority of them come from homes where fathers and mothers are under-employed in low status occupations and their educational level is considerably below national norms.

1. *Occupation of Parents.* It is interesting that 22 percent of the students indicated that they did not know what kind of work their fathers did. This could mean that the fathers were not living in the household or that they were ashamed to report the kind of work, if any, their fathers did.

Among those who did indicate the occupations in which their parents were engaged, 80 percent reported that their fathers were employed in some blue collar occupation; 68 percent said that their mothers were engaged in some sort of blue collar or service work. It is important to note that 51 percent of the fathers and 58 percent of the mothers held the lowest level, most insecure and unremunerative jobs. Therefore, according to information furnished by the students themselves, plus information secured from administrators in these colleges, between 70 and 80 percent of the students in the sample colleges come from homes of working class parents.

Of course, the best indication that the majority of them come from poor homes is the evaluation of the economic status of the families by the students themselves, which is supported by information parents furnished school authorities. According to the most reliable information available, 37 percent of the fathers earned less than $5,000 a year, while 30 percent earned from $5,000 to less than $10,000, only 5 percent earned an annual salary of $10,000 or more. This means that 28 percent did not estimate the incomes of their fathers because they either did not know, or because their fathers were unemployed, disabled, retired or deceased. In any case, this 28 percent expected no substantial support from their fathers. According to these data, then, the median annual income of the fathers of students in the sample is between $4,000 and $5,000.

It is a well established fact that Black mothers have always played a very essential financial role in the support of their children. They have traditionally supplied the degree of additional encouragement—spiritual and economic—needed to get their children through school and college. Some observers are convinced that the major reason Black females are better educated on the whole than males is that many mothers often push their daughters into preparing for occupations which would make them independent. Another thing to remember: Black women as a group hold the lowest level, poorest-paying jobs in American society. This is true even on an individual community basis. Despite this, they play a major role in the educational support of their children. Most of the students with whom we talked acknowledged that their mothers were able to make relatively small financial contributions to their education, but it was often the essential margin that made it possible for them to attend college.

It is evident from data furnished by the students that most of their mothers are not able to make a substantial financial contribution to their education. According to their reports, 40 percent of the mothers earned less than $5,000 a year. About 15 percent earned $5,000, but less than $10,000 a year. Only 1 percent earned $10,000 a year and over. This leaves 44 percent of the mothers who were either housewives, unemployed or deceased. Actually, 32 percent of the students classified their mothers as housewives. In some cases we found that mothers in the housewife category worked part time on service jobs or were, in reality, partners with their husbands who were engaged in farming. Therefore, the individual income of these mothers is either very small or invisible. Essentially, then, 44 percent of the students in these colleges can expect no significant financial help from their mothers because, according to the best estimates available, the mothers of students in the sample colleges have an average annual median income of only about $3,000.

When we combine the incomes of the fathers and mothers, we get a somewhat healthier picture of the economic status of the homes from which the students are recruited: fifty-nine percent (59%) of the homes had a combined income of less than $5,000 per year; 31 percent earned between $5,000 and $10,000 per year, and about 10 percent had a combined income of $10,000 per year and over.

The general economic status of the homes from which the students are recruited varies somewhat from college to college, but the difference is not significant unless we compare the highest average at one or two colleges with the lowest average at another. For instance, at one extreme only about 60 percent of the students in an all women's college came from blue collar homes where parents are engaged in manual or service work. At the other extreme are rural-oriented colleges where practically all of the students responding to the questionnaires came from working class homes. Also, whereas almost a third (31%) of the women's college students came from homes where the combined incomes of the parents is $10,000 and over, less than 5 percent of the students from rural-oriented colleges came from such homes.

In trying to assess the importance of the parents' income for the higher education of their children, it is necessary to consider a basic intervening variable—the number of children in the home. We found that a majority of the Black students in the sample colleges came from families where there are four or five children. The statistical average is four children per family, with 48 percent of the families having five or more children; 18 percent of the homes have eight or more children. It should be remembered that, on the whole, families represented in these colleges are about 30 percent larger than the average American family. This means that some of the families with annual incomes between $8,000 and $10,000 still find it difficult to pay the high cost of sending their children to a private Black college.

Another point: more than a third, actually 36 percent, of the students come from broken homes. Their distribution according to family structure is as follows:

Parents' Marital Status

Living together	64%
Divorced or separated	17%
Father deceased	12%
Mother deceased	4%
Both parents deceased, reared by relatives, etc.	3%
	100%

Students indicated at least four different types of broken homes. The most frequent was divorced and separated parents. In some instances, students reported that their fathers were deceased when in fact their fathers were simply unknown to them. Whatever sociological classification of broken homes may be used, one economic fact stands out: the median annual income of homes where the father is not present is considerably lower than for homes where the father is present—just $3,500 compared with the overall median of $5,000.

In any case, according to the most reliable information available, only 15-20 percent of the students came from homes where their parents were financially able to pay their expenses in a private Black college. Even some of these would have to make difficult sacrifices in order to do so. Another 20-25 percent of the students came from homes where parents could afford to pay a substantial proportion, but not all, of their college expenses (from 50-75 percent). Between 75 and 80 percent of all students came from homes where parents could not afford to send them to a private Black college without very substantial aid. When asked to name the source(s) of their support, just 20 percent of the students indicated that their parents paid all or nearly all of their college expenses. All of the other students had to find other sources of funds to pay some significant proportion of their expenses. Among the most reliable sources they identified were loans, scholarships, gifts from organizations or religious denominations, and individual employment. Many of the students had received funds from all available sources. One student voiced the complaint of many when he said: "When I graduate from here I'll owe everybody who will lend me money. I'll be working for others for the first five years."

Almost half of the students depended to some extent on earning money to help pay their college expenses. Between 7 and 8 percent of the students held what amounted to full time jobs while carrying a normal schedule of courses; they worked off campus from 20 to 40 hours per week. An additional 29 percent of the students held part time jobs on the campus. Little time and energy were left for the achievement of academic excellence, to say nothing about participation in extra-curricular activities.

The fact that Black colleges recruit the vast majority of their students from the lower socio-economic classes is their most distinguishing characteristic. Their commitment to provide higher education for academically and economically disadvantaged Blacks has some unique inherent problems not normally encountered by white colleges. The central problem is this: traditionally private white colleges, like colleges and universities throughout history, were established primarily for children of the elite or "ruling" families and for the more talented, ambitious, fortunate children from the upwardly-mobile middle class. While the admissions policies of these colleges are much more liberal today, these policies are still relatively rigid. They are still middle class oriented in that they avowedly prefer to recruit their students from complimentary affluent homes. Their admission policies clearly suggest that, for the most part (though in recent years they have been frequently disillusioned), they expect their recruits to bring with them a firm commitment to established middle class values, the advantage of superior high school education, and impeccable standardized tests credentials.

Black colleges have never enjoyed the luxury of admitting only those students adjudged to be middle class or middle class oriented, and, as we shall see later, few of their recruits have impeccable high school and test credentials. The very opposite is more often true: the great majority of students enrolled in the sample colleges come from the wrong side of the tracks, so to speak. They are products of lower socio-economic class homes, usually trained in the lowest ranking high schools, and socialized in a disesteemed Black sub-culture which differs in some important respects from middle class white culture.

The truth is, Black colleges have always had to practice modified open enrollment. While they have succeeded in establishing some fairly stable admissions practices whereby students with the best academic records are admitted first and those with the more doubtful credentials are admitted only to secure the number of students desired for the freshman class, their admissions policies have remained flexible. There have been times when the academic potentials within a given student body have been much higher or lower than at other times.

This type of open enrollment policy on the part of Black colleges is a major reason why they have never received the measure of academic respect and recognition they deserve. This is certainly a characteristic that Jencks and Reisman singled out as an indication of their inferiority.[14] It is not surprising, then, that at the present time the possibility of open enrollment policy being adopted by an increasing number of influential, prestigious colleges and universities throughout the nation is causing great alarm in some conservative quarters. Many top educators, politicians, and just ordinary alumni contend that such a policy, whereby a high school diploma will guarantee admission to college, would certainly corrupt academic standards and the colleges' traditional exclusiveness.[15] Yet, despite strong voices to the contrary, the philosophy of open enrollment is being cautiously adopted in one form or another. Since Black colleges have always practiced a form of open enrollment, this may be an innovation in higher education in which they, with proper funding and improved staffing, can lead the way. This could be these colleges' greatest, most far-reaching contribution to the democratiziation of higher education in American society and to emerging educational systems in so-called developing societies. The challenge is to make open enrollment work while maintaining high academic standards.

Education of Parents. Another indication that the vast majority of students in the sample colleges are recruited from lower socio-economic status homes is the fact that their parents are poorly educated according to normal expectations in American society. This can be seen in Table 1.

Table 1
Education of Parents

Level of Education	Father	Mother
	%	%
Elementary school or less	33	17
Some high school	24	27
Business or trade school	5	5
High school graduate	19	26
Some college	8	10
College graduate	6	9
Graduate and professional degree (s)	5	6
Total	100%	100%

To some important extent, the amount of education received by the individual is the most reliable measure of his socio-economic potential in American society. It is perhaps *the* most important determinant of social status in the world of Black Americans. Accordingly, we may conclude that from half to two-thirds of the students in the sample come from lower socio-economic class homes. That is, 62 percent of the fathers and about half of the mothers have received less than a high school education. Just 27 percent of the fathers and 36 percent of the mothers are high school graduates or college dropouts. This leaves just 11 percent of the students whose fathers are college graduates and 15 percent whose mothers are college graduates. Only 5 percent of the fathers and 6 percent of the mothers hold graduate or professional degrees. A negligible number holds the doctorate in any field.

Looked at from a national point of view, we find that parents of students in the sample are not nearly as well educated as parents of white students in American colleges. For example, only 38 percent of the fathers of students in our sample have a high school education or beyond, while 74 percent of white college students' fathers are high school graduates or beyond. The differential is somewhat less pronounced, but still great, when we compare the schooling of mothers. Eighty percent of the mothers of white college students had graduated from high school or beyond.[16] For students in our sample, just 51 percent of the mothers were high school graduates or beyond. It is interesting to note that both white and Black students come from homes where the mothers are on the average somewhat better educated than the fathers. This is much more pronounced, of course, when we compare the education of fathers and mothers of students in our sample.

Again, we may underscore the fact that the education of parents of students in the sample colleges indicates that these colleges do in reality practice open enrollment. Except for an apparently slight preference for students whose mothers are somewhat better educated than the average Black American woman, the students are recruited from homes that are representative of all social classes characteristic of the Black population in the communities in which tier parents live.

As we have noted, students in the sample are mostly first generation college people. This has far-reaching interpretative significance. One category of data may serve as an illustration: only 18 percent of the students reported that their parents played the major role in helping them choose a college (2% indicated the father and 16% the mother). In other words, 82 percent of the students did not rely upon their parents to help them decide what college to attend. Analysis of the data on this point reveals that the higher the educational level of the parents, the larger the proportion of students who cited them as the "most" important persons helping them decide to attend a given college. Only 6 percent of the students whose parents have elementary school education or less said their parents were most influential in helping them choose a chollege, compared with 34 percent of the students whose parents are, themselves, college graduates. According to data the students furnished, instead of advising their children themselves,. some parents had them seek the counsel of high school teachers, counselors, and so forth, whom they regarded as better qualified.

One important reason, then, why some of the students did not have their parents help in the selection of a college may be that they did not regard their parents as being sufficiently informed to give them such advice. There is, of course, an additional sociological interpretation: children in socio-economically deprived homes must often grow up early in order to assume adult responsibilities quickly. Therefore, choosing a college without the benefit of their parents' advice may be simply a logical extension of their conception of adulthood.

In-depth interviews with students revealed another important role parents played in helping their children decide upon a particular college. On the one hand, non-college parents were more likely to see a college education from afar and to regard all college degrees as equal. When asked about the role of their parents in helping them select a college, students from such homes usually concurred that their parents were basically pragmatic in that they were concerned with how much it would cost to attend a given college compared to others, and how long it would take to graduate and get a job. No student in this category reported that their parents were primarily concerned with such intangible qualities as the prestige of the college, its faculty, or even its academic standards. On the other hand, college educated parents, though also concerned about the tangible, pragmatic aspects of their children's education, seemed primarily concerned about the quality of education they could expect in different colleges. Usually such students reported that they and their parents went through months of agonizing before a given college was finally chosen. Some even went with their parents to visit a number of colleges before making a decision. Quite often college educated parents emphasized special reasons for wanting their children to choose a particular college. The strongest such reasons were that a given college is their (the parents') alma mater, that it would be best suited to the student's ability or past academic achievements, that it would provide valuable social contacts, or that the college is prestigious.

It is very significant that just 6 percent of the students indicated that college recruiters played a major role in their choice of a college. After talking with students and officials in the sample colleges about recruitment policies and practices, it seems fair to conclude that on the whole their present recruitment programs are ineffective and seldom evince any innovation or real imagination. These programs are poorly financed, routine, and poorly organized. Almost none is designed to counsel with parents. This is badly needed since, as we have pointed out, many parents simply are not qualified to give their children the advice they need in selecting a most suitable college.

Religious background. On the whole, students in the sample came from church-oriented homes. About 90 percent reported that one or both of their parents belonged to some church. Prac-

Table 2

Religious Preference of Parents and Students

Religion	Father %	Mother %	Student %
Methodist (all branches)	25	25 ·	24
Baptist	53	50	50
Episcopal	2	2	4
Presbyterian	2	2	4
Lutheran	2	2	4
Other Protestants	4	4	4
Catholic	6	7	11
Jewish	1	—	1
Not stated	9	12	6
Total	100%	100%	100%

tically all of the students indicated that they attended church regularly as children.

Traditionally, Black church-related colleges have recruited students without regard to religious background. This continues to be the practice, as can be seen in Table 2 above regarding Black Methodist colleges.

The large majority (75%) of students in Black Methodist colleges came from other than Methodist homes. Half of them were Baptist and the others reported membership in just about all other Protestant denominations found in their communities. So far as could be ascertained, this pattern is characteristic of all Black church-related colleges. That is, they generally recruit students with little or no obvious preference in regard to their denominational affiliations.

Generally speaking, students in these colleges remain in the denomination of their parents; only a few students in the sample changed to other denominations. Interviews with students who had already changed their religious affiliation or were planning to change some time in the future, revealed two distinct reasons for change:

Social mobility. Some students were reared in what might be classified as low status churches, or even cult-type churches. These students seem to have the most complicated struggle in the establishment of a satisfactory religious identity. Quite often they were reared as fundamentalists insofar as religious beliefs and practices are concerned, and, for the most part, they acknowledged that they continue to feel more comfortable in that type of religious atmosphere. Several with whom we talked expressed the desire to remain loyal to the churches of their parents, yet they were usually ambivalent because they felt that other college people would "look down upon people who go to ghetto churches," a student leader expressed it. He also added that "many instructors make slurring remarks about the preachers, members and services of ghetto churches." Such students are likely to renounce religious practices altogether or join avowedly higher status churches in the college community.

Protest. Most of the students in the sample were highly critical of organized religion in American society. They seemed especially disillusioned with what one group agreed to be the "bourgeoisie posture" of the Black church. Thus, whereas most of them claimed some church affiliation, a large number had no sustained involvement in the programs of any given church. When asked how often they attended church, students gave the following answers:

Regularly (at least once a month)	50%
Occasionally	30%
Seldom or never	14%

The proportion of students attending church regularly varied to some extent from college to college. Generally speaking, students in rural-oriented colleges attended more regularly than students in the urban-oriented colleges. However, on each of the campuses from a third to half of the students with whom we talked expressed some measure of dissatisfaction with the Black church, and non-attendance at church services seems to be their means of protest.

Another more positive means of protesting against what many students regard as socially inept denominations is to join the militant Black Muslim movement. Only a few students (less than 1%) in the sample colleges were bonafide members of the Black Muslim religion, but a larger number were apparently quite sympathetic with the basic ideology and programs of that movement. A group of student leaders agreed with a spokesman who said:

> I go along with about everything they stand for. They understand the depraved white man better than anybody else. They also know better than any other Black group that Black people must look out for themselves. The only thing I don't like is that they try to put down everyone who disagrees with them. I don't like dictators.

Despite the small number of Black Muslims in the sample student bodies, they have played a considerable role in undermining traditional religious beliefs, spreading the doctrine of racial separatism, and increasing students' distrust of the Black middle class. Another point: there was no evidence that the Muslims, as a group, played a significant part in the anti-administration, anti-college demonstrations which took place on some of the campuses. Interviews we had with members of this group indicated that they were primarily community-oriented and spent little time or effort in campus politics. Evidently they are well-disciplined and do not feel as free as other students to participate in poorly-defined campus demonstrations.

There has been a drastic decline in the religious life on the campuses of private Black colleges. Only 23 percent of the male students and 25 percent of the female students in the sample reported that they participated at all in the religious life of their campuses. This decline in religious activity was noted by most college officials, especially college chaplains. They generally agreed that insofar as viable religious behavior is concerned "god is dead" on their campuses. Their opinion was based upon the fact that, for the most part, students refuse to attend regular religious services and manifest no sincere interest in carrying on traditional religious activities on the campus. Almost all college officials reported that students flatly rejected the moralizing and preachments inherent in most traditional religious services, and such services have little or no sustained student support. There was no evidence that students on these campuses were turning to esoteric cults and unorthodox religious behavior as is the case on some large white university campuses. In fact, campus leaders usually expressed considerable distrust of religious unorthodoxy and radicalism such as that expressed by community religious cults and the Black Muslims.

NOTES

1. Earl J. McGrath, *The Predominantly Negro College and Universities in Transition* (Bureau of Publications: Columbia University, 1965), pp. 22-23.

2. The actual number of Black students enrolled in college is not known. Estimates vary greatly. The figures cited seem to be the most

plausible. Some colleges seem to "pad" their enrollment by including special students.

3. *The Social and Economic Status of Negroes in the U. S. 1970:* Report No. 394, p. 83.

4. *Public Negro Colleges: A Fact Book*, Office of Advancement of Public Negro Colleges (Atlanta: March 1971), pp. 5-6.

5. Informal reports on the social adjustment of Black students in white colleges as made to staff members of this research have since been validated by a systematic study made by Professor Charles V. Willie of Syracuse University entitled "Black Student Life on White College Campuses" (Unpublished manuscript, 1971). See also Gilbert Moore, "The Dot and the Elephant," *Change Magazine*, Vol. 4, No. 3, April 1972, pp. 33-41. The author points out that the "378,000 Black students attending white institutions in 1970 amounts to a paltry three per cent of the 8,000,000 . . . in the national student body."

6. Michael Meyers, "The New Black Apartheid," *Change Magazine*, Vol. 4, No. 8, October 1972, pp. 8-9.

7. Christopher Jencks and David Riesman, "The American Negro College," in the *Harvard Review*, Vol. 37, No. 1, 1967, pp. 21-22.

8. Robert K. Merton, *Social Theory and Social Structure* (Glencoe, Illinois: The Free Press, 1949), pp. 20, 182-183, 475-490.

9. See James S. Coleman and others, Equality of Educational Opportunity (Washington: U.S. Department of Health Education and Welfare, U.S. Office of Education, Government Printing Office, 1966).

10. Daniel C. Thompson, "Our Wasted Potential," *The Dillard Bulletin*, Vol. XXIV, No. 4, April 1960, p. 1.

11. *The Social and Economic Status of Negroes in the United States, 1970*, Report No. 394, p. 81.

12. E. Franklin Frazier, *Black Bourgeoisie* (New York: The Free Press, 1957).

13. Daniel C. Thompson, "The Civil Rights Movement—1968," in Pat Romero, *In Black America*, p. 75.

14. *Harvard Review*, Vol. 37, No. 1, 1967, pp. 24-25.

15. For a provocative discussion of open enrollment, see Timothy S. Healy, "Will Everyman Destroy our University"; and Alexander W. Astin, "Folklore of Selectivity" in *Saturday Review*, Vol. 52, December 20, 1969, pp. 54-58, 68-70.

16. Alan E. Boyer and Robert F. Boruch, *The Black Student in American Colleges* (Washington, D.C.: American Council on Education, March 1969), p. 18.

5.

The Students: Campus Scene

The essential nature of the unique open enrollment policies characteristic of the sample colleges is exemplified by their
actual admissions requirements. Thus, a careful examination of
the academic background of the students revealed two basic interrelated policies:

*Little or no deterministic value is placed upon national stand-
ardized test scores.* This fact is particularly evident with regard
to the Scholastic Aptitude Test (SAT), which is widely used by
colleges as a major device in the selection of students. Though the
mean score of students in the sample colleges varies somewhat
from one college to another and from year to year among students
in a given college, none of the colleges seems to have an established cut-off score. In each of the colleges the mean score of the
student body is quite below the 400-500 usually regarded as a
minimum admissions requirement by private colleges in the nation.
While the scores made by individual students in these colleges
range from the lowest possible (200) to the middle 600s, the
average in each college is in the 300s. The record shows that in

one college no student in the 1969-1970 freshman class had a score above 300. In another college there were just two freshmen who had scored in the 600s. A score of 600 or better is rare among these students.

All in all, only about 10 percent of the students in the sample colleges had scored as high as 400-500 on the SAT. When asked to interpret this fact, admissions officers pointed out several reasons why these colleges rely so little upon SAT scores in the selection of students. All admission officers called attention to what they regarded as essential weaknesses in the SAT. They agreed that it is weighted in terms of middle class norms, biased in favor of students with urban experiences, and not designed to test unique abilities or measure academic motivation. Furthermore, practically all administrators and teachers who commented about the use of standardized tests in the selection or ranking of Black students gave many convincing examples to prove that such tests are too often invalid. They pointed to students who did very poorly on standardized tests, yet later achieved great academic success in college and subsequently in graduate and professional schools. They tended to concur, however, that, as a rule, their students who made the highest scores on the SAT, or some other standardized tests, usually made the highest grades in college.

It is interesting to note that despite the well-thought-out criticism officials and teachers in the sample colleges directed against the SAT as a valid admissions instrument for Black students, these colleges continue to use it and acknowledged that they desire to have a much larger number of students who make high scores on it. All of the colleges offer some special inducements to high school graduates with average or above average SAT scores. For example, at least one of the sample colleges has a special scholarship program whereby full scholarships are extended to high school graduates who score 500 or more. Such students can retain this scholarship for four years if they maintain a "B" average or above. Also, one of the bitterest complaints voiced by administrative officers and teachers in the sample is that their colleges are losing out in competition with traditionally white colleges for top Black SAT performers. One academic dean lamented:

We are getting fewer and fewer students who make good scores on the SAT. Already local Black high school seniors who score in the 400-500 range are automatically offered scholarships by white colleges. The most disconcerting thing is that if they would come here we would put them in our honors program, yet they go to white colleges where they are likely to be regarded as "high risk" students.

Consequently, while all of the sample colleges would like to have a larger number of students who have high SAT scores, high school graduates with very low scores are admitted without prejudice.

Insofar as the students' high school records are concerned, private Black colleges seem to have a kind of gradient admissions policy. That is, students with the higher grades are admitted first and then the grade standard is lowered almost point by point, until the particular college has admitted at least the minimum number of students desired for the freshman class. From time to time, these colleges have lowered the cutoff level of high school standing to the point that a high school diploma *per se* is sufficient credentials for admission. Therefore, according to certain achievement tests (particularly the California Achievement Test), the great majority of students in the freshman class perform on an achievement level considerably lower than that expected of high school graduates. For instance, in 1969-1970 the average freshman in the sample colleges was about two years below the national norms, or about 10th grade level, insofar as reading and mathematics skills are concerned. This estimate, of course, varied from one college to another and among students in the same college at different times. The highest average was reported for students in one of the colleges between 10th and 11th grade in reading achievement and 9th and 10th grade in mathematics skills. The lowest average was for students in another college who scored 8th or 9th grade in reading and 6th or 7th grade in mathematics skills.

SCHOLARSHIP

A proper evaluation of the academic performance of students in the sample must naturally take into account the fact that 92 percent are products of public schools. Fully 90 percent graduated from all Black high schools located in the South, which are still notoriously inferior by regional and national standards. About 7 percent of these students are products of church controlled schools, mostly Catholic, and just 1 percent are graduates of private high schools. In addition, 35 percent graduated from small high schools with less than 100 members in their senior class; 50 percent came from medium size high schools, with from 100 to less than 400 members in their senior class; and just 15 percent came from large high schools with 400 and over in their graduating class. The fact that a majority of students are products of segregated public high schools in rural counties and small cities in the South strongly suggests that they are hardly as academically and socially sophisticated as would be expected of youngsters socialized in large cities, and graduates of high schools meeting at least normal standards. In order to acquire an acceptable, standard college education they must have special programs and excellent instruction designed to bridge these gaps.

When asked to compare their average grades in high school with those they received in college, the students were distributed as follows:

Table 3

Grades in High School and College

Average Grade	High School %	College %
C	22	62
B	63	36
A	15	2
Total	100%	100%

This student self-evaluation points up again that the sample colleges are generally open to all high school graduates. On the one hand, despite the general inferiority of the high schools represented, 22 percent of the students in these colleges graduated on or near the bottom of their high school classes. On the other hand, 19 percent of the students received some kind of honors or awards from their high schools.

It is very important to note that the academic standards maintained by the sample colleges are apparently much higher than those in the high schools from which their students are recruited. The two extremes on the scholarship continuum illustrate this. For one thing, only 22 percent of the students averaged Cs in high school, yet 62 percent of them were making Cs in college. At the other extreme, while 15 percent of the students made As in high school, only 2 percent were making As in college.

Finally, when students were asked how well they thought their high schools had done in preparing them for college they answered as follows:

Did a very good job	25%
Did a fairly good job	58%
Did a poor job	17%

During interview sessions several students discussed their high school preparation at length. Even those who praised their former high school usually pointed out certain serious deficiencies in their training. Perhaps the most frequently mentioned weaknesses were: their high schools did not prepare them to study independently; their reading had been too narrow; they had too many inefficient teachers, especially in mathematics; and the physical plant and facilities in their high schools were inadequate.

In order to get the students' evaluation of the quality of academic life on their campuses, they were asked to identify what seemed to them to be the main orientation of their fellow students. Only 24 percent felt that students on their campuses were mainly serious students who were anxious to get the best education available. The largest proportion of students (40%) felt that their fellow students were primarily interested in simply getting the necessary credentials to qualify for some vocation after college, and 36 percent insisted that most of their fellow students were mainly interested in the social life and non-academic activities on the campus.

During many interviews with students and teachers we probed into the essential nature of the academic life and atmosphere of the campuses visited. For example, knowing that most of the students came to these colleges with serious reading problems, we talked with many students and librarians in all of the colleges about students' reading habits. So far as we could ascertain, only from a fourth to a third of the students use the college library frequently or attempt to do any serious reading or research beyond minimum class requirements. About half seldom use the library unless they are preparing some assigned written report or term paper, and perhaps a fourth never use the library for any sustained period of time. The librarians were generally convinced that a large proportion of the students—maybe the majority—have not learned to use the library effectively.

According to information from several authentic sources, students in the sample colleges may be divided into three well-defined academic categories:

The intellectually oriented. From 10 to 15 percent of the students may be classified as serious intellectuals. They were determined to succeed in college and qualify for graduate or professional school. Generally they expressed great concern about the quality of education they were receiving in their particular colleges. They were quick to praise those they regarded as good teachers and to criticize those they classified as poor. The intellectually oriented students usually volunteered to evaluate the curriculum they were pursuing and always offered suggestions about how it might be improved.

The pragmatically oriented. At least a majority, maybe even two-thirds, of the students with whom we talked and about whom we acquired extensive data were crass pragmatists. Just about all of the attitudes they expressed concerning education in general and their own education in particular were pragmatic. To them, a college degree is important because directly or indirectly it is a necessary credential for acquiring a good job.

Ironically, the rigid pragmatism some students evinced tends to militate against the attainment of their singular occupational goal: in their pursuit of a degree rather than an education they usually avoid taking enrichment courses or courses in other disciplines unless they are specifically required for the degree. Even when they must take such courses they do so under covert or overt protest, and tend to perform in a more or less perfunctory manner. The result, of course, is that they seldom get more from such courses than passing grades. Consequently, pragmatic students generally do very poorly on standardized tests where a command of broad areas of knowledge is expected. The outcome is inevitable: failure to pass required tests prevents most pragmatic students from qualifying for the graduate school in which they could be prepared for the occupation of their choice, or for a satisfactory job immediately upon graduation from college.

The anti-intellectuals. From 20 to 25 percent of the students in the sample were avowedly anti-intellectual. Most of those interviewed made no attempt to conform to accepted standards of speech or academic logic. Instead they often used slang and cliches, preferred colloquialisms, and deliberately rejected logic and reason in the discussion of issues.

Very few of these students manifested any sincere interest in the content of the courses they were taking or even in the broader fields in which they were majoring. They generally refused to participate in discussions of current intellectual issues which were of interest in the broad college subculture unless those issues impinged directly upon them as individuals.

Some of these students were hard pressed to verbalize why they decided to attend college in the first place. When prodded they gave superficial reasons such as pressure from some family member; "it was the thing to do;" "some of my good friends were going to college;" "I couldn't find a job;" or "I had a good offer of financial assistance." All agreed that they wanted a college degree but expressed some serious dissatisfaction with having to work so hard to get it. Evidently, they seemed to dislike all teachers who insisted upon maintaining high academic standards and saw little value in the "hard courses" they were required to take.

Students in this category constitute the so-called difficult fifth in their colleges. They made up the bulk of those who were usually described as unmotivated, disinterested, undisciplined, and maladjusted among the students. They were prone to challenge all of the existing rules, regulations, requirements, and traditions of the college. They were always prominent, enthusiastic followers, and occasionally leaders, of any movement where students were agitating for changes in academic regulations, the abolition of precise academic standards, the repealing of social regulations, and the harassment of administrators and teachers.

ACADEMIC CLIMATE

Competition is a basic theme in American culture. As a rule, success-oriented individuals experience continuous pressure from others with whom they are in constant competition, directly and indirectly, for jobs, influence and special privileges. This is especially true of individuals who attempt to achieve and maintain middle class status: middle class status must be repeatedly validated and nurtured by more success. The relentless pursuit, then, of higher and higher status, with all of its inherent tangible and intangible rewards, has been the chief characteristic of middle class persons. The middle class person can never afford to "rest on his laurels," as it were. In a sense, every success is expected to lead to another greater success in a sort of endless series.

Nowhere is competition more pronounced than on the traditional college campus. There one can find competition in its rawest forms. Actually, the competitive ethos in American society generally comes to focus in the college. It is manifested in recruitment practices and continues all the way through to graduation and eventual graduate school or occupational placement. During this process students are never allowed to forget the nature and consequences of their competition. The successful college student is usually an individual who has been socialized to vie for grades, recognition, honors, scholarships, rankings, and so forth. Therefore, one sure indicator of the academic viability or academic climate on a given college campus is the degree to which students are aware of and respect each other as competitors. With this proposition in mind, students in the sample were asked to estimate the degree of competitiveness they felt prevailed on their particular campuses. They answered as follows:

A great deal	19%
A fair amount	52%
Little or none	29%

The degree of competitiveness experienced by students varied to some extent from one college to another and also according to the particular departments in which students were registered. Generally speaking, students in colleges in the larger cities were more conscious of competition from college students at large and from fellow students than were those in colleges in the smaller, rural-type communities. Also, a somewhat larger proportion of students in the natural sciences, for example, were more conscious of academic competition than were those registered in other fields.

The fact stands out that 71 percent of the students were evidently pursuing their education in these colleges in an unnaturally easy, relaxed, nonchalant academic atmosphere. This brings to focus two inherent qualities of academic life in the sample colleges: one, the great majority of these students are not success-oriented in the traditional middle class meaning of the concept; two, these students do not feel particularly threatened by the academic standards and requirements that prevail in. their colleges. Therefore, according to certain key teachers on each of the campuses, some of their most capable and talented students make no sustained effort to succeed in college beyond the mere passing of a required program of courses. They seem naively unaware of the relationship between success in college and success in the larger society. This may be due to the fact that a third or more of them were reared in homes where the family was forced to accept public welfare for some extended period of time and they are having their college education paid for out of federal funds (total financial aid package). It may be that despite the inconveniences and humiliations associated with welfare in this nation, extended experiences in homes and programs supported primarily by welfare may lead children to devalue industry and develop a distorted concept of success.[1]

In order to get a deeper look into each college's academic ethos, we asked student leaders to discuss the atmosphere which characteristically prevailed among their fellow students. It is important to note here that elected student leaders are among the more academically competent students in the sample. Their average grades were about "B−" compared with the low "C" average maintained by the students on the whole. Their higher average grades were due to a process of selection whereby most of them belonged to Greek Letter organizations which usually require better than average grades as a qualification for initiation. Further, colleges usually require about a "C+" average of students who run for elective offices. We can assume, then, that authorized student leaders would be the most reliable group of interpreters of the academic atmosphere that generally characterizes their campuses. Despite some minor differences, they tended to agree that about a third of students in their colleges were unprepared for college work when they were admitted, unwilling to perform on the highest academic level of which they are capable, shy away from "stiff" courses when possible, are often apathetic, and too often attempt to get by or simply pass their courses instead of engaging in the hard work and discipline expected.

ACADEMIC MAJOR

Just about all of the students (92%) had definitely or tentatively decided upon a major field when the study was conducted. Most had decided upon a major even before coming to college, especially those who planned careers in business, education, nursing and medicine. Interviews with several of these students revealed that the large majority had selected major fields leading to specific occupations without benefit of proper high school counseling. They were prone, then, to select mostly fields into which Blacks have traditionally gone. This is one reason why some college counselors advise students to wait until the sophomore year to choose a major. In any case, there is much changing of majors during the college years; fully 20 percent of the seniors had changed from their first choice of a major. The changes were due to two primary factors: some students discovered that they did not have the aptitude for the first major selected, and most benefitted from college counseling about occupational opportunities in other fields.

For decades most students in Black colleges majored in formal education in preparation for teaching in some public school system. Public school teaching, even now, is the most available profession for which Black students, particularly in the South, may aspire. Until recently, most other professional pursuits were more or less closed to Blacks in the South either because of segregation or the prohibitive cost of professional preparation. This inadvertently resulted in a situation whereby some of the most able Black students eventually gravitated to public school teaching. Again inadvertently, the fact that some of the most brilliant Black graduates went into public school teaching is no doubt a primary reason why the notoriously discriminated against Black public schools have been able to turn out a goodly number of highly motivated, and often well-trained, students who went on to do well in college and subsequently developed into competent professionals and leaders.

The occupational optimism generated by the sustained civil rights movement of the 1960s and favorable civil rights legislation is clearly reflected in the students' selection of academic majors. They are distributed as follows:

Table 4

Academic Majors

Major	Male %	Female %
Business Administration	24	13
Education	11	20
Humanities	10	14
Natural Sciences	23	14
Social Sciences	26	25

Records from the registrars' offices in the sample colleges support the data in Table 4: during the last five years or so the proportion of students majoring in education and preparing for public school teaching careers has steadily declined. The proportion of students selecting business administration has constantly increased.[2] Further, though certain occupations in American society are still thought of as male and others as female pursuits, there is a definite tendency for an increasing number of students to ignore these designations in their choice of an academic major. Of course, some occupations such as nursing and home economics are still monopolized by women, and the proportion of men majoring in business administration is still twice as large as for women. The proportion of women majoring in education is still twice that of men, yet the sex ratio in the traditional major areas shows a definite trend toward equalization: more women are preparing for once male designated occupations and more men are majoring in education and the humanities. The largest number of students on all campuses are majoring in the social sciences. This is especially true if we include business administration, which is also regarded as a social science in the sample colleges. The largest department is sociology, which is attracting some of the most militant, able students. The fresh attraction of sociology is due largely to the fact that Black students are more than ever socially conscious. A growing number of them are beginning to define relevancy in terms of basic social problems and social change. More and more of them are accepting the principle of involvement as a cardinal social value. Even students who major in other fields usually elect some social science course—particularly those which deal with social problems and the Black experience.

ACADEMIC OUTLOOK

Most of the students in the sample are graduates of segregated high schools which prepared them poorly for successful competition in college. Yet despite this glaring handicap, a significant number of them were optimistic about their chances of going beyond the college degree to the completion of graduate or professional education. This can be seen in the table below:

Table 5

Plans for Post-Graduate School

Stage of plans	All Students	Sex		Grade Average		
		M	F	C	B	A
	%	%	%	%	%	%
Definitely yes	21	30	17	15	32	40
Probably yes	49	43	50	49	57	50
Uncertain or no plans	30	27	33	36	11	10
Total	100%	100%	100%	100%	100%	100%

About a fifth of the students definitely planned to continue their education beyond college. About half desired to do graduate study, but felt that they would not have the financial resources to do so or that their grades were too low. As a rule, male students were more optimistic or ambitious than female students and students with higher college grades were more optimistic than those with lower grades. Nevertheless, a significant proportion of students (70%), regardless of sex or grade averages, aspired to acquire a graduate or professional degree if they could manage to do so.

The fact that 15 percent of the "C" students definitely planned to do graduate work, and another 49 percent still entertained some desire to do so, strongly suggests that they were not reality-oriented. Interviews with several students revealed something about the nature of their unrealistic optimism. Some who graduated from high schools where they had experienced little or no sustained academic competition tended to remain uncommonly naive about general academic values and standards which prevail in higher education. They knew, for example, that high grades would make it easier for them to get into graduate or professional schools, but many believed that a strong letter of recommendation from a college teacher or official would be sufficient to guarantee their acceptance, regardless of how low their overall grades would be upon graduation from college. Others manifested an almost complete disregard for academic rules and established standards. Somehow they appeared to project this lack of respect for established standards and regulations to all college and university officials. They often implied that all they needed to do in order to get into a graduate school of their choice was to have enough money to pay the expenses. When reminded that just about all graduate and professional schools recruit only those students who make honors grades in college and who score high on selected standardized tests, one student evidently voiced the opinion of others in the group being interviewed when he said: "That's pure racism. Those tests were designed for whites—not us. We are going to change all of that." This and other such statements implied that some students in the sample were optimistic about attending graduate school because they believed that certain rules would simply be set aside for them. There were students with the lowest grades who seemed confident that they would be admitted to some of the most prestigious graduate schools in the nation.

As a rule, the higher the classification of the students the more realistic they were about their chances of going on to graduate school. Thus, when students on all academic levels were asked about their intention of going on to graduate school after college the following pattern emerged:

"Definitely yes"

Freshmen	50%
Sophomores	35%
Juniors	27%
Seniors	11%

This increasing realization of their academic inadequacies is no doubt a major reason why the morale of students in the sample seems to get lower and lower as they proceed through the levels of classification toward graduation. Many students, particularly upper-classmen, manifested great anger with their college. Somehow they blamed their college for their own failure to qualify for some good job or for the graduate school of their choice. Thirty-eight percent (38%) of all students, and 61 percent of those with low grades (C− and below), complained about the content of courses they were required to take and/or about their teachers. One student attempted to give a summary interpretation of what he claimed to be the majority opinion among students on his campus: "These students are not fools. They know that most of their courses are irrelevant. Even when we get into a good course the teacher is usually lousy. I know some really good students who have just given up. They don't even try anymore."

When asked to rate the teachers in their college and those in their particular major disciplines, the students responded as follows:

In the College		*In their Discipline*	
Generally Superior	24%	Generally Superior	34%
Generally Average	35%	Generally Average	60%
Generally Inferior	41%	Generally Inferior	6%

While the students were much less critical of teachers in their major disciplines than they were of the teachers in their college on the whole, they still gave a majority of their teachers very low ratings. Interviews with a cross section of students revealed that in some instances they attempted to give a fair appraisal of their teachers. In other instances, students were obviously using their teachers as scapegoats for their own failure to measure up to what they discovered to be more or less rigid academic standards.

STUDENT-TEACHER RELATIONSHIP

The basic rationale for the small college is that it provides maximum opportunities for students to benefit from contacts with teachers. It is believed that sustained interaction between students and teachers will considerably enhance the students' chances of achieving academic success. It is then indeed significant that at the time of the study there was a critical alienation between many students and faculty in the sample colleges. When the students were asked to give the number of teachers with whom they had developed a personal, face-to-face relationship they gave the following responses:

With none	46%
With only one	15%
With two	15%
With muَe than two	24%

This distribution did not differ significantly according to the students' sex, classification, or academic major. Self-imposed alienation from faculty members seems to be a widely shared norm among these students. It is, however, very important to note that 71 percent of the students with "A" and "B" grades reported having personal relationships with more than two faculty members. This suggests a rather high correlation between academic success in the college and sustained personal contacts with teachers. Also, since graduate and professional schools, as well as most future employers, will want two or more in-depth recommendations from former teachers, positive relationships with teachers may also influence subsequent occupational success.

It was not always clear whether certain students' good academic performance was due to their close association with teachers or whether teachers consciously or unconsciously selected the better students with whom to develop this kind of sustained relationship. There does seem to be a sort of interaction syndrome according to which good students are more likely to seek out teachers, who respond by encouraging them to interact. It appears that good students are more likely to feel comfortable with teachers than are poor students, and their feeling of ease in interaction facilitates a responsive *esprit de corps* whereby the student-teacher relationship becomes a rewarding experience.

Ironically, students with the most serious academic problems are called upon to perform a most difficult task: they are expected to keep up with better students, which in itself may be too demanding, and they have the added disadvantage of not having the sustained personal assistance of their teachers, which is likely to be available to their more academically prepared competitors. One key problem, then, in the sample colleges is that students who most need help and understanding from their teachers are too often precisely those with whom teachers are least capable of developing sustained, fruitful relationships. In each of these colleges there was a group of alienated students, from a third to half of the student body, who seldom or never had any meaningful personal relationships with their teachers. Some never participated in class discussions, visited teachers' offices or even spoke to teachers on occasions of accidental encounters. According to department chairmen, in too many instances these alienated students either drop out altogether or stick out their college years to become undistinguished, bitter alumni. Characteristically, it has been the more fortunate fourth of the students who establish sustained interaction with their teachers who go on to graduate and professional schools.

STUDENT SUB-CULTURE

Though student bodies in the sample colleges differ in some respects from one campus to the other, and there are some significant, fundamental differences among students on each campus, the essential nature of student culture is really quite similar on all of the campuses. There are two distinct yet interrelated general reasons for this. First, today's youth have inherited and participated in the most tremendously well-organized, expensively propagandized, influential youth sub-culture that ever existed. The traits of their unique culture pervade every area of American life—from styles of dress to sex patterns, from entertainment to international politics. Second, no matter where Black college youth were reared, they tended to experience almost the same unique pattern of socializing influences. All have been conditioned to respond in a more or less patterned way to various instances of racism, and have experienced unnatural social restrictions because of their Blackness. Therefore, students in the sample have had a double base on which to develop a strong, distinct sub-culture. In the first place, youth culture has been accentuated by a full generation of war. In the second place, there has been constant pressure for Black unity which is an inevitable by-product of segregation and ensuing racial revolution. The viable sub-culture of Black students is manifested in every aspect of campus life in the sample colleges and is undoubtedly the strongest force for change in higher education, especially where Black colleges are concerned. Let us look at a few of their evaluations, beliefs, organizations and general styles of life.

Opinions about their colleges. Almost all of the students expressed some degree of ambivalence or indecision about the college in which they were enrolled. When asked to give the main reason why they chose their particular colleges they answered in this way:

Scholarship available	16%
To be with friends	10%
Close to home	18%
Good academic reputation	31%
Felt they could make better grades there	21%
Its religious affiliation	4%
	100%

Interviews with a cross section of students did, in fact, underscore the validity of the questionnaire data just presented. For example, while just 16 percent said that a scholarship offer was the most important reason for their choice of a college, at least half of them indicated that financial considerations figured heavily in their decision. The vast majority of students said in interviews that, although one reason for their choice was crucial, at least two of the other listed factors played important parts. It is interesting that just 18 percent cited "close to home" as the determining factor. The conclusion is that, as a rule, students are quite willing to leave their local communities to attend college if such is economically feasible. Many local students, especially females, told the interviewer that they would have preferred to attend a college outside of their communities. A large number of off-campus students said that they chose the college in question primarily because it was away from their home community. Several who said that they chose their college because it is close to their homes hastened to explain that this was more a family than an individual decision. Such choices were usually made because parents felt that it would be more economical to send their children to a college close to home than it would be to send them away where room and board would be more costly. Others simply wanted to keep their children at home with them.

A fifth of the students chose the sample colleges primarily because they believed that they could make better grades in them than in other available colleges. Some readily acknowledged that they would have enrolled in some other Black or white college but were afraid that they could not meet the entrance requirements or maintain reasonably high grades. Statements made by representatives on each of the campuses suggest that the lack of academic self-confidence on the part of Black high school graduates is a much more constant factor in their choice of a private Black college than the statistics indicate.

It is interesting that less than a third (31%) were primarily concerned about the academic reputation of their chosen college. Time and again students revealed a naive conception of a college education. Many evidently felt that a college degree, no matter where it is earned or how low one's average grades may be, is equal to any other such degree. To them it is a sort of union card which qualifies one for white collar and professional employment and insures high social status. Consequently, their choice of a college is not necessarily determined by that college's reputation of scholarship, but rather on how likely it seems to be to graduate in the four years allotted.

The widespread ambivalence and confusion on the part of students about their choice of a college are further revealed by the data in Table 6 which show the pattern of answers to this question: if you were graduating from high school this year what college would you choose?

Table 6
Present Choice of a College

Choice	All Students	Juniors & Seniors
	%	%
The same college	40	39
Another Black college	41	40
A white college in the South	4	4
A white college out- side the South	11	13
Would not attend at all	4	4
Total	100%	100%

It is very significant that the vast majority (81%) of the students would still prefer to attend a Black college. Nevertheless, more than half of them were unsure or dissatisfied with their choice of the particular Black colleges in which they were enrolled. These students cited several expected reasons (a sort of well-established student line) why they were more or less dissatisfied with their colleges. One might select a number of students at random on any one of the sample college campuses and predict their list of criticisms of the college in question with a great degree of accuracy. Some of these criticisms will be valid, some overstated, and some blatantly unfair. However, a close reading of their complaints reveals that there are some very critical aspects of life on these campuses which are diminishing these colleges' viability and might eventually render them academically impotent altogether. Among the criticisms most frequently cited are the following:

1. *Unclear goals.* Practically all students interviewed, whether individually or in groups, concurred that the primary goals of their college are unclear. That is, the goals are viewed as poorly defined, anachronistic, or contradictory. The most fre-

quently cited dilemma was the integrationist vs. separatist controversy. Some students felt that while their college avowedly believes in an integrated society, for example, it makes little or no effort to attract white students. Others said that while their college is dedicated to teaching Black students, its teachers and programs often demean the Black experience. One bitter student leader put it this way:

> The main goal of this college is to take ignorant Black people and change them into middle class white people. In a sense it is a great white melting pot where we are to lose our identity in the name of God and mankind. We have a different dream. We have a dream of developing competent Black people who are proud of themselves and their Black heritage.

The criticism offered by this student is also reflected in the general questionnaire data. Students were asked to evaluate the extent to which their college emphasized the heritage and culture of Black people. They responded as follows:

Too much	3%
Just about enough	20%
Not nearly enough	77%

Obviously only a handful of students felt that their college was giving too much emphasis to the Black experience, and just a fifth were satisfied with the amount of time and effort given to this type of experience. The great majority were very critical of their colleges because they felt much more emphasis should be given to the study of Black people—their history, culture and present socio-economic condition.

Since interest in the Black experience was avowedly a cardinal value in the students' sub-culture, they were asked to indicate the extent to which they would want their college to deal with the history, culture, and problems of Black people. They answered in this manner:

(a) A totally Black-oriented curriculum   15%
(b) Integrate Black Studies into every relevant
        departmental program   35%
(c) Institute a separate department of Black
        Studies   32%
(d) The college should place more emphasis on
        all ethnic and racial groups in the U.S.,
        including Black people.   15%
(e) No special emphasis should be placed on
        Black Studies.   3%

The fact that 97 percent of the students felt that their college should place more emphasis upon Black Studies than is now the case is of signal importance. This was their most salient criticism. It is also significant that this opinion was uniform among all student bodies and did not differ significantly in terms of race, sex, social background, or academic classification. White students in the sample had about the same range of opinions as Black students, and there was little or no difference in the pattern of opinions expressed by freshmen or seniors, male or female. Interest in the Black experience is certainly a central value in the student subculture. Therefore, it is indeed surprising to find that, in 1970, 76 percent of the students had never had a course in Black Studies; 18 percent had had only one course (one semester), and just 6 percent had had more than one course. This, despite the fact that all of the colleges offered at least one course in the history, culture or literature of Black folk. Thus, the question naturally arises—were these students sincerely interested in Black Studies or simply conforming to what was a popular demand?

2. *Lack of respect for Black culture.* Not only were most students critical of their college's general lack of offerings in Black Studies but they were also unhappy with their college's apparent disinterest in the Black experience as such. In order to change this posture and at the same time express their protest, students have written articles for various publications emphasizing the need for more attention to Black culture and unity. One of the unique examples of this was done by a group of students at Clark College who called themselves *"Pride"* (*People ready in defense of ebony.*)

Their publication was called *Your Mama Is Black*. This was an obvious attempt to stress the essential unity and integrity of Black people and their culture. The name of the publication is a phrase taken from a Black ghetto game called "The Dozens." The students' use of this phrase underscored their demand that the Black college's main goal should be to train students to participate in Black society for the benefit of Black people. The main goal should not be "to make them think and act white and educate them away from their poor Black brothers and sisters," as one of the student writers put it.

On another level, students in the sample colleges have instituted programs designed to emphasize their Afro-American heritage. These programs have taken the form of lectures, seminars, musicals and various types of exhibitions. One of the best organized of these programs was initiated by the "Afro-Americans For Progress," a group of students at Dillard University. These students instituted an Afro-American Festival which ran for an entire week during each of three academic years. Some nationally known entertainers and scholars rendered their services free or for mere expenses. During these festivals, students arranged art exhibits, concerts, theater productions, readings, forums, lectures, and one or two free-swinging, more or less impromptu, "Coffee Houses." All of these experiences were deliberately designed to reveal and extol the creative genius of Black people: "A glorification of Blackness," as stated by one of the leaders. Student leaders opened all of their programs to the public and saw to it that there was participation by "ghetto artists." Many school children attended the scheduled programs with cooperation from public school officials.

3. *Vocational goals too narrow*. Another of the students' criticisms of the goals of their college is: they claim that in spite of statements to the contrary, their colleges still endeavor to prepare students for a very narrow range of occupations. Some students are particularly concerned about this, because all evidence points to a more open job market for Blacks. On this point a female student remarked: "This college still assumes that all a Black woman can do is teach, and that all Black men must find jobs among Black folk. This simply isn't true . . . The administration and

faculty talk integration while they prepare us for segregation, forever."

Students want to prepare for a greater variety of vocational options. Male students, particularly, expressed great interest in new, developing vocations in the general fields of electronics, communications and management.

4. *Contradictory goals.* In one way or another, students on all of the campuses complained about what they see as contradictory goals of their college. Perhaps the most frequently cited is that regarding the colleges' avowed goal of leadership training. On the one hand, they contended that their colleges constantly remind them that they are to develop into knowledgeable, responsible leaders, while on the other hand they are often denied the opportunities needed for such development. Some students illustrated this accusation by pointing out that the authorized student government had no inherent power to make any meaningful change in the way of life on campus, and that student representation on powerful college committees was only "token at best and we are always overwhelmed by the faculty and administration." The student continued:

> If they want us to be good little children doing what our elders tell us to do, then they should say it outright. We would know then exactly where we stand. But no! They play games with us. They tell us we are taking part in a real democratic process, yet we are not a part of important decisions.

According to the students, despite the much-publicized student power movement, the faculty and administration are still solidly in control of private Black colleges. When students were asked to evaluate the extent to which their college officials controlled the lives of students, 82 percent indicated that they exerted "too much control"; only 18 percent thought that the degree of control was about what it should be.

Furthermore, 67 percent of the students felt that their college systematically punished students who did not conform to what the students regard as conservative white middle class norms. About half of them (48%) believed that most of their fellow students usually conformed to the college's conservative traditions and administrative rulings. It is significant, however, that a third of the students disagreed with this conclusion. This was particularly true of student leaders at one of the colleges. They generally conceded that "the faculty is not with it." That is, the faculty is "brainwashed" and very disturbed about the college's break with old traditions and they "just manage to tolerate us." On the whole, however, they felt that in spite of faculty disapproval they were allowed the degree of freedom necessary to "relate meaningfully to one another and the problems and culture of Black people." These students were especially proud of the courses offered in Black Studies in their college. They boasted that they were a closely-knit peer group and that a researcher from the University of California at Berkeley who had spent some time on their campus reported that "the students (at this college) have an extremely high sense of social awareness." Summing up, a student leader stated, "students here demand that fellow students should be real. One can't make it here unless he's for real." By being "real" he meant the very opposite of formal or class conscious attitudes and behavior.

While it is true that student leaders in the sample colleges seemed more aware of the relationship between student power and student responsibility than the non-leaders, college administrators tend to agree that there seems to be an increasing number of students representing all segments of the student body who are developing a strong sense of responsibility to compliment the increasing amount of freedom and authority they have attained in private Black colleges. In just about all instances where students have been accorded important decision-making functions, they have acquitted themselves as responsible citizens in the academic community.

5. *Church-relatedness.* Students in church-related colleges frequently expressed confusion about the nature of church-relatedness. Some felt that their college was primarily concerned about how it could prepare and encourage students to go into the ministry or other religious pursuits. Noting that only a few students were preparing for such vocations, a student exclaimed:

"My, the church is really getting fleeced. This is no preacher factory. That's for sure!"

Another student, who said he was known as a Black militant, volunteered this opinion: "This college is a missionary effort to brainwash Black people." He added:

> White society is afraid of bad niggers. The white power structure supports colleges like this where we can get good moral and religious training so that we can help them keep the *field niggers* from overthrowing their precious establishment. They are not interested in love. They are interested in self-preservation.

Many students interviewed, perhaps a majority, saw no real difference between their church-related college and any other college. Apparently, they have had no reason to consider the more subtle ideological foundation of their college beyond a few general statements made from time to time by some college official or visiting preacher. None could recall ever having a seminar or sitting in a formal meeting where the concept of church-relatedness had been examined. Rather, some students reported instances where college officials and teachers had attempted to de-emphasize their college's church-relatedness.

6. *Academic program.* Practically all students interviewed expressed some degree of dissatisfaction with the course offerings in their particular college. A student leader in one of the colleges made this observation:

> The toughest problem we (the students) face here is the outdated curriculum. We are required to take courses that are simply not relevant to the age in which we live or the kinds of problems we must face in this century—to say nothing about the problem of being Black. Yet we get nowhere when we try to get old courses dropped or new courses added. Getting changes in our curriculum is like winning a Supreme Court decision.

There was more or less general agreement with this expressed point of view among students in the sample. They emphasized four distinct categories of criticism of the academic program:

(a) They often complained that they did not get ample opportunities to express themselves in classes. Some said that this was due to the fact that most teachers consumed all of the class time by lecturing and little or no time was left for discussion. Others blamed large classes where a student could attend every day and still never get a chance to express himself. A few students cited authoritarian teachers who almost never listened to students or did not respect their opinions.

(b) A group of student leaders insisted that the course offerings in certain major fields were too shallow and criticized one-man departments. Thus, while a few students in all of the colleges boasted of rich offerings in their major, other students in the same college called attention to the fact that only the absolute minimum number of courses was offered in their major fields and that certain basic subjects were not offered at all. Several students who were seriously planning to go on to graduate or professional schools expressed fear that they were not being adequately prepared to pursue graduate training in their chosen fields. They felt that it might be necessary for them to take certain additional undergraduate courses before qualifying as bona fide graduate students, and that they would have special problems in trying to catch up with fellow graduate students.

There were students who had excellent grades in the subjects they had taken, yet made very low scores on national or regional standardized examinations. Some concluded that this was due to the fact that they had not been able to take the courses needed because these courses were not offered in their college.

(c) Another dimension of relevancy desired by an increasing number of students is the opportunity to do field work. They frequently expressed a desire to relate to the Black ghetto. One female student voiced a general complaint when she said:

> This college is still an island in the community. It has no
> real relationship with the people in this community. The

Black poor regard us as snobs. Our instructors act like
the masses are just evil, dirty, unfortunate people with
whom we should not come in contact.

We (the students) don't see it that way. We know that if
our education is to be worth anything we must work
with the Black poor. They need us and we need them.
This college must realize that it is a part of the community—or it is nothing at all. Relating to the people is
what a true education is all about.

The sincerity of this expressed desire is underscored by the
fact that deans of students reported that students on their campuses were, in fact, volunteering to work in Black ghettos in much
larger numbers than before. Students in the social sciences and the
humanities, especially, argued that certain of their courses should
include field work and observations as an integral part of the requirements. Also, students were beginning to open many of their
own campus activities and programs to non-college youth.

(d) The most frequent criticism students expressed about the
academic programs in their colleges was that too many courses
are "irrelevant or unnecessary."

Much of this criticism no doubt reflects the rigid pragmatism
of the students noted earlier. There was a definite tendency for
them to reject any course or academic procedure which did not
contribute directly to their competency in the specific occupations
they planned to enter or was not expressly required for admission
to their intended field of graduate study. As a rule, the
pragmatically oriented students objected to any required course
outside of their major and minor academic interests.

As we have discussed, there is a persistent, even threatening,
demand by students for additional courses in Black studies;
however, there is also convincing evidence that even when such
courses are offered the vast majority of students will not enroll in
them unless they are required to do so. Despite the fact that all of
the sample colleges offered at least one course in Black studies
each year (some colleges offered several), 76 percent of the students had never elected to register for such a course.

Teachers frequently complained that students in their colleges hardly ever elected to take any course regarded as a hard subject and deliberately avoided exacting teachers. When given a choice they mostly elected easy courses and the most sympathetic teachers. This was sometimes frustrating if a teacher suddenly decided to raise academic requirements in an allegedly easy course and hold students to rigid standards. This unexpected change in scholarship demands was one cause interviewers cited for widespread frustration and teacher castigation on the part of students. Thus, while it is true that much of the students' criticism of the academic program in their colleges was unfounded, their general agreement on certain areas of criticism strongly suggests that private Black colleges must make some revolutionary changes in their curricula if they would be more relevant to the needs of their students specifically and the demands of modern urban technological society generally.

LEADERSHIP

In order to better understand the quality and posture of student leadership in the sample colleges all students were asked to name the historical leader they admired most, and the leader who lives or lived in their own lifetime whom they admired most. The answers they gave to these two questions suggested at least four significant characteristics of their own leadership ideology and social commitment:

1. They had very little sense of history. As a rule they made no distinction between history and the present and often named the same leaders in each category—they usually ignored history altogether. Just 2 percent of the 2,342 students named such great historical leaders as Mohandas K. Gandhi, Abraham Lincoln, Thomas Jefferson, or Jesus.

There was, in fact, a strong anti-history attitude prevalent among the students. Though 6 percent indicated that they admired Black militant leaders in history such as Nat Turner, Marcus Garvey, and W.E.B. DuBois, and 20 percent named such Black historical giants as Frederick Douglass, Booker T. Washington and Harriet Tubman, interviews showed that they did not really identify with them in any meaningful way. Seldom did students say specifically what they admired about the leaders they selected. They almost never revealed any personal leadership philosophy or position which they had borrowed from Black historical leaders, or which had influenced them. Often the very opposite was true. For example, after indicating that they admired such personages as Booker T. Washington, Mary McLeod Bethune, or some well known Black scholar or writer, they would proceed to enunciate certain of their own beliefs and practices which were diametrically at variance with the central ideology and activities of these leaders. Therefore, some of the student leaders interviewed were quite baffled when they were asked pointedly: "Exactly what do you admire about the leaders you just named?" In some instances the interviewees answered this question in a contradictory manner by pointing out a number of things about the leaders which they did not admire. Even when they felt called upon to defend, so to speak, a leader they had cited, theirs was more an apology than a vigorous endorsement. This leads to another of the students' leadership characteritisics.

2. They were not hero worshippers. Despite the fact that today's Black students are likely to be more iconoclastic than hero worshipping, of all the leaders in history and in their own lifetime they might have named, 55 percent of those in the sample named Martin Luther King, Jr., 16 percent named John F. Kennedy, and 7 percent named Robert F. Kennedy. No other single leader received as many votes from the students as did these. Significantly, all three of these leaders were regarded as champions of a new social order in which all races would live and work together in harmony. Dr. King especially tended to transcend history, race, religion, nationality and age in the evaluations of the students. There was just about unanimous agreement among the students that these three leaders were martyrs for the cause of civil rights. (The Kennedys were honored because somehow students identified them with the philosophy of Martin Luther King, Jr.).

The students' identification with these three assassinated leaders was apparently quite genuine. Despite the loud, often vulgar, rhetoric about Black power, hate whitey, violence in the street, and apartheid—ghetto style, which was prevalent on these campuses during the time of the study, Martin Luther King, Jr., who is the greatest symbol of non-violence and the philosophy of brotherhood the Western world has produced, was by far the most admired leader by students in private Black colleges. This was pointed out in the following editorial:

> Following the assassination of Dr. Martin Luther King, Jr., many persons expected violence to overtake the country, particularly in Atlanta, Dr. King's home and the center of several 'Black power' groups. While it is true that violence did engulf several American cities, including our nation's Capital, Atlanta was noticeably free of strife. Clark College students had a major hand in the orderly funeral of Dr. King and the general attitude in the city that further violence would damage the contributions that Dr. King made to Negroes and all Americans.[3]

On that occasion Clark students organized what they called "Operation Respect." They wrote and distributed flyers throughout the Black community which advised:

> Riots hurt me and you Baby . . . Dr. King stood for love and understanding among men of all races and creeds . . . If we truly respect him, our responsibility, therefore is to see that his dream becomes a reality. Violence is not and cannot be the answer. (April 8, 1968)

Although Black students are not often hero worshippers, Dr. King comes closest to being a hero to them than any other person either in history or during their lifetime. He was the one leader about whom every student leader interviewed volunteered an opinion. It is also significant that hardly any student rejected his philosophy of non-violence or impugned his strategy *per se*. Instead his student critics blamed the "white racist establishment", as some phrased it, for whatever failures King may have experienced. This was succinctly voiced by an avowed Black militant, a dedicated Black Panther. He said wistfully: "King was a good man. A great Black leader. More than any other man he gave this racist society the method to change itself and the blue-print of what it should be. They wouldn't listen. They killed him. Now it's our turn." Despite much violence and rumors of violence in Black ghettos throughout this nation, and violent rhetoric and disrupting demonstrations on the campuses studied, the student sub-culture still valued non-violence as a strategy for effectuating change. The vast majority held that they would turn to violence only as a last resort. When asked to express their opinions about student protest and demonstrations on their own campuses, the students responded as follows:

Strongly approve of all of them	24%
Approve of those that did not destroy property	56%
Disapprove of methods used	20%

During interviews, even students who approved of violence as a necessary strategy because "this nation is violent-oriented" as one student put it, flatly rejected violence against persons or destruction of property on their campuses as proper means of bringing about change. Actually, all but one of the twenty student leaders who had led or participated in disruptive protests and demonstrations on their campuses insisted that such activities were a last resort. They seemed anxious to establish the proposition that if they could have gotten results in any other way they would have done so. They described what they regarded as a series of unsuccessful attempts to effectuate changes by peaceful means.

It was not always clear whether students who led demonstrations on their campuses were really sincere about preferring other measures. It is important, however, that they felt compelled to convince their fellow students that the changes sought could be realized by no other means. A few leaders themselves may have preferred disruptive, insulting tactics to more orderly procedures, but they reasoned that the masses of students would not support so raw an approach except as a last resort—an ultimate strategy. While actually engaging in psychological pressure, character

106

assassination, boycotts, and violent rhetoric these campus leaders gave indirect sanction to non-violence in the sense that they attempted to convince fellow students that they would have preferred non-violence over the indelicate pressure methods they were in fact advocating. Here again was a sort of indirect acknowledgement of the essential rightness of the principle of non-violence as enunciated by the students' most admired leader—Martin Luther King, Jr.

3. Students expressed little or no admiration for the most successful, established Black leaders who symbolized Black protest and progress during the 1960s. Only four of the 2342 students, for example, indicated that they admired Thurgood Marshall, the great Black stalwart of the civil rights movement for twenty years or more—now a U. S. Supreme Court Justice. He was successful in winning more civil rights cases before that august body than any other lawer in its history. One might have expected that Justice Marshall would have eminently qualified as a folk hero, yet he was more or less completely ignored by the students. They also conspicuously omitted naming other Black leaders who have had great success as pioneers in the established white world: just 3 percent of the students indicated admiration for such outstanding leaders as Ralph Bunche, Carl Stokes, Edward Brooke, Robert Weaver or even James Farmer, who was a popular leader of the once militant CORE, and at the time of the study was the highest ranking Black leader in the Nixon administration. When they were asked as individuals to express their feelings about such persons they generally concurred with a statement made by an honor student at one of the colleges. He said, concerning a so-called Black "first" who has had considerable success in competition in the society at large:

> All Black men are not Black. Since Black people have been raising so much hell and threatening to burn down their cities, the white establishment has been looking for representative Black leaders to display before the Black masses. They want us to believe and teach Black children that if we behave like good little darkies someday we, too, might feast at the table with nice white folk.

107

They take some of our most able Blacks and lose them
in the white establishment. Most of them belong to the
new breed of house niggers.

On the whole, students were quite ambivalent about Black
leaders who are successful in the society at large, which they often
refer to as the white establishment. On the one hand, they boasted
about successful Blacks and seemed to experience considerable
satisfaction in identifying with them. After all, this is the basic
rationale for their insistence that all schools should require students to study the history and achievements of Black Americans.
Yet, on the other hand, their deep distrust of the white establishment—which they described as "corrupt, phony, oppressive,
brutal and inherently anti-Black"—led them to suspect all persons
identified with it, even their own Black leaders. While lauding
some successful Black integrationist, for example, students also
expressed fear that he will be used against them in a sort of "Super
Tom" role. This fear was brought out by contrast in several com-
ments students made about Adam Clayton Powell. They were
often somewhat cautious about identifying with him as a person,
but they obviously admired him for standing up for Black people.
A female student exclaimed: "Even when other Black leaders, like
college presidents, were running scared, Powell was doing his
thing. He never knuckled under to white people. He has never
acted like a rabbit."

Not only were the students skeptical of Black leaders who
have become a part of the white establishment, but they seldom
expressed admiration for powerful leaders of Black civil rights
organizations. Not more than 3 percent of the students named
such key Black contemporary leaders as Roy Wilkins, Whitney
Young, Rev. Ralph Abernathy, Roy Innis, or Charles Evers.

Whenever we talked with student leaders we attempted to
find out why Black youth were generally disenchanted with
powerful civil rights leaders who have given so much of themselves and their talents—even at great risks to their lives—in their
efforts to improve the lot of Black Americans. We received many
responses. They ranged all the way from unreasoned emotions:

"They don't care about the ghetto Blacks. They just want to keep their own jobs looking after us 'field niggers'," as put by one student, to thoughtful respect and appreciation voiced by another:

> Whatever really sound progress Black people have been able to make in this country, from liberating court decisions and civil rights legislation to better jobs and better schools was engineered and masterminded by Black men like Marshall, Young, Wilkins and King. However, we have gone beyond them now. We want more than paper rights, token integration and a full stomach.

The several statements made by student leaders may be summarized into six broad categories:

First, students felt that Black men who now head powerful and respected civil rights organizations have lost their charisma. These men are thought of more as racial entrepreneurs, business executives, and political strategists than as folk leaders.

Second, Black militants often contended that the traditional civil rights leaders are assisting the white establishment in preserving a decaying, unjust system of human relations that must be utterly destroyed before Black people can secure their dignity and freedom. A group of Black Muslim students expressed it this way:

> They accuse us of trying to destroy the American social system. We don't have to. It is rotten, and has been always unjust and racist. Left to itself the system will succumb to a long-overdue death. Misguided Black men are trying hard to make the system last; thus they have joined the enemy of their own people.

Third, to many students the more established Black civil rights leaders identify with the white-dominated middle class. They are suspected of having the same kind of snobbery they claim to be characteristic of white persons in the middle class. This attitude was expressed by a student who described herself as culturally deprived. She was explaining why students did not attend a program at which a well-known civil rights leader was the speaker. She concluded:

> He was just like most other Negro leaders. He just came to criticize us because we don't dress and talk and act like white middle class kids. They don't respect us. They call us crude and a disgrace. They tell us we must act like white folk if we want to succeed in life. I don't believe that.

In one way or another, this criticism of traditional Black integrationists was voiced on all of the campuses. Their stance regarding race relations was questioned by a growing number of disciples of Blackness among the students, who insisted that they wanted to be left alone to "do our own thing." They didn't want to be white, as they put it; rather they seemed to have been convinced that the best society is one where there is racial and cultural pluralism. Some emphatically rejected the melting pot theory of race relations.

Fourth, students were cautious about identifying with well-known Black militants. Since there were a few students on all of the campuses who openly admired and regularly propagandized the impatient restlessness and iconoclastic, violent qualities symbolized by extremist Black militants, it is somewhat surprising that only 2 percent of the students in the sample named celebrated Black revolutionists among the leaders they most admired. Among the militants named by this 2 percent were Nat Turner (leader of a celebrated slave revolt), Stokeley Carmichael, Huey Newton, and H. Rap Brown, Black militants who had exerted significant influence on Black youth of their generation. This was true despite the fact that at the time of the study Black militants were very prominent in mass media and given wide acceptance on college campuses.

Interviews with students strongly indicated that it could be a dangerous mistake to assume that since they do not particularly

110

admire certain Black revolutionists as individuals they are necessarily disciples of non-violence. Rather, most students with whom we talked felt that the riots and threats of riots which were still prevalent during the time the interviews were held (1969-1970) had a very definite place in the Blacks' struggle for freedom and dignity. They often insisted that the only times when peaceful civil rights efforts were successful were when there was an imminent danger of racial violence and serious social disorder.

Although no leader came nearly as close to being a hero to the students as did Martin Luther King, Jr., conversations with them revealed great admiration for the manliness, poise and style of Malcolm X and Julian Bond. A group of student leaders agreed that they admired these men over such leaders as Nathan Hare, militant college professor and editor of *The Black Scholar*, and Eldridge Cleaver, at that time presidential candidate of the militant Peace and Freedom party, at one extreme and Roy Wilkins and Whitney Young at the other. The first two leaders, they reasoned, want revolution but offer little or no estimable program for making society better. They accused the latter two of disavowing a true revolution and placing too much faith in the willingness of white people to accord Blacks the freedom and justice they seek. Many students felt that Malcolm X and Julian Bond offered logical ways out of this dilemma. That is, Malcolm X advocated complete racial separatism where Blacks would determine their own destiny, and laid out a definite plan to achieve this end. Bond, they felt, had logical proposals for the achievement of Black unity and political power.

Student leaders on each of the campuses were anxious to weigh the merits and possibilities of Malcolm X's brand of separatism against the concept of integration with Black power and dignity they read in Julian Bond's pronouncements. While they respect both points of view, the vast majority of students in the sample look forward to an integrated society. This can be seen in the responses they gave to this question: "Which of the following do you feel would be the best or most workable pattern of Black-white relations in this country?"

111

	Now	In the Future
	%	%
Racial Separatism	18	8
Completely Integrated	82	80
The way it is now	7	12

No matter how bitter and angry these students may have been with white America, they still hoped for an integrated society where all races will be equal in status, power, and opportunity.

Fifth, students voted in surprising numbers (26%) for local Black leaders, often including family members. It is not easy to know what this phenomenon indicates. However, it does call dramatic attention to a long neglected fact: the Martin Luther King, Jr., approach to civil rights activism, which necessarily involved strong support from the local community, functioned to create and legitimize some outstanding local Black leaders. In the past, only occasionally did a local minister or teacher emerge as a strong, respected Black community leader and there was, of course, little opportunity for Black persons to emerge on the economic, political or racial ladder to the level of national leadership. Today, increasingly young indigenous Black leaders are emerging in all large urban ghettos and are demanding the right to speak for their own people and help them control their destiny. This has manifested itself in the loud insistence on community control and Black unity by certain Black leaders, which sometimes sounds a lot like the rhetoric of white supremacists. There is some reason to believe, then, that Black youth are beginning to look to their own communities for leadership, and that fewer and fewer of them accept the leadership of national figures legitimized by the white establishment. This is no doubt a fundamental reason why local Black political candidates are experiencing wide success in large urban communities throughout the United States.

Sixth, somewhat less than one percent (0.9%) of the students acknowledged admiration for contemporary white leaders. Except for Hubert H. Humphrey, Edward M. Kennedy, Lyndon B. Johnson and the Rockefellers, no other national white power figures were named by more than five of the total sample of students. None named their local governors, mayors, and so forth.

The students did not ignore white leaders in their interviews. There was hardly any student who did not volunteer to single out local and national white leaders for some degree of vilification. Certain white power figures such as George Wallace, Strom Thurmond and even President Nixon, were cited by all of the students as examples of the opposition Black people experience in this society as they press for first-class citizenship. Thus, the fact that they did not name white political figures among those they admired definitely indicates their disenchantment with the white establishment, not their ignorance of it.

STUDENT LEADERS

One primary aim or purpose emphasized by all the sample colleges is to discover and develop knowledgeable, responsible leaders. These colleges do, in fact, encourage student groups in which potential leaders may emerge and grow. Thus, there are several chartered student organizations on each of the campuses. One college, for instance, recognized 34 student organizations. The avowed purpose of this policy is to give every student an opportunity to discover his leadership potential while contributing to the life of the total campus. Students were asked to indicate the extent to which they participated in certain key student organizations. Their responses are summarized in Table 7 (page 114). As can be seen in this table, only a small proportion of students in the sample colleges may be classified as leaders. According to the most reliable information available, that furnished by personnel deans, the student leadership class is made up of about 5 percent of the students in the sample colleges. This means that, as a rule, there is an interlocking leadership whereby campus leaders are likely to hold leadership positions in several organizations. For example, one student leader interviewed was president of five campus organizations and was an officer in a few others.

Student leaders complained about the widespread apathy on the part of the masses of students. Their complaints were well

Table 7

Extent of Participation
In Selected Student Organizations

Extent of Participation	Religious	Government	Greek Letter and Student Groups	Black Unity
	%	%	%	%
Leader	8	4	6	2
Member or participant	17	29	17	8
Non-member or non-participant	75	58	77	90
Total	100%	100%	100%	100%

founded; in most instances a mere handful of students carried the burden of organizational life on each of the campuses. This is best revealed by the lack of support given the key student organization—Student Government. More than half of the students do not participate at all, despite the fact that they are automatically members by virtue of being students. In most cases, only a few student officers plus a handful of officer-aspirants attend any meetings of the student government "unless some hot issue like a campus protest is being discussed, or maybe when we gather to listen to candidates for office," as attested by student leaders on all of the campuses.

Fraternities and sororities dominated leadership on all but two or three of the campuses. Non-Greek letter students complained that in one way or another fraternities and sororities manage to have their members elected to most leadership positions. Several students blamed fraternities and sororities for the general state of student apathy. They claimed that non-fraternity or sorority students had simply lost interest in campus affairs. Thus, about a fourth of the students who are well-organized usually set the leadership tone and direction on these campuses.

So far, Black militant student organizations have very few enthusiastic leaders and almost no sustained membership. Yet, despite this, the leaders are relatively influential in the management of campus life. On occasions, especially during protests, members of unauthorized Black militant student organizations on certain campuses have emerged as the spokesmen for all of the students—superseding the authorized leaders of the student government.

There are several religious groups on each of the campuses. They usually represent the various denominations to which the students belong. Each one, of course, has a hierarchy of offices. An examination of these organizations indicated that most of them were largely inactive and almost totally ineffective in significant campus leadership.

Finally, we found that the students enrolled in private Black colleges were recruited from every major religious, familial, geographic, and social segment of the Black community, plus a sprinkling of non-Black students. These student bodies represent all levels of student qualifications, motivations, attitudes, and philosophies existing in the larger Black society. Furthermore, their commitment to higher education, professional development and social problems varies in somewhat the same manner as that found in the larger society. In a very real sense, students in the sample colleges are truly representative of the total American social system in a way that is not expected on the campuses of traditionally white colleges. Educating this democratic selection of students is the greatest challenge faced by this group of colleges. To paraphrase Abraham Lincoln's classic Gettysburg Address, we might conclude that a century ago private Black colleges were "dedicated to the proposition that all men are created equal" and equally deserving of the highest level of education this nation could provide. Yet higher education in this society was established for, and has generally remained a privilege available to, those from the most fortunate socio-economic backgrounds. Indeed, in recent years this philosophy has been revitalized by certain conservative laymen and repeatedly voiced by high ranking political figures. Consequently, the challenge before private Black colleges during the 1970s—indeed the challenge of academic democracy itself—is that they are again called upon to prove that any college "so conceived and so dedicated can long endure." Like democracy, this proposition in regard to higher education is yet to be proven. Since private Black colleges as a group have been always mass-oriented, it would seem historically just if all concerned sectors of this nation—public and private—would support these colleges in their avowed belief that higher education can be truly democratic in the selection of students while maintaining the highest standards of academic excellence.

NOTES

1. Daniel C. Thompson, "The Socialization of Upward Bound Students," an Unpublished Research Report (1970).

2. The same trend is characteristic generally. In 1955-56 "Education accounted for 66.2 percent of all bachelors' degrees. Today it accounts for only 34.8 percent." See *Public Negro Colleges: A Fact Book*, p. 5.

3. The lead editorial which appeared in the *Atlanta Constitution* on April 11, 1968.

6.

The Faculty: Social Characteristics

A century ago James A. Garfield is reported to have said: "The ideal college is Mark Hopkins on one end of a log and a student on the other."[1] Since then, the whole system of higher education in this country has experienced many significant change. Apropos to the present interest is the fact that the "log" in Garfield's theoretical formulation is today a costly scientifically-designed air conditioned building furnished with very expensive academic technology. The "student" is a much more complex, restless, powerful personage, and the symbolic "Mark Hopkins" is likely to be a highly-trained specialist whose academic and/or entrepreneurial interests extend far beyond the individual student. Nevertheless, careful, reflective analysis of the essential core of "The Ideal College" today reveals that the central fact of higher education is still the student and the teacher. The learner and the learned. This is especially true of Black colleges.

We have already noted that the great majority of students in private Black colleges are products of inferior public schools and grew up in socio-economically disadvantaged communities. Since

Table 8

Education of Parents of Teachers

Amount of Education	Father	Mother
	%	%
Elementary or less	38	35
Some High School	6	8
High School or Trade School	24	29
Some College	4	8
College Degree	15	16
Advanced Degree	13	4
Total	100%	100%

Table 9

Occupation of Parents of Teachers

Occupation	Father	Mother
	%	%
Blue Collar	51	28
White Collar	4	3
Small Business Owners and Managers	10	1
Professionals	29	16
Retired or Housewives	6	52
Total	100%	100%

this is so, these students need to be taught more or less individually by the most highly qualified, expert teachers if they are to overcome a lifetime of accumulated academic and social handicaps. Therefore, a constructive evaluation of the present status and future potentials of the sample colleges must necessarily include a

118

close look at the teachers who occupy, as it were, "the other end of the log."

Social Origins. Though somewhat more diverse as a group, the individual social origins of teachers, especially Black teachers, in the sample are quite similar to the social origins of their students. This includes place of birth, social status of parents, socialization experiences, and the fact that most of them were also products of inferior public schools. These similarities of social origins are indicated in Tables 8 and 9 (page 118).

We see, then, that the great majority of teachers came from homes that were generally like these from which their students were recruited. Approximately three-fourths of the teachers came from homes where one or both parents had dropped out of school before graduation and more than half were/are engaged in blue-collar occupations. Further, approximately two-thirds (64%) of the Black teachers were born in small towns and rural communities. This is also true of one-fourth (24%) of the white teachers. Again like the students, approximately 80 percent of the Black teachers were born in the South and so were a third (35%) of the white teachers.

The socio-economic backgrounds of most teachers in the sample colleges, and Black teachers in particular, should have eminently prepared them to identify, even empathize, with their students. It turned out that this was not always the case. For instance, teachers born on farms were likely to be as critical of, or as sympathetic with, their students' shortcomings as were teachers born in large cities. Likewise, teachers reared in middle class or professional homes tended to be about as tolerant of the manners of their students as were teachers who were reared in lower class families. Teachers born in the South were as prone to criticize or defend student protest as were non-southerners.

Perhaps the one thing that distinguished teachers in these colleges from many of their students is the fact that as a group they have been extremely success-oriented. Some have overcome just about every conceivable handicap in their drive to succeed "American style." This is a major reason why some cannot understand at all the widespread academic apathy on the part of their students. They become quite disturbed when students do not take full advantage of opportunities to succeed. They are emphatically intolerant of students who do not prepare their assignments promptly, spend too much time with social activities, and/or "fritter away their time" in any way.

Practically all of the Black teachers with whom we talked anxiously volunteered to tell us how difficult it was for them to acquire a higher education. They talked about having worked their way through college and how they made all manner of sacrifices to qualify as college teachers. They characteristically compared their own hardships with the "subsidized education of today's college student . . . No wonder we have so many who are lazy and unambitious," as a highly respected educator expressed it. Teachers commonly mused about how much more successful they might have been if they had been subsidized and otherwise assisted in the manner of today's students.

It seems, then, that the similarities between the social origins of teachers and students often resulted in intolerance as well as sympathetic understanding. Teachers who have struggled hard for an education and for whom an advanced degree was a magnificent obsession, so to speak, may understandably find it difficult to be sympathetic with the nonchalant, non-competitive academic attitude which often prevails among their students. For example, when asked to describe the majority of students in their colleges, teachers answered in the following manner:

They are mainly interested in preparing for a vocation.	65%
They are mainly serious students who want to learn and prepare for graduate and professional school.	16%
They are mainly interested in social life and activities.	19%

Furthermore, when asked to evaluate the competitiveness of their students, they answered as follows:

A great deal	10%
A fair amount	51%
Little or none	39%

As the figures above indicate, the vast majority of teachers did not respect the academic dedication and efforts of their students. Only 16 percent of the teachers apparently approved of the academic climate that prevailed among their students. As liberal arts teachers, just about all of them condemned the narrow vocational concept the great majority of their students have of a liberal arts education, and they were obviously proud of students with professional aspirations that presuppose graduate training. At least 39 percent of the teachers expressed disappointment and frustration because so few of their students manifested this ambition. They loudly lamented the fact, succinctly expressed by one teacher, that "college teaching today is terribly frustrating. Negro students talk about the virtues of Blackness and perform as inferiors."

Not only do most Black college teachers have a genuine feeling of pride because they have managed to overcome great socio-economic handicaps in the acquisition of an education; they are also proud of the social status they have acquired. This is a normal response because Black college teachers hold very high status in the Black community. Almost thirty years ago, Gunnar Myrdal observed: "Practically all Negro college teachers are upper class," and this is one respect in which "the American Negro world is strikingly different from the American white world."[2]

Even now, when Black college teachers find themselves increasingly competing with a new breed of Black professionals representing non-academic pursuits in a rapidly expanding Black middle class, they are, as a group, still accorded very high social status. This is perhaps a basic reason why many Black teachers in the sample were very critical of the "rough, uncouth manners of today's Black militants," as a woman department head put it. Not only do the majority of students deviate from the academic norms as internalized by college teachers generally, but, even more disconcertingly, they often deviate from the middle class manners most of the teachers associate with the academic subculture. This point was emphasized by the president of one of the sample colleges in a public address. Essentially he argued, "I object to the assumption which seems to be prevalent among our students that we show pride in our race by uncombed hair, avoiding the use of soap, and crude manners." He went on to advocate and express approval of the personal appearance and general manners which were characteristically exhibited by Black students in the first protest demonstrations under the leadership of Dr. Martin Luther King, Jr. At that time, they scrupulously behaved in an impeccable middle class manner.

Statements as quoted above seem to indicate that the real nature of the gap that exists between teachers and students on the Black college campus is basically due to social class values. In a sense, each group is trying to impose its social values upon the other.

Sex Composition. During the spring semester of 1969 there were 614 full-time teachers in the sample colleges. Of this number, 58 were on special assignments, such as directors of special programs, visiting professors, and so forth. There were 556 regular full-time teachers. Of these, 233, or approximately 42 percent, were female and 323, or 58 percent, were male. On the surface this appears to be a more democratic sexual distribution than one would expect to find in American colleges generally. As a matter of fact, those in the modern women's rights movement regularly protest against what they insist is unequal, discriminatory employment of female college teachers. However, underneath this facade of democracy is the fact that all of the administrators of the sample colleges acknowledged that they would have preferred a larger proportion of male faculty members. They tended to concur that the real reason for the more or less democratic balance between the sexes on their faculties is that, as a rule, female teachers are more available and their beginning salaries are usually lower than equally qualified male teachers are willing to accept.

An examination of the faculties of these colleges throughout the 1960s suggested that they were becoming increasingly female. If this trend continues, private Black colleges, like the traditional faculties in public schools, will soon become predominantly female. The increasing proportion of female teachers *per se* in the sample colleges does not mean that the overall quality of these faculties is either improving or deteriorating. Measured by any standard, some of the most competent teachers in each of the colleges are female. The actual threat to faculty quality is much more subtle. We can only begin to understand the nature of this threat by considering the underlying reasons why these colleges are recruiting a larger and larger proportion of female teachers. The most obvious reason, of course, is the fact that, generally speaking, women's salaries in this society are considerably lower than men's, even when occupational competency and experience are held constant. Despite enabling legislation, women as a group simply have not been able to demand equal salaries.

Very involved with the question of salary is naturally the degree of bargaining power the individual teacher commands. A teacher's bargaining power is a function of degree of training, prestige of colleges from which degrees were received, experience, scholarly production, status in the profession, and the quality of charisma possessed. In some instances, the bargaining power of prospective female teachers is quite weak even if they rank high in the qualities just listed. This is often due to a common situation whereby a husband, for example, accepts a position in a city and his wife, as is socially and legally expected, accompanies him. As a university trained person, she may have no opportunity for satisfactory employment in the new community except at a given Black college. Therefore, her bargaining power is compromised. Such women often accept teaching positions in Black colleges despite the very low salaries offered them.

What is true of migrant professionals is even more valid when applied to university trained females whose husbands are solidly established in a given community. Even the most highly trained wives of such men may seek positions in local Black colleges because none are available to them in local white colleges. Since there is little or no freedom of professional choice these women, too, have weak bargaining power. They are likely to accept salaries considerably below those demanded by male teachers with comparable credentials but who are potentially mobile, or free to accept an appointment in some other section of the country.

There is another easily available source from which the colleges draw a goodly number of female teachers—the public school system. Here a sort of "Peter Principle"[3] seems to operate, according to which certain of the more successful public school teachers are promoted or recruited to college teaching. Some 20 percent of the female teachers in the sample were once teachers in public schools. Usually such recruits are natives of the communities in which the colleges are located. Their potential mobility is low because of multiple ties and deep roots in the local community. The bargaining power of these native daughters is weakened and they too often accept salaries considerably lower than their formal training and experience would ordinarily demand.

There are, then, several subtle reasons why the constant increase in the proportion of female teachers in the sample colleges may well indicate a decline in the overall quality of the faculties. Basically, one reason stands out: an accumulation of information indicates that in a significant number of cases teachers were recruited primarily because they were easily available and not because they were deemed to be the most promising professional prospects. While some such recruits go on to become truly creative teachers, others simply hold their jobs from year to year. They perform their professional roles in a more or less routine, lackadaisical manner. A department head summed up what seems to be a prevalent attitude about this small but persistent group of female teachers on each of the faculties. He said:

> They are forever housewives or society matrons. The female dimension of their personalities is always dominant. Even in the most formal academic situations they behave more like housewives than skilled professionals. Most of them shy away from any duty or involvement that might interfere with family affairs.

To reiterate, according to any valid criteria of a good teacher that may be acceptable—formal training, experience, the ability to communicate with students, creative scholarship or professional dedication—some of the best teachers in the sample are female. Conversely, some of the most unambitious, effete teachers are male. The central question is not the male-female balance of the faculties but the essential quality of the teachers composing them. *The main contention is that the overall quality of the faculties in private Black colleges is deteriorating because, among other considerations, these colleges are sytematically recruiting teachers* (male and female) *who can afford to accept low salaries rather than those with high professional competence.* That is, recruitment practices are too often geared to availability rather than determined needs. Consequently, some key, academically sensitive posts are filled by non-professionally oriented female teachers simply because circumstances conspire to undermine their bargaining power. (The concept non-professional as used here is meant to describe the teacher who does not strive for classroom success, who does not regard teaching as a calling but simply as a job, and who is relatively unconcerned about his/her professional image or standing.) They often get relatively little from the college and give little in return.

Racial Composition. About a third of the teachers in the sample colleges are white, or non-Black. The range is from approximately 25 percent in one college up to 50 percent in another. Historically, these colleges have never been the focus of racial controversy; yet at the time of the study (1969-1970) a distinct racial polarization characteristic of American society had become manifest on their campuses. More and more students were becoming suspicious of white teachers. On each of the campuses there were students who charged that some of their white teachers manifested ancient missionary attitudes and generally assumed traditional paternalistic stances in their dealings with them. On at least one campus there was a prevalent assumption expressed in a student petition that "white teachers are generally inferior teachers. Otherwise, they would not select Black colleges, since they despise us (Black students) anyway." While only 16 percent of the students in the sample colleges expressed distrust and bitterness about white teachers, there were many, perhaps even a majority, who seemed convinced that to some important degree white teachers as a group do not and perhaps cannot understand the nature of the Black experience.

It is no accident that the wave of skepticism about white teachers began to take form simultaneously with the new interest in Afro-American history and culture. This was a natural consequence of what may be described as a distinctly Black approach to history. It is essentially a subjective approach—an attempt to discover in the history of Black folk a legitimacy for Blackness, a validation of the Black identity and presence in history. In other words, it is a search for the uniqueness of the Black experience. Some critical students with whom we talked acknowledged the academic authority of certain white teachers (for example, students were aware that some of the outstanding authorities in Black history are white scholars); however, they tended to reject white teachers' insight into, and/or their interpretation of, the Black experience. Black students often insisted that very few of their white teachers, regardless of the extent of their academic knowledge, had the *verstehen* or depth .of comprehension necessary to creatively grasp and effectively communicate the unique dimensions and subtle qualities inherent in the history and culture of Black folk.

A group of students in a class on "The Sociology of Black Americans" was pressed to explain why they felt that white teachers can hardly comprehend the depth and meaning of Black history while certain Black teachers are acknowledged, widely acclaimed authorities on white history. Their responses varied widely and reflected several points of view which proved to be difficult for them to verbalize convincingly. However, their many statements emphasized three basic explanations:

1. They insisted that almost all white people have been socialized to believe that Black people are inferior. One student described this process as a "lifetime of constant brainwashing" designed to instill the belief that Blacks are inherently inferior and whites are basically superior. Another student said "white parents begin to teach their children to avoid and despise Black children along with their toilet training." As a result, the students generally agreed that "belief in the inferiority of Black people has been

126

instilled in the minds of most white people since their infancy, and that this belief is as ingrained and sacred as their beliefs in freedom, democracy, and God," as one student expressed it in a group discussion.

Students who defended this point of view insisted that just about all white children have internalized the belief that their racial identify, as such, makes them superior to Black people and that they are unlikely to discard that belief because it is so deeply rooted and also flatters their ego. Therefore, they held that even surface changes in the attitude of white teachers toward Blacks would require systematic counter-brainwashing. The students speculated that most of the intimate friends of white teachers are prejudiced toward Blacks and that the doctrines of white supremacy and racism are articulated to some important degree by the various groups and institutions with which these teachers are associated. Thus, one student government leader averred:

> Even the few white teachers who grudgingly come to accept Black students as normal human beings always revert to their old ways of thinking the moment some student does not conform to their own standards. They turn out to be just another brand of white liberals who are always looking for a super nigger. If you are not super you got to be inferior.

A young Black professor endorsed these students' evaluation of most white teachers. He felt that the main barrier to white teachers' comprehension of the Black experience is deeply rooted racial prejudice reinforced by insulated ethnocentrism.

2. Lack of sustained contacts with Blacks. One of the students called attention to a fact alluded to frequently: the system of race relations in this country, North and South, is carefully and rigidly designed to protect whites—particularly children—from any but absolutely essential contacts with Blacks. Barriers between the races exist under the guise of economic, political, social, educational, residential, legal, and religious rights. No matter what kind of barrier, the result is always the same: most white people, including those who teach in Black colleges, have grown

up and taken their places in American life without ever having had any but temporary, peripheral, secondary contacts with Black people. Thus, the student insisted: "A real cultural gap exists because white teachers know little or nothing about the Blacks they try to teach. The worst part is they try to cover up their own ignorance by trying to make us (Black students) look small."

Not only did students complain about white teachers' lack of past contacts with Blacks, but some white teachers also claimed that their white colleagues do, in fact, protect themselves as much as possible from contacts with any Blacks except those in their classes. One white teacher made this comment about his white colleagues:

> I don't know of anyone but myself who ever takes an opportunity to visit a Negro home, church, a social gathering of any kind, or even Negro faculty members. Most of them try to live in all white neighborhoods. I know of none, and come to think about it that includes me, who is a bona fide member of a Negro religious, civic, social or fraternal organization.

Small wonder, then, that Black students, who are pushing for the teaching of Black studies as a basis of growing Black pride, often accuse white teachers of having only shallow, even distorted, knowledge of the Black experience. A female senior put it bluntly: "They don't teach us. They teach books."

3. White teachers tend to view the Black experience from a white historical and cultural perspective. This seems to be the fundamental reason why Black students questioned the ability of white teachers to comprehend the Black experience. Their remarks generally reflected an uneasy suspicion that white teachers would naturally judge Black experiences and achievements in terms of white middle class standards and values, and not in terms of the inherent meaning and nature of Black history and culture as such. A vocal student leader contended that "white teachers have white heroes, not Black heroes; they identify with white generals, not Black revolutionists."

Blacks, as a group, have never really trusted white people's insight into, and appreciation of, their experiences. This is cogently and succinctly expressed even in an old Negro spiritual—"Nobody knows de Trouble I've Seen." It is a central contention of practically all young Black intellectuals and the so-called Black militants. It is also evident that many whites share this doubt, because from time to time white authors or researchers contrive experiences designed to put themselves, as it were, in the Black Man's skin in order to get better insight into the Black experience, which they acknowledge cannot be achieved in any other way. However, as might be expected, Black students vented their strongest wrath against white teachers who insisted that they understand and appreciate the Black experience. One student in the class just mentioned insisted that "a person must be born Black and have Black ancestors who were slaves, disesteemed and lynched, in order to really appreciate what being Black is all about." This conviction was expressed in one way or another on all campuses.

Finally, as we have noted, there seems to be a sort of anti-history bias on the part of Black students. This phenomenon was manifested in their choice of heroes, as discussed above, and is frequently cited by high school and college teachers. The students interviewed did throw some light on this prevalent attitude. In one way or another, they expressed the feeling that history, generally, has been written to enhance and reinforce white people's high esteem for themselves and to de-emphasize the role of other nations—particularly that of Black individuals and nations—in the making of history. In the words of one student "They are hung up on their own superiority and always view other people as playing a sort of supporting or obstructionist role." Thus Black students are prone to believe that their white teachers and the texts they use are likely to view the Black experience from a white superiority perspective and evaluate it within a white-oriented frame of reference.

Some Black teachers felt called upon to defend their white colleagues. They claimed that Black students had become oversensitive and prejudiced. College presidents and deans also seemed to have felt it necessary to come to the defense of white teachers on their faculties. Some of the presidents were deeply concerned about the students' opposition to white teachers: all agreed that some of the most effective teachers on their faculties were white and feared that students would drive them off and make it difficult to recruit others. Reinforcing this concern was the fact that all administrators with whom we talked were disturbed by the shortage of potential Black faculty recruits. They reasoned that the only way they could get the number of qualified teachers demanded was by recruiting whites. Consequently, they were apparently doing everything possible to offset the effectiveness of student criticism.

There were, of course, some Black teachers and administrators who concurred with students' criticism of white teachers. Some of them pointed to instances where white teachers manifested negative attitudes toward Blacks ranging all the way from avoidance to contempt. All in all, the preponderance of statements made by teachers and administrators tended to support the general opinion of students. At least four distinct types of white teachers emerged from their evaluations:

The dedicated professional. On all of the campuses there was at least one white teacher, sometimes more, whom Black teachers and students singled out as a "good" teacher without reservations. It was interesting that some students who were most outspoken about the shortcomings of white teachers on the whole were anxious to extol the competency and dedication of individual white teachers. This apparent contradiction led the interviewers to conclude that the students were not objecting to white from a racial point of view, but to the much more subtle "white attitude" of their teachers.

The missionary type. The concept of the missionary originally referred to ethnocentric persons representing an allegedly superior culture who were professionally engaged in the enlightenment of people representing an allegedly inferior culture. This concept is very complex when applied to teachers in the sample colleges. We may identify three ideal types of missionary:

(a) The traditional missionary who has the proclivity, or the calling, to uplift underprivileged, "primitive" peoples. Ordinarily they would serve in some foreign country in Africa or Asia. For personal reasons or lack of proper connections, some with this bent decide to be "home missionaries;" a few of them seek positions in Black colleges. As a rule, they are accused of being condescending and paternalistic in dealing with their students. They are likely to regard just about all of their students as culturally deprived or culturally different. For example, a highly educated and widely respected white head of an English department in one of the sample colleges contended that "all Negroes, without respect to education and many other cultural standards, are part of a culturally different group." She defined the central problem as that of "removing them from the culturally different category."[4]

The rigid ethnocentrism inherent in the academic stance just cited was attacked by Charles J. Calitri who charged that teachers are too often guilty of attempting to impose the values of educated white, middle class Americans upon Black youth from big city Harlems. He said:

> We tell them they must speak as we do, read as we do, follow our customs, and adopt our moral values. We attempt to impose our music and art upon them and insist that they admire our technology as if the very differences that make them what they are, individuals in their own right, make them less than we instead of only different.[5]

(b) The guilt-motivated missionary who may have superior training, yet deliberately selects Black colleges because he/she tends to share guilt for the ways white Americans have treated Black Americans. Theirs is a sort of atonement for historical sins. Characteristically, these teachers "bend over backwards," as some put it, in their efforts to uplift Black students. Many of them are believed to give students flattering grades, promote various types of uplift programs, and feel called upon to go beyond the call of duty to help students. There is a tendency for them to be apologists for the shortcomings of Blacks and they never seem to give up trying to instill white middle class values and attitudes in Black students.

Students object to this type of missionary primarily because they are regarded as white middle class chauvinists. Whatever they teach, and in all of their contacts with students, they always seem to emphasize the rightness of traditional white middle class culture and inadvertently the inferiority of the Black experience. They usually manifest tolerance, but not genuine respect, for Black people and their culture.

(c) The Peace Corps type missionaries are usually young white teachers in Black colleges who seem to be motivated by the desire to do something significant to uplift the race. Conversations with a sample of them indicated that they have somewhat the same kind of honest desire to bring civilization to Blacks as some of the idealistic young people who join the Peace Corps. Just as the latter do not plan to remain among the "primitives" longer than a year or two, so these young white teachers plan to teach in Black colleges just long enough to satisfy their consciences.

Some college officials feel threatened by the presence of these young idealists. One college president said:

> Though they are bright young people, they do more harm than good because they try to change everything about the college. They feel that they already know more about how to educate Black youngsters than do our more experienced teachers who have given their whole lives in colleges like these.

According to this president the central characteristic of this type is identification with students in criticism of the Black college. They almost always latch onto student protest efforts whether they concern internal, national, or international issues. Most of them dress like the students, prefer to associate with students, and can be counted upon to join with students in any assault against tradition in the colleges where they are serving.

While I am not certain that this is characteristic on all campuses, on the particular campuses studied this type of idealistic white teacher has been subjected to as much criticism as the other missionary types. Students accuse them of being inwardly conservative in the sense that they want to change the Black college into a kind of white college, not to make it a part of the Black revolution. In other words, while white idealists concur with Black students that they do not like Black colleges the way they are now, they are likely to disagree with the students on what kind of colleges they would have them become. Thus, after initial union with Black student protesters, white idealists frequently incur the wrath of both administration and students. They often find themselves unwanted and unloved by all segments of the college community. Several expressed hurt and disappointment with Black colleges because they felt that they had been rejected by the very people they sought to help. These are the teachers who generally terminate their associations with Black colleges after very limited tenure. One such teacher, in explaining his pending resignation, expressed a general sentiment of this group when he said: "I am leaving this college because I have become disillusioned. I cannot help the students and I am opposed by the faculty. I am going to spend the rest of my time becoming a good scientist." Too often, white idealists quickly become ineffective as teachers in the Black colleges; after a short tenure most of them tend to move on to white colleges. According to Georg Simmel's formulation, this potentially very mobile group remains "strangers" in Black colleges.[6] This is primarily because their lack of stable identity with the Black experience is soon detected and usually results in their rejection and alienation by those they sincerely desire to help.

The young white scholar. On each of the faculties in the sample colleges there is a relatively small number of able white teachers who have recently graduated from prestigious white universities. For the most part, they are professionally ambitious and subject matter oriented. Some who have not received their doctorates attempt to do what amounts to full time teaching in a Black college while taking graduate courses in a local university. Others teach in the Black college while writing their doctoral dissertations. In any case, soon after the doctorate is completed they usually find employment in white colleges.

There are, of course, young white scholars with doctorates on practically all of the faculties of Black colleges. A few seem unable to find satisfactory appointments in white colleges and accept positions in Black colleges until they are able to find more desirable appointments in white schools. In a sense, they simply use Black colleges as a stepping stone in their professional advancement. There are others, of course, who apparently find great professional satisfaction in teaching in Black colleges. A few with whom we talked prefer to stay in these colleges and resist the brain drain attractions of prestigious white schools because they find their work personally satisfying and challenging.

The academic reject. Both students and teachers contended that too many white teachers accept positions in Black colleges because they have been unable to secure or retain suitable employment in white colleges. Some of these individuals have personal problems that undermine their professional competency, while others are academically inept. Yet, despite their shortcomings, Black colleges must often depend upon them to fill essential vacancies or to provide terminal degrees necessary for accreditation. There are some who believe that this might be the largest group of white teachers in Black colleges since they have been traditional objects of recruitment due to their weak bargaining power.

There are white teachers in some of the Black colleges in large urban centers like New Orleans and Atlanta who manifest little interest in the colleges as such, but accept positions in them because they are attracted to the cities. They ordinarily have little or no basic interest in the programs of the college or the development of their students. They perform formally required professional roles and return to their private lives in their segregated white neighborhoods. Seldom do they become a part of the college by developing identity with the students, teachers or alumni.

It is apparent that there are also Black teachers who would fit well into any one of the categories mentioned above. They, too, may be divided into dedicated professionals, social class missionaries (as opposed to religious missionaries), young idealists who want to change the whole academic system, and academic rejects who are unable to find comparable employment elsewhere. All academic segments of the college campuses frequently cited such types among their Black teachers. As we shall see later, with the brain drain operating as it is today, and many of the best teachers being recruited by white colleges, there is an eminent danger that the proportion of academic rejects on these campuses, without regard to race, will increase rather than decrease. The recent displacement of highly trained space scientists and the alleged over-supply of young Ph.D.s may offset the negative forces mentioned here if these colleges find the resources and develop complimentary programs to take advantage of this opportunity.

Training. Approximately 25 percent of the teachers in the sample colleges hold the doctorate; 65 percent hold the master's as the highest earned degree; and about 10 percent have only earned a bachelor's degree. An examination of the holders of the doctorate reveals that they are unequally distributed among the colleges. Nearly a third of the schools have less than 20 percent of their teachers holding the doctorate. Approximately a third of them have 20-25 percent of their teachers with doctorates, and another third claim to have 26-40 percent of their teachers holding a doctorate. In 1970-1971, only a few private Black colleges had 50 percent or more of their teachers with doctorates.

There is one very important variable to consider in the comparison of the number of teachers holding doctorates in the various colleges: a relatively weak faculty may have a larger number of doctorates than a relatively strong faculty. This is because no matter how small the college, it usually offers degrees in approximately 15-18 standard departments or fields. Thus, a doctorate heading each of the departments, where there are only two or three teachers in each, would mean a relatively high proportion on a faculty of 50 or 60.

As is well known, a certain proportion of teachers must hold the doctorate in order for the college to receive regional accreditation. Generally, a college is expected to have at least 40-50 percent of its teachers with terminal degrees in order to qualify as a "good" college. Despite small faculties, none of the colleges in the sample has the stable proportion of doctorates deemed desirable. A few of the colleges attempted to bridge this gap by recruiting part time and retired teachers who hold the degree. There is also a widespread practice of recruiting displaced foreign teachers who have some type of doctorate from foreign universities. A comparison of the types of terminal degrees held and the courses taught by foreign teachers frequently showed no correlation at all. In one college, for instance, a teacher with a Doctorate in Jurisprudence was serving as chairman of the Department of Foreign Languages. There were other instances in which teachers held doctorates in engineering or some other discipline not even offered by the college, but were listed as bona fide members of a departmental faculty.

The examples just cited are not spurious but basic to an evaluation of the faculties in these colleges, and strongly suggest that the quality of the faculty in terms of terminal degrees may not be nearly as sound as an objective listing would lead one to believe. The central question in this connection is: does the number of doctorates on a given undergraduate college faculty indicate anything definite about the overall quality of teaching? The accreditating agencies, honor societies, and all other agencies involved in higher education in this country hold to the general proposition that the larger the proportion of doctorates on a faculty, the stronger the faculty. Therefore, colleges with relatively few doctorates, as is true of most private Black colleges, must by definition be rated academically inferior.

Recently, however, there is a persistent demurrer; Black students are increasingly questioning this proposition. One student leader emphatically insisted that "The Ph.D. degree is a phony degree. It has no meaning at all in a Black university." This student leader was demanding that his college employ more Black teachers and/or teachers that understand the Black experience. He wanted the college to prefer Black teachers, "even without any degree at all but who are able to communicate with Black students over some phony Ph.D. from a so-called research university." Other students expressed about the same point of view. In one way or another, a representative number of students on each campus contended that they wanted teachers who could communicate regardless of their credentials.

While only a few nationally respected educators agree with the Black students just quoted, there is a growing feeling in academic circles that we need at least another type of Ph.D. The present Ph.D., some hold, denotes competency in a narrow field of specialization which often has little or nothing to do with the day by day subject matter dealt with in the classroom. The degree connotes more about research ability than the quality of teaching skills needed in undergraduate colleges, particularly Black colleges.

The argument continues to rage about how relevant the Ph.D. is to the teacher's ability to communicate in the classroom. It is interesting, however, that nobody claims that the Ph.D. prevents communication. There is still the widespread conviction that "no exact equivalent of the Doctor's degree exists, as is well recognized by everyone who has earned such a degree . . . Experience does not equal it, nor do years of graduate study, however long extended."[7] So long as this belief persists, colleges in the sample will have little choice but to exert greater efforts in the recruitment of a larger proportion of teachers with the doctorate. Especially desired by students and administrators are Black teachers with the doctorate. At this time, there are only a handful—not nearly enough to fill even the key academic positions in Black colleges. Even the most militant Black students are coming to realize this. Therefore, on all of the campuses visited, even students who would disclaim the traditional virtues of the Ph.D. were demanding that more Black Ph.D.s should be added to their colleges' faculties. This same desire was underscored by all of the college administrators. Some administrators said they were willing to pay such persons more than they would ordinarily budget for teachers because the need for Black teachers with the doctorate transcends the need to improve the faculty as such. Not only does the Black Ph.D. professor enhance the academic status of the college, he symbolizes racial equality and intellectual attainment—examples of which are so badly needed by Black students experiencing an identity crisis. The Black Ph.D. functions to refute the mentally inferior stereotype with which the race has been shackled. This secondary meaning of the degree "endows it with a significance which has no counterpart outside the academic life of Negroes."[8]

Teachers in the sample with the master's as their highest earned degree represent practically every major university in the nation. Also, depending upon the college's location, a significant number of masters degrees was taken at Black universities. The actual proportion in this category ranges from about 10 percent at a few colleges to 20-25 percent at other colleges. It is interesting, however, that practically all of the teachers with only master's degrees awarded by Black universities have done further study at white universities. Somehow they seem to be seeking academic legitimacy as well as advanced learning from white universities.

It is not possible to arrive at a reliable evaluation of the academic preparation of teachers just by citing their highest degrees. In a sense, they are much better prepared than the statistics would indicate. For example, 75 percent of the teachers without the doctorate have done some post Master's studies or attended special seminars and workshops designed either for academic credit or solely to enhance their teaching competency with no determined academic credit specified. Fully a third of the teachers have completed a year or more of formal graduate studies beyond the Master's. Included in this category are teachers, 19 percent of the sample, who have completed all course requirements for the Ph.D. This means that they have completed all requirements except one or more of the traditional hurdles—comprehensive examination, foreign language qualification or the dissertation. The most interesting teachers in this category are those who have completed all requirements except the preparation of an acceptable dissertation. There seems to be three general explanations for this:

1. Very often teachers in this group are professionally ambitious and try very hard to succeed in their colleges. Some, deliberately or unwittingly, find themselves involved in extensive committee assignments, special programs, student affairs, scrupulous planning for class assignments, and, in some instances, time-consuming administrative duties. Interestingly enough, teachers in this group are often among the most valuable teachers in their colleges. Not only are they good teachers but they are also quite dedicated. Some of them become so involved with the college's programs and with their students that they are reluctant to take the time off necessary to complete requirements for the degree. These are the ones who are most likely to attend some graduate school summer after summer and spend an unusually long time in the preparation of a dissertation.

2. There are teachers in this category who seem not to possess the skills in research and writing necessary to prepare an

acceptable dissertation. Some of these teachers have written draft after draft only to have it rejected. Despite the fact that some universities have dissertation seminars for Ph. D. candidates, these teachers seem totally unprepared to do the independent research required.

3. On each of the faculties there were teachers who had completed formal courses for the doctorate and simply dropped out before the final hurdles were completed. Interviews with some of these teachers established that they originally fitted in one of the two categories above. For one reason or another, they postponed the completion of the degree requirements or apparently were not able to do the kind of independent work necessary.

Among the teachers who only need to complete final academic hurdles for the doctorate are those whose value to their colleges has been established and rewarded. Without the degree they are among the highest ranking, most influential and best paid teachers in these colleges. Thus, the usual incentives to acquire the degree are mitigated. Incidentally, interviewers got the impression that they represent the most administratively oriented, conservative faculty members in their respective colleges. It is likely that this conservatism may be due largely to the fact that successful non-doctorate teachers in a given college are afraid that their value to their particular college is not transferrable to a similar position elsewhere. Therefore, their bargaining power is relatively weak.

Perhaps the most difficult to evaluate among faculty members are the 25 percent or so who receive the master's degree but never make any tangible effort toward a doctorate, or even to improve their knowledge in their given disciplines. Quite often department heads and deans singled out such teachers as dependable, competent, or reliable. They were also often cited as unambitious, bad influence but has tenure, obstructionist, and so forth. All in all, it seems that some teachers in this category, who do not usually qualify for the top positions on the faculty, either attempt to establish themselves as good teachers or become political allies of those who hold decision-making positions in their college.

Finally, in each of the colleges there are teachers who have no advanced degree. According to established faculty policy they do not qualify for an academic rank. College administrators seldom violate this policy unless there are extenuating reasons. Generally, these teachers are confined to academic activity areas such as coaching or the fine arts where individual skill and talent are uncommonly required. Occasionally, however, the colleges find it necessary to fill strictly academic positions with teachers having only the bachelor's degree. Such teachers are usually accorded non-academic ranks such as instructional assistant, lecturer, or program director. In instances where their worth to the college is established, they may be accorded the rank of Instructor.

Since the employment of teachers with only the B.A. degree violates academic policy, we made special efforts to get some concrete information about them from administrative officers. From what information we could obtain, theirs, maybe more than for any group of teachers, was merit employment. They had demonstrated competency in their fields and were seldom employed on the basis of credentials only. As a result, they usually made substantial contributions to the academic programs of the colleges comparable to that of other teachers with superior academic credentials.

Experience and Tenure. In terms of college teaching experience the faculties in the sample colleges present what may be regarded as a normal, desirable pattern of distribution: 25 percent were new professional recruits, having had less than three years of college teaching; 34 percent had from three to ten years experience; and 41 percent had ten or more years experience when the study was made. Consequently, there was the potential of a creative overall balance in terms of experience. The median years of college teaching experience among those in the sample was approximately eight. According to established regulations of the American Association of University Professors, seven years should be regarded as a sort of average for professional maturation. Therefore, the faculties in this study represent the ideal insofar as experience is concerned. There is a healthy proportion of young teachers added each year (8%), which should assure a constant inflow of new ideas and viability. At the same time, at least half of the teachers have had enough experience to qualify them as mature professionals, with sufficient wisdom to incorporate and channel the new ideas and vitality of young faculty members into constructive endeavors.

While it may be expected, even hoped, that there would exist some significant measure of creative disagreement between the younger and older teachers in these colleges concerning academic philosophy, procedures, and issues, the situation in some actually amounted to disruptive conflict. Some of the most ambitious, competent younger teachers accused older colleagues of being ultraconservative, anti-progressive—even anti-student. Some of the mature, influential teachers accused their younger colleagues of being nonprofessional, anti-administration, too student oriented, and generally disruptive of academic order. Most of the time the conflict between the younger and the more mature teachers was kept *sub rosa*. From time to time, however, the differences surfaced and revealed deep-seated antagonisms. Apparently the issue that most frequently brought out faculty division and conflict was student protest or demands.

Generally speaking, younger teachers were more prone to identify with the students and offer them some measure of support. The more mature teachers were more likely to insist upon academic order and the preservation of traditional academic standards. Nevertheless, this division among them was by no means constant and fine. According to any criterion of liberalism-conservatism, teachers representing all levels of experience may be classified in a kind of gradient pattern. That is, very few new recruits could be placed at the extremely conservative or rightist end of the continuum and their proportion increases as we move toward the liberal or leftist extreme. The opposite pattern seems to be characteristic of the mature teachers: few of them may be classified among the very liberal and their proportion increases as we move toward the conservative extreme.

It is interesting to note, however, that very few teachers, new recruits or mature, could be classified as radical or ultra-conservative. During normal times the great majority of teachers seem to espouse a more or less moderate or analytical stance toward all basic issues regarding the academic situations of which they are a part. This includes almost all orderly changes that are proposed or in process. However, during times of trouble or crises, a polarization process is likely to occur. More and more younger teachers move toward the left and more and more of the mature teachers move toward the right. Naturally, the longer a crisis lasts the more distinct and dysfunctional the polarization becomes. In one of the colleges where there had been a prolonged student crisis, there was openly expressed conflict among teachers. Some hotly defended the conservative stance taken by the president, while others defiantly identified with the very militant stance of the students. In other colleges where student demands had been disruptive there was a distinct polarization among teachers. On each of the campuses there was or had been a handful of young teachers who had become active leaders in student protest, and about the same proportion of mature teachers manifested an even more rigid conservatism than did their presidents or their boards of trustees.

The balance of experience among teachers on the whole does not exist regarding tenure on a given faculty. A third or more of the teachers (36% of the sample) may be classified as itinerants. As a rule, they remain only two or three years at a given college and then move on to another. Frequently teachers in this category volunteered to inform the researcher that they did not desire to pursue their future professional careers in the colleges where they were located and that they were actively seeking positions elsewhere. Therefore, while only 8 percent of the teachers were in their first year of experience, fully 21 percent were in their first year in their particular colleges. Also, almost half of the teachers (46%) had been in their present colleges less than three years when the study was made.

From the point of view of the academic renewal and change so urgently needed in the colleges, the fourth (24%) of the faculty with ten years and over tenure in their present colleges constitute the most significant segment. If there is a power structure in these colleges, it is composed primarily of teachers from this group. They certainly form the most stable and dependable core of the faculty. Most of those with whom we talked saw their own professional careers intricately bound up with their college. As a rule,

142

deans, divisional and department heads, and special program directors belong in this category. They are usually the ones called upon to chair important faculty committees and to perform the numerous chores which seem to be necessary to carry on the functions of the college. This is especially true in colleges where the president has served for several years. It is not uncommon for a few selected teachers to function in several major capacities simultaneously. For instance, a teacher in one of the colleges was head of a division, head of a key department, head librarian, plus chairman of two faculty committees and a member of two or three others. He also attempted to engage in research and writing. A teacher in another college was head of a division, director of an important federally funded program and chairman of three faculty committees. These heavy non-teaching assignments are typical. In each of the colleges there were a few teachers who were saddled with very heavy responsibilities. Margaret Dabney, a research assistant for this study, referred to these teachers as "work horses."

According to the most reliable information available, the main reason a relatively few teachers were responsible for the lion's share of academic, administrative, and organizational chores is simply that, for one reason or another, there were very few teachers on these faculties with the combination of experience, tenure, training, and dedication to qualify them for important academic responsibilities. This was the major explanation given by almost all of the presidents of these colleges: all expressed the desire to recruit additional teachers who are qualified and willing to assume important academic and administrative responsibilities.

One of the most persistent challenges facing the colleges in this sample is to find means whereby new recruits, the highly mobile or itinerants, and the more mature teachers can, in a creative manner, blend new, even revolutionary, ideas with tested practices. So far, attempts to achieve this goal have been generally unsuccessful. For the most part, each of the colleges spends only two or three days at the beginning of the academic year in some version of a faculty workshop, retreat, or conference. These are attempts to introduce new recruits and to provide them with some basic facts about the nature and procedures of the college's programs. As a rule, a few formal papers and discussions are presented regarding certain selected issues in higher education generally or the individual college. The faculty also usually reviews some highlights from the student and faculty handbooks. While all teachers concurred that these pre-academic year conferences are helpful, they tended to agree that they are insufficient in that they present old problems and traditional approaches, but fall far short of achieving anything near a functional consensus among the faculty on basic issues. And little or nothing is ever said about badly needed innovations and how they might be achieved.

One college has a mid-winter conference at which the orientation of new recruits is extended and where perennial academic issues and problems may be discussed at length. The teachers involved insisted that even this added effort is not enough to achieve the degree of faculty understanding and consensus needed. It may be that at least during this revolution in higher education generally, and the sub-revolution in Black colleges in particular, faculty seminars need to be established in each college so teachers and administrators can meet regularly to analyze issues and problems common to them. If such seminars are carefully designed, as was true in at least one of the colleges, they might achieve two very necessary, interrelated goals: a broadening of the teachers' knowledge about developments in higher education generally, and the achievement of a greater consensus and cooperation among the faculty *per se*. Certainly, extended formal discussions involving all faculty members should precede the kind of revolutionary changes these colleges need to make.

NOTES

1. Frederick Rudolph, *Mark Hopkins and the Log* (New Haven: The Yale University Press, 1956), Preface.

2. Gunnar Myrdal, *An American Dilemma*, p. 694.

3. Laurence G. Peter and Raymond Hull, *The Peter Principle* (New York: William Morrow & Co., Inc., 1969).

4. Lou LaBrant, "The Goals for Culturally Different Youth," in *Improving English Skills of Culturally Different Youth*, U.S. Department of Health, Education and Welfare, Office of Education (1964), pp. 22-23.

5. "The Nature of Values," in *Improving English Skills of Culturally Different Youth*, pp. 3-4.

6. Georg Simmel, *Sociology*, translated and edited by Kurt H. Wolf (Glencoe, Illinois: The Free Press, 1950), p. 401. See also Daniel C. Thompson, *The Negro Leadership Class*, pp. 49-52.

7. Melvin E. Haggerty, *The Evaluation of Higher Institutions* (Chicago: University of Chicago Press, 1938), p. 3.

8. Daniel C. Thompson, "Teachers in Negro Colleges: A Sociological Analysis", Ph.D. Dissertation (Columbia University, January 1956), p. 37.

7.

The Faculty: Professional Duties

The primary function of any educational institution is the dissemination of knowledge. The teaching function is given different emphasis according to the type of institution; as a rule, the smaller or more elementary the educational institution, the more emphasis it places upon teaching over other academic activities. Yet, even in the major universities or research centers, classroom instruction, preparation for classes, directing student assignments, and evaluating student progress should ideally consume the greater part of the academician's professional time.[1]

Teaching is especially significant in the colleges in our sample, due largely to the fact that most of the students enrolling in them come from inadequate high schools and socio-economically disadvantaged backgrounds. Many of them have hardly mastered even the most elementary level of reading comprehension and disciplined reasoning. Thus, in addition to regular classroom teaching, the effective teacher in these colleges must devote a great deal of time to out-of-class, face-to-face instruction. Despite the fact that teaching is most essential, only a small proportion of teachers in the sample seemed to regard it as a calling, in the sense that they are totally committed to it. There were at least six different attitudes toward teaching expressed by the teachers interviewed:

1. *High morale teachers*. A few teachers, about 5 percent, may be classified as high morale teachers. They are enthusiastic about teaching and communicate this to their students. These are the teachers with charisma who are said to "turn on" their students. Students enjoy going to their classes and benefit greatly from their instruction.

2. *Good teachers*. Between 30 and 40 percent of the teachers in each of the colleges are classified as good teachers by their students and colleagues. They differ from the high morale teachers in that they seldom turn students on, yet they have a reputation for being thoroughly familiar with their subject-matter areas and for dealing patiently and fairly with their students. Perhaps the most frequent criticism of teachers in this category is that they tend to be too bookish.

While all academic deans and department heads acknowledged that these teachers are indispensable to the academic programs in their colleges, they are seldom inspired or inspiring as teachers. All too often they are the proverbial unsung heroes on campus, seldom receiving any recognition or honor from their students or colleagues. They are essentially subject-matter centered and not student-centered. Such teachers are often undervalued even by top administrative officers. For instance, one president described such a teacher on his faculty as a "good second man." He meant that this teacher could do the teaching, but he needed someone else to do the creative thinking necessary to challenge students and develop his department. This was despite the fact that this man had a larger proportion of students going on to graduate school than any of his colleagues.

3. *Rusty teachers*. According to the most reliable data gathered by use of questionnaires, interviews, and information supplied by students, teachers and administrators, about 20-30 percent of the teachers in the sample colleges may be classified as "rusty." They perform their duties in a more or less routine man-

ner. Some of them have been teaching the same set of courses for years, and have accumulated extensive notes, bibliographies, and examinations that they use year after year with little or no revision. They are conservative teachers in the sense that they continue to use traditional methods of communication (almost exclusively lectures), established approaches to knowledge, and maintain the same attitude toward students that has prevailed in higher education for decades.

College officials are almost always ambivalent about rusty teachers. In the first place, a large proportion of them already have tenure and it is difficult or impossible to dismiss them because moral turpitude is seldom involved. Furthermore, since there is no established criteria of a good teacher, it is usually quite difficult to prove in an objective manner that a given teacher is not adequately performing his role. For example, one college administrator confided that his college was "stuck" with a professor who had ceased to be effective in the classroom. Yet professional incompetency could not be proven, and so the college was forced to buy up a year remaining on his contract with the understanding that he was not expected to teach that year. Actually, practically every college president with whom we talked suggested that he would like to replace certain rusty teachers but had no definitive cause for dismissing them or no applicants who could replace them.

4. *Outwardly mobile teachers.* As suggested earlier, 20 percent or more of the teachers regarded their present position as merely a stepping stone on their career ladder. Although it is not usually a rational decision, these teachers in effect begin their careers in a given Black college and are ever ready to accept new appointments in other colleges, if by doing so they can get an increase in salary, rank, and/or academic status.

These are the teachers who are usually the first to respond to overtures from college deans and department heads in other colleges who urgently need to recruit additional faculty members. They are likely to move from one college to another every two or three years. One such professor said, "I'm always looking for greener pastures." If loyalty to the college and commitment to student advancement are regarded as among the criteria of a good teacher, outwardly mobile teachers do not qualify. Their conception of a career is selfish in that they are exclusively interested in their personal success, with little apparent concern for the services that they may be able to render to the development of their students or their college in the larger sense.

Another version of this outwardly mobile group concerns the motivation of a number of teachers who are not necessarily interested in transferring to some other college, but rather in acquiring some administrative position within the present college. The important point here is that they want to get away from teaching as such. A dean in one college guessed that "just about every Ph.D. and tenured teacher in this college is bucking for my job."

Insofar as training, experience, and the ability to communicate with students are concerned, outwardly mobile teachers may be among the most competent in the college. In fact, some of them rationalize their readiness to change positions precisely in terms of their alleged professional superiority. What mainly disqualifies them as good teachers is the emphasis they place upon their own professional advancement, while having little or no serious concern for the students they teach. So far as we could ascertain, they are not often among the truly creative teachers.

5. *Professional misfits.* A relatively small number of teachers, about 4 or 5 percent, indicated that they really do not like teaching. The younger teachers in this group openly acknowledged that they are seeking non-teaching positions. The older teachers frequently reminisced about some different career they would have chosen if today's opportunities had been available earlier in their lives. This is especially true of certain Black teachers, some of whom spoke with great envy of former students who are earning larger salaries than they and have acquired high social status. They expressed bitterness about the fact that they have recent graduates who chose careers in industry or government and earn more money the first year out of school than they earn after ten years or so of teaching. Apparently some teachers communicate this dissatisfaction to their students; this approach would tend to undermine the students' respect for college teaching and could be one reason why there continues to be a shortage of

competent Black college teachers. They do not present attractive, viable models.

6. *Uncertain professionals.* Though the actual number will vary from one college to another, the available data suggest that about 5 percent of the teachers in the sample are still quite uncertain about their choice of a teaching career. Some expressed disappointment regarding the profession, indicating that it does not offer the self-fulfillment they expected. Some had hoped that they would have been able to accomplish more in the development of students, and that the teaching career would have been more challenging than they found it to be. Not only were they disillusioned with the performance of their students, but they felt unrecognized and unappreciated among their colleagues and in the larger community. One teacher voiced this complaint:

> I have taught in some of the best Black colleges. I have turned out students who are among the most successful people in the nation. I have a Ph.D. degree. Yet, despite all of my achievements I am not known outside of narrow academic circles. (Figuratively) I am the original person about whom James Baldwin wrote—*Nobody Knows My Name.*

No doubt one of the main reasons why so many teachers have ceased to strive for excellence is the fact that only 25 percent of those in the sample believed that the teaching role *per se* is recognized and rewarded by their colleges. This belief was underscored by an academic dean who confided:

> Some of the best teachers in this college go unnoticed and unrewarded year after year. They are taken for granted when extraordinary problems arise. They can be counted upon to make their contribution. They are dedicated to the point of devotion. Yet there is no day set aside for their recognition. Some of the best teachers here have made important contributions to this college, to the profession itself and to the community, of which even their closest colleagues are not aware. The greatest

irony of all is that some of those who do not have the degree (Ph. D.) are among the lowest paid teachers on the faculty.

As suggested before, one reason why good teaching in these colleges is likely to go unrecognized and unrewarded is that there is no acceptable criteria according to which "good" or "bad" teaching can be determined. There are no clearly defined academic standards which teachers are expected to maintain in their individual courses. To a very large degree, each teacher is left pretty much alone to conduct his classes as he wishes and to set whatever norms of achievement he believes to be best suited to his students. There are times, then, when this very much valued academic freedom becomes academic anarchy. There were teachers in all of the colleges who recognized this to be so. Some of the more dedicated complained about the lack of professionalism and uncertain, indefinite academic standards maintained by their colleagues. When asked why they did not attempt to correct this they generally indicated that they were afraid that objective standards of teaching might destroy the academic freedom they all treasured. Consequently, teachers are reluctant to develop criteria by·which they and their colleagues should be judged, while at the same time they recognize the need to differentiate good teachers from bad.

It should be noted that the problem of teacher evaluation is not peculiar to the sample colleges. It is a national problem of the first magnitude. For decades educators have tried to devise means of evaluating teaching as a necessary step toward rewarding good teaching. Some advocate that students should rate teachers, while others would have teachers rated by a committee of "master teachers" or by deans and department heads. There are also those who feel that each teacher should be given objective criteria to rate himself/herself. Nevertheless, despite all proposed approaches, the teaching role still can not be effectively evaluated. Evidently the vast majority of teachers simply reject any standard by which their performance may be judged. Almost all teachers with whom we talked rejected student evaluation because they felt that their students were either incapable of judging teaching, likely to be prejudiced against certain teachers, or would be too complimentary or critical of certain teachers on purely personal grounds. Teachers also generally resist being evaluated by their colleagues, whom they fear might attempt to use their own methods and styles of teaching as norms according to which they would render judgement. Consequently, on one ground or another, most teachers resist any standardized measurement of their professional competency and skill. There is a widespread feeling among them that teaching is essentially a communications art, and therefore defies objective evaluation. If this is so, then it follows that the professional teacher should be free to pursue his role in his own individual style. As long as this proposition is accepted as valid, some good teaching will continue to go unrewarded, and too much poor teaching will continue to be tolerated.

No matter what the reason, one thing is certain: there is little highly structured, standardized teaching in the sample colleges; each teacher is generally free to pursue his role as he likes. This is particularly true insofar as kinds and amount of outside reading, individual student research, and laboratory experiments are concerned. A given teacher may require much more or much less than another teacher in the same subject, or the same teacher may vary assignments from year to year. To the extent that this is so, students in these colleges will hardly acquire the uniform set of information necessary to make high scores on well-known standardized tests. Consequently, it is not at all surprising that the vast majority of students and teachers in these colleges are supercritical of standardized tests. As a rule, Black students refuse to accept their scores as a fair measurement of their abilities and achievements, and teachers refuse to accept the performance of their students as valid indication of their teaching competency.

At first blush, the outsider is likely to agree with those critics of Black colleges who insist that, as far as academic standards are concerned, these colleges should be declared "disaster areas," as characterized by Jencks and Reisman. A more open-minded examination, however, may reveal that private Black colleges actually represent a sort of bastion of true academic freedom and liberalism in higher education. Despite the fact that they tend to accept national norms, they, more than any other group of colleges, have continued to defy the pressure of rigid standardization which has become a prevailing hallmark of modern education. Actually, it is the cult of standardization about which college youth today are expressing great unhappiness; they constantly protest standardized social, moral, academic, and political patterns. They especially renounce the formalism and rigidity reflected in traditional academic procedures and standards. One student leader angrily accused what he termed the "academic power structure" of attempting to make "carbon copies of today's generation . . . The national standardized tests really say that 'either you must be like every other college student or there is no place for you in this society'."

An increasing number of college students, representing even the most prestigious colleges and universities, are denouncing what they hold to be enslaving standardization and formalism characteristic of higher education in this nation. They are demanding open enrollment, wider academic freedom, relevancy, the elimination of standardized tests, less rigid curricula, and a more functional interpretation of teacher competency.

It may well be that the relatively flexible academic standards characteristic of the sample colleges need to be refined and reformulated so that they may be widely applied in higher education. Eventually all colleges may have to do what Black colleges have always done—make their entrance requirements, standards of academic performance, and teaching methods and styles liberal enough to meet the needs of students who will be increasingly recruited from all segments of American society, not just from the white middle class.

It is already quite clear that when students are democratically recruited, no single standard of excellence can be effectively applied to their performance or, for that matter, to the methods of teaching them. The sample colleges, like the society at large, are becoming too complex and multi-purposed for their efforts to be judged by a few simple, sovereign objective tests. Since Black colleges have been forced, historically, to experiment with flexible academic procedures and standards, it may be that they have some definite contributions to make to higher education as it gropes and stumbles into this complex urban, nuclear age. Black colleges' audacious experiments in the education of students other colleges deem uneducable might be the most effective guide to the colossal task of democratic education in this and all other nations, especially under-developed ones. One thing is certain: teaching is the key to success in this area.

RESEARCH

There is just about unanimous agreement among educators that college teaching is considerably more effective if it is closely related to research. The central problem arises in attempting to arrive at a proper, optimum balance between these two basic academic functions. There are two ideal approaches to the balance of teaching and research:

First, a college might deliberately employ teachers who are experts in the classroom and other teachers who are experts in research. While this approach might be the most efficient organization of specialized talents, coordinating these two specialties in the education of students would still constitute a major problem to be solved.

Second, both research and teaching would be expected of all teachers. Consequently, a given teacher's professional welfare would be determined by his competency in both areas. This is essentially the policy adopted by some of the more prestigious colleges, where the teacher is expected to "publish or perish." This is, in fact, their functional definition of the scholar.

Until now, effective research has been narrowly conceived as that exercise which leads to publication. Accordingly, there are very few scholars in Black colleges. Where this study is concerned, we find that only 5 or 6 percent of the teachers in the sample had ever published a book; just 12 percent had contributed to any published work, and a mere 4 percent had ever published in a scholarly journal.

There are several reasons why teachers in Black colleges do not ordinarily engage in scholarly research, as defined by top professionals in their academic disciplines:

1. Research or creative scholarship is not usually expected of teachers in Black colleges. Certainly none of the colleges in our sample exerts pressure upon its teachers to do research. Only one or two of the deans in the sample listed creative scholarship among their colleges' expectations of the full professor. None of the deans and only one of the department heads interviewed suggested that creative scholarship might be a key reason for an increase in salary or promotion in rank. Even more significant, only 10 teachers (2.5 percent of the sample) felt that research or creative scholarship was important to their professional welfare in their colleges.

2. Little or no time is alloted to do research. During the course of this study, we talked with several teachers who were obviously top scholars in graduate school and still manifested potentially prolific, brilliant minds. They generally talked at length about areas of scholarship which were of burning interest to them. These interests ranged all the way from extensive research projects they would like to conduct and new approaches to the fine arts, to demonstration projects relating to teaching and administration. Yet seldom had any of these scholars actually produced in their fields of special interest.

Ironically, teachers who were apparently most capable of creative scholarship were precisely those who were often too busy to engage in it. Only 1 percent of the teachers had ever had a leave of absence to do research, and just 2 percent had ever had their teaching load reduced so that they could engage in creative scholarship. Furthermore, for one reason or another, the sabbatical leave is not an institutional practice in the sample colleges. Only 2 percent of the teachers had ever had a sabbatical leave, and it seems that even these leaves were usually due to non-academic, extenuating circumstances—maternity, work on special projects, or illness. Only one teacher in the entire sample had ever received a sabbatical on full salary with the understanding that he was to pursue his own academic interests.

3. All Black colleges experience some important degree of cultural isolation. While only about half of the colleges are actually physically isolated from the mainstream of cultural life in this nation, all of them suffer from significant to almost total

isolation from the larger academic community. Two-thirds of the teachers in the sample indicated that they had little or no sustained contacts with their white counterparts in the communities in which the colleges are located or in the larger academic disciplines in which they specialize. This situation, combined with the fact that most of them are in small or one man departments, means that, for all practical purposes, the vast majority of teachers in the sample get no sustained intellectual stimulation from top-flight scholars in their own specialized fields. One scholar voiced the feeling of several when he said: "Sometimes I have good ideas, but I have no one to discuss them with. My colleagues are simply not interested in research and writing or anything outside of their immediate classroom concern. We do not discuss ideas; we talk shop."

What this teacher described is a problem of cultural isolation where the individual teacher in the Black college may not be just the only specialist in his college, but in some instances the only one in his community with training and interest in a specific discipline. For example, a psychologist in one of the colleges was the only such specialist on the faculty. In at least half of the colleges located in small communities, a psychology professor might well be the only psychologist in the community. The same could be true of other academic specialists.

It is a truism that great civilizations have developed at the crossroads of culture, where men of learning meet and stimulate one another. What is true of civilizations on the whole is certainly true of institutions of higher education. Ideally, the college or university is a community of scholars. It follows, then, that during this age when academic specialization is so pronounced, it is likely that the kind of stimulation needed for creative scholarship in a given discipline pre-supposes sustained interaction with fellow specialists. The lack of such stimulation is undoubtedly a major handicap for certain teachers in Black colleges.

4. The great majority of teachers are not formally prepared to carry on top-level creative scholarship. As noted earlier, approximately 75 percent of the teachers do not have the doctorate. Some of them are engaged in dissertation research, while others have given up the research necessary for the doctorate. There are

still others who have never even attempted to pursue the doctorate because they feel that they are not qualified to do the necessary research. Therefore, for whatever reason, only a relatively few teachers in the sample colleges have demonstrated the ability required to become creative scholars by the current definition in academic power circles.

5. Practically all of the teachers lack funds to participate in extensive creative scholarship. While more than a third of the teachers (37 percent) indicated a desire to do research and 17 percent said that they were actively engaged in some type of research, only 15 percent said that they had any funds designated for research. A close look at those engaged in research revealed that 58 percent were working on projects designed to satisfy degree requirements. This means that only 28 of the 400 teachers in the sample, or about 7 percent, were engaged in non-degree research projects, and they were engaged in studies designed to provide broader understanding of their colleges (self-studies) or research related to classroom-oriented projects. A negligible number was engaged in what was termed pure research.

It is very significant to note that only six, or at most ten, teachers in the sample were engaged in the kind of research that could develop into reports in which scholarly journals would be normally interested or which might be published later as a book. Therefore, there seems to be a vicious cycle: professors in Black colleges seldom get funds to support research because these colleges have no research tradition; the colleges have no research tradition because the professors have no money for released time and expenses to carry on meaningful research.

6. Black college teachers, like other members of their race, have experienced constant complex forms of discrimination. Directly or indirectly, there was hardly any professional society which did not discriminate to some degree against its Black members. Black members were seldom included among their officers and were rarely invited to present papers or to publish in their official organs.

The president of one of the largest professional organizations attempted to explain this phenomenon. In essence, he said that almost all officers in his organization had been drawn historically from faculties in major universities noted for their rich research tradition. These officers in turn selected editors of the society's journals who solicited papers from other scholars they knew in similar universities. Since Black professors seldom published enough to be classified as scholars, they were not elected as officers of the professional society, and were not regularly invited to present papers at annual meetings or to submit papers for publication. Even now, very few teachers in Black colleges are given the opportunities and challenges to participate in creative scholarship as conceived by national professional societies.

Because they were discriminated against in the larger world of higher education, Black scholars formed their own scientific societies and published their own official organs. A few examples of such official organs are: *The Journal of Social Science Teachers, The Journal of Negro Education, Phylon, The Journal of Negro History, The Journal of Human Relations, The Negro Year Book,* and *The Black Scholar.* An examination of some of these scholarly journals will show that, according to any criteria of excellence, many of the articles reflect the highest standard of scholarship. Despite this, their works remain buried in the sense that other scholars writing on the same subjects seldom cite these articles in their bibliographies. Consequently, Black scholars who regularly publish in these journals are very likely to remain unnoticed by their colleagues in the larger academic world and unrecognized by their professional societies.

Just as Black scholars have had great difficulty in having their papers published in scholarly journals, much of their larger research efforts have been abortive when it comes to getting books published by prestigious publishers. This difficulty may stem to some extent from the quality of research involved, yet there is accumulated evidence that a constant factor that must be considered is the relatively low prestige of Black colleges and the fact that, even now, only a few Black scholars have been accorded the professional status prestigious publishers seem to demand. Thirty years ago Logan Wilson called attention to a form of discrimination from which Black scholars suffer:

Despite the fact that material submitted for publication from, let us say, Yale or Princeton, may not be better than that submitted by an unknown from a second-rate college, it usually *looks* better to the editor or reader because of the institutional prestige and authority behind it.[2]

What Wilson noticed in regard to discrimination against low prestige colleges is, of course, eminently apropos when we talk about low status Black colleges and their professors.

In order for teachers in Black colleges to make a unique yet significant contribution to research, at least two interrelated approaches might be seriously considered:

First, the research concept should be broadened so that it will not be enslaved by publication in established professional journals. Teachers would be encouraged to do research that would enrich their classroom performance but may not add significantly to knowledge in their discipline at large. Actually, such research may be a simple validation and extension of knowledge already widely known, its main purpose being to train students in the explication of research theory, methods and presentation. In this way, greater emphasis would be placed upon continuities in research which are needed, yet often neglected, in certain disciplines. Another kind of valuable though limited research might deal specifically with indigenous community groups according to well-known theoretical and methodological procedures.

One of the most overlooked opportunities to do meaningful yet limited research is in the area of social change. In every community where Black colleges are located the issue of social change is paramount. Sometimes it involves the increase or decrease in population, the increase of Black voters, school desegregation, equal employment, the use of public facilities, or racial conflict. Studies of these processes could yield valuable knowledge about the nature of social change which would provide students and teachers with opportunities to develop and refine basic research methods and theories. The main object would be teaching and the expansion of knowledge for the benefit of the students and teachers involved—not necessarily for publication in national journals or books. It could be an effective procedure for the accumulation and continuity of knowledge in a given discipline and might also produce valuable information for intelligent social action.

Second, certain Black colleges might become valuable subresearch centers. Despite some outstanding research done by individual scholars, southern colleges and universities have, for the most part, lagged far behind top institutions of higher education outside the South. This gap might be narrowed if certain Black colleges are provided resources to participate in meaningful research. Much of this could be done in consortia arrangements with established research centers.

It is hardly possible to understand the intricate fabric of American political structure and the varying, unstable social and cultural patterns in this country unless systematic research is done in certain southern communities which have so far been neglected. It is even more improbable that we can understand the Black experience just by studying a few large Black ghettos immediately adjacent to prestigious research-oriented universities, because every significant aspect of the Black experience in Chicago, New York etc. is colored to some extent by the constant flow of migrants from southern communities of varying sizes and different sub-cultural patterns. The enclaves migrants set up in large cities outside the South tend to perpetuate key aspects of their native, regional and community ways of life. These more or less intact cultural enclaves exert some definite measure of influence on the total life of the larger community to which they have been transplanted, from police methods and political behavior to the distribution of power and wealth. It is only reasonable, therefore, that a scientific understanding of our basic social institutions must necessarily include a great deal more knowledge about their southern roots than is now the case. It is not just the small communities in the South that have been overlooked and omitted when it comes to scientific social research, but large cities as well. Far too few comprehensive studies have been made of the political, economic and social life of such cities as Atlanta, Houston, Birmingham and New Orleans where Black colleges are located and could serve as research centers.

161

Black colleges generally, and the sample colleges specifically, have reached a very critical stage in their development. They need to re-define their purposes and reformulate their philosophies if they would make the level of contribution in their second century that they were able to make in their first. In order to fulfill their original mission it would seem to be both necessary and feasible for foundations, government on all levels, and private philanthropy to sponsor joint research between affluent universities and certain of these Black colleges. Some of them could become centers where university students and visiting professors might work side by side with students and teachers in Black colleges. This could lead to new and fruitful patterns of mutual aid between the university and the small college.

PARA-ACADEMIC ACTIVITIES

In addition to the regular classroom teaching and research which comprise the primary role of the college teacher, there is a wide range of secondary or para-academic duties which are also performed. While every administrator in the sample colleges acknowledged that these are essential activities, none of them could report that teachers who engage in them were given proper recognition or rewards for worthy performance of such duties.

There are several para-academic activities inherent in the program of a viable college. These activities include non-academic consultation and guidance of students, participation in civic and community organizations, off-campus consultation services, and participation in professional organizations. Such activities in Black colleges are particularly important because these colleges are not in the mainstream of higher education; the academic and social backgrounds of the vast majority of their students may be classified as disadvantaged, and they ordinarily need a great deal more guidance from teachers than would be necessary for students from more affluent backgrounds. Much of it is due simply to the students' need for meaningful relationships outside their peer groups. A small percentage of teachers (between 5 and 10 percent) reported that they spent several hours a week in non-academic consultation with their students. Such sessions are used by students to discuss almost any issue or problem which concerns them personally, ranging all the way from their military draft status to courtship and marriage. Frequently, teachers come out of such sessions exhausted. One teacher reported that she had spent most of an afternoon listening to a young man's description of family problems which included a brother's dope addiction, conflict between family members, and his sweetheart's pregnancy. Another teacher had spent several hours on different days attempting to help a student resolve problems relating to his health and his need to prepare for final examinations. Some teachers expressed great frustration and even depression because the students with whom they related had problems for which there were no apparent solutions.

Another level of para-academic duties performed by teachers is loosely categorized under the role of advisor. All student organizations are expected to have at least one teacher-advisor. As we have noticed, there are usually 25 or more student organizations on each campus. This means that teachers on small faculties like those represented here would be quite busy as advisors to student groups. Some teachers either deliberately avoid such assignments or are unacceptable to student groups. The result is that a relatively small number of interested teachers assume most of the responsibility for the advisement of student groups.

During recent years college students generally, and Black students in particular, have been demanding that their colleges become more relevant to the communities in which they are located. Many teachers in the sample agreed with this demand, and a few of them have always actively participated in civic and community organizations. Some have run for and won public office, served on civic commissions, offered themselves as speakers on public occasions, and participated in a wide range of community and civil rights organizations. While these duties are not classified as strictly academic, they do in fact extend the professional services of the teacher and enchance the image of the college in question. One college president expressed this belief: "Teachers' active concern and involvement in community affairs is the best form of publicity a college can get." Here again, only a relatively small number of teachers are actively engaged in community and racial betterment. Insofar as we could ascertain, only 3 or 4 percent of the teachers in private Black colleges are regularly involved in community projects or programs.

At one time, only a few Black college presidents were called upon to function as consultants to governmental, philanthropic, and business organizations. This situation has changed so that now most Black presidents and many mature teachers in these colleges are being selected as advisers or consultants. Several of the teachers with whom we talked had spent a large proportion of their time traveling, consulting and writing reports for various types of organizations during that academic year. In most instances, they were selected because they were experts in some aspect of the Black experience. Since some honest attempts are being made to improve the condition of Black people, there has been an increasing demand for such experts in both the private and public sectors of American life. This is one concrete indication that Black college teachers are slowly but definitely becoming a part of the mainstream of intellectual life in this nation. Some of them have gone far beyond their colleges in terms of racial integration, and very often sit as equals with other intellectuals representing renowned colleges and universities. As one such consultant averred— "It is a strange feeling to be well known as an individual by nationally-recognized scholars who have never heard of my college."

Black scholars have perennially felt the need for support from their professional societies. In the past, only a selected number were reluctantly accepted as equal participants in national professional organizations; in some instances they were actually excluded. In response to this there sprang up Negro professional organizations representing just about every major academic discipline—including Black honor societies. In recent years, however, Black professionals have been accepted more liberally by erstwhile white professional societies. At the time of the study, 75 percent of the teachers in the sample claimed membership in some professional society. Their membership was generally passive; 60 percent attended meetings fairly regularly, and just 11

164

percent said they were active participants, having read papers before such groups or held some official position. There were also teachers who had been invited as speakers or panelists on organizational programs other than their professional societies. In all, a third (34 percent) had participated in professionally oriented organizations within a three-year period.

Despite the fact that para-academic activities are essential to a viable faculty and one of the best indications of a college's true academic quality, colleges in our sample have made little or no provision to formally recognize and reward such activities. As much as is being said about the need for student guidance, the college's relationship to its community and the nation, and the necessity for teachers' involvement in professional societies, it is alarming to note that none of the teachers in the sample indicated that their colleges formally expected them to carry on such activities. Furthermore, none felt that such activities would be directly rewarded by their college. As one teacher phrased it "My college allows teachers to participate in off-campus projects provided that they do not interfere with their academic duties." At least 10 percent of the teachers were convinced that the administrators in their colleges tended to frown upon teachers' involvement in off-campus activities of any kind. This opinion was indirectly validated by three college presidents who expressed some fear that teachers so involved might either neglect their academic responsibilities or reflect negatively upon the image of the college.

THE PROBLEM OF FACULTY MORALE

Morale may be defined in terms of the attitude one has regarding his work. It is largely influenced by the degree of security and self-fulfillment a person receives in the performance of his occupational duties. Morale is intangible and not easily measured, yet all employers are likely to agree that it is a definite asset that is reflected in the quantity and quality of the worker's production.

Several definitive studies have shown that the morale of a given professional is largely determined by two sets of conditions:

the degree to which he likes or dislikes the work he does, and the outside conditions which constitute the environment in which he works.[3] It follows, then, that morale within any group will be unstable because it is the function of a complex of forces. For instance, as we noted earlier, from 70-75 percent of the teachers in the sample indicated that they were satisfied with their choice of a teaching career. Ordinarily, then, the great majority *should* be high morale teachers. However, only about 5 percent of the teachers in the sample definitely manifested what may be regarded as high morale at the precise time of the study. The question arises: what are the basic factors contributing to the debilitatingly low morale among a large number of teachers? We must look for the answer primarily within the professional environment of the teachers, the general conditions which define the teachers' role and influence their professional well being. Among the most important of these conditions are salary, rank and tenure, teaching load, professional status, the brain drain, student power, administrative style of the president, and powerlessness.

Salary. Money income or salary is important to the professional man, because of what it can buy, and because it is a symbol of recognition or degree of professional success. The truly successful man in the social sense of the term is one who has attained economic well-being and social recognition in some chosen occupation. The professor in most Black colleges is generally ascribed the status of an outsider in both the non-academic world and in the broader academic profession. His chances of getting recognition and acclaim for his work are considerably more limited than are those in the academic profession at large. To the extent that this is so, money income would be a more independent symbol of success for teachers in Black colleges than would be true of teachers in the more prestigious universities where the status of the institution rubs off on the individual teacher and enhances his professional status and his chances for professional advancement.

Although salaries in the sample colleges varied significantly according to sex, academic rank, training and academic duties, in 1969-1970 the median salary for all teachers was just $8,333.[4] This is about 12 percent less than in public Black colleges, and from 12-20 percent less than for white colleges in the same states.

The beginning instructor's salary in the sample was $7,000, both for male and female beginning teachers. However, male teachers holding the ranks of assistant and associate professors earned on the average $8,000 and $9,500 respectively, $500 more than female teachers in the same ranks. It was quite surprising, then, to discover that female full professors on the whole had a median salary of $12,000, $1,000 more than the male professors in the sample.

After careful analysis, it seems that the primary reason why female professors earned higher average salaries than male professors is that highly qualified Black male professors tend to be drained off to other colleges much more frequently than their female counterparts. Consequently, female full professors who have remained in these colleges have a somewhat longer tenure, more formal training and are otherwise better qualified than the male professors who remain. Despite this, female teachers are more likely than males to remain at the minimum rank and salary level. Only 6 percent of the females in the sample had reached the level of full professor, while 27 percent of the male teachers held this rank. It is likely then that the females who persevered through the ranks have proven their value to the colleges in which they were employed. Top administrative officers in each of the colleges volunteered to cite certain female teachers they deemed indispensible to the programs in their colleges. As a rule, the female professors seemed to have been more readily available to direct special programs, conduct enrichment laboratories, and to pinch-hit for some other professor on leave or whose position had not been filled.

The more plausible explanation for the higher average salaries among the female full professors is the brain drain of professors from Black colleges. In most instances, it is the male professor who is drained off; if there are a male professor and a female professor with comparable professional qualifications, the male professor is much more likely than the female to be recruited to some other college. Females also cannot solve family ties as easily as their male counterparts. This means that female professors often inherit top positions left vacant by male colleagues.

Despite somewhat significant variations in salary among the teachers, on the whole, all of the teachers in the sample are underpaid. Only one percent of the teachers earned $14,000 and over, and all of these held administrative positions, such as division chairmen and deans. No teacher without administrative duties during the academic year 1969-1970 reported as much as $14,000 salary. Without doubt, low salaries are the fundamental reason why the morale of many teachers may be characterized as very low.

Rank and tenure. It is a well-known fact that professional advancement or promotion in rank is of crucial importance for the morale of the teacher. The college, like other bureaucratic structures, is expected to have definite criteria according to which its personnel should be promoted in rank. Despite this fact, teachers in the sample colleges were obviously confused about the basis upon which academic rank and tenure were determined. Teachers, even in the same college, disagreed widely on what they regarded as the most important criterion determining rank and tenure. The largest proportion, 36 percent, agreed that no consistent policy was followed in the granting of promotions and the according of tenure. Some of the teachers, 11 percent, insisted that their professional welfare was more or less arbitrarily decided by the president of their college, who usually hired, promoted, and fired as he willed.

Only 19 percent of the teachers had permanent tenure. One-third (32 percent) were on one year contracts, 11 percent had 2-5 year contracts, and 38 percent indicated that there were no definite tenure practices followed by their colleges. Theoretically, the fact that so few teachers had tenure seemed not to be the fundamental reason for the low morale; it seemed rather to be due to the uncertainty which prevailed among teachers about their professional future. Almost half (47 percent) indicated that they did not know what criteria determined promotion or tenure.

Records of interviews with teachers are literally full of their criticism of the rank and tenure practices in their colleges. It was obvious that some of the most critical teachers had failed, themselves, to make satisfactory professional adjustments, and their criticisms may be somewhat biased. However, several teachers who had evidently succeeded in the profession endorsed this criticism. It seemed to have been a prevalent feeling among the teachers that their top administrators were constantly looking for someone else to replace them. This was true even among the most secure, tenured teachers. While they were not afraid of being fired as such, they were afraid that they would be replaced in their present positions—demoted—if their colleges found enough funds to significantly improve the faculty.

Some of the professional insecurity expressed by teachers was no doubt unfounded. It is hardly possible to recruit enough new, allegedly superior teachers to replace those without tenure. Besides, since there is no established policy of recognizing good teachers, much of their insecurity may be due mainly to uncertainty about their value to the college and the estimate of the administration.

Yet, there is reason to believe that in some cases their feeling of insecurity was well-founded. Administrators in each of the colleges expressed a desire to improve their faculties, and they usually suggested that one sure way to do so is by replacement. They obviously considered all ranks in their plans to improve their faculties. This is implied in a question asked by one of the presidents, and which was apparently on the minds of others: "How do you get rid of a faculty member with permanent tenure? If only I knew, I could get rid of some dead weight." The insecurity experienced by most teachers in these colleges does loom as a major reason for low morale.

Teaching Load. A third of the teachers had teaching loads regarded as "heavy"—more than twelve hours. More than two-thirds (68%) of those without administrative responsibilities had two or more very large classes of 50 students or more. Presidents of the sample colleges generally regarded 15 hours as a normal teaching load. While most deans questioned this principle, they apparently felt called upon to sanction it. When discussing the assignments of teachers on their faculties, they often volunteered to explain why a given teacher was not carrying a "full load"—15 hours. If a teacher had less than 15 hours he was likely to be pinch-hitting in some administrative position, responsible for time-consuming committee functions, such as a self study, or had a number of very large classes. After discussing this pattern with a number of such teachers, one of the interviewers characterized them as "overworked". That is, when their teaching loads were reduced they had been assigned non-teaching duties which were more time-consuming than teaching the course(s) they gave up.

Though teachers generally complained about too heavy work assignments, it was hardly this problem as such that contributed to their low morale. It was, rather, differential, or what some labeled discriminatory, teaching assignments that apparently contributed to low morale. Some teachers felt that their assignments were heavier than other teachers, or that they had been deliberately assigned the most difficult or unrewarding classes. For example, one teacher complained: "Because I am a new teacher they give me the largest, dullest classes and let their old friends get the best classes." Another teacher said: "I am expected to serve on any number of committees and run errands in addition to my regular heavy class load." Again, a teacher who was cited by the president and some students as an excellent teacher was quite unhappy because, as she put it:

> Teachers in my department are either inexperienced or dull. Students will only take their classes when forced to do so. Instead of requiring them to enroll in these teachers' classes they (the dean and division chairman) put them in my sections because they seem to be afraid of the students and allow them to do anything they want. As a result, they work me to death while the other teachers do very little. The worse thing about it is that some of these teachers make more money than I do.

An academic dean offered a fundamental reason why some teachers are over-worked while others are given comparatively light assignments. According to him, there are relatively few good, talented teachers: the majority are mediocre. In the colleges' attempt to provide the highest level of teaching possible, they often penalize their most talented, conscientious teachers in the sense that they are assigned the lion's share of the teaching and non-

170

teaching duties. This frequently results in low morale among the very teachers the colleges must rely upon most.

Professional status. Almost all of the teachers with whom we talked expressed some real concern about their professional status. Perhaps half of them either felt that their academic rank was lower than it should have been, or were uncertain about their future status. Some of the younger teachers were worried about what they believed to be the lack of opportunities for solid professional growth. They complained about the lack of time and necessary support to engage in the type of research or creative scholarship necessary for competition with top flight teachers in their particular disciplines. A young Black Ph.D. put it this way:

> I love this college. It is my alma mater. I like what I have been able to do for my students. I am sometimes amazed with the students' development. They deserve whatever I can give them. But what about my future? Where can I go from here? For example, one of my classmates (Black) didn't get his degree until a year after I got mine. He stayed on at the University to work with his major professor. He has a book coming off the press this fall and has already had a promotion in the University. Where do I stand? Nothing has changed for me.

Not only was there considerable anxiety about the lack of opportunities for creative scholarship, but there was even wider complaint about the very limited funds available for travel and participation in professional societies. Consequently, some of the most able teachers in the sample are simply not known by their peers in the profession at large. They realize that this is a barrier to their professional growth and some were anxious to find ways to establish sustained and meaningful contacts with their counterparts in other colleges and universities. In the meantime, they feel professionally inhibited.

The brain drain. Very closely related to the teachers' concern about their professional growth is their disturbance over the so-called brain drain plaguing Black colleges. Some of their most

171

able and promising teachers are being recruited to white colleges. This is indeed a major problem threatening the quality of faculty in the sample colleges and could result in diminishing their future status and role in the world of higher education.

Another serious dimension of the problem of the brain drain is that it tends to undermine the morale of the more stable teachers. When it is widely believed that the best Black teachers are recruited to white colleges, an unnatural question arises about teachers who are not so recruited. Why do they remain in Black colleges? Some of the best qualified, successful Black teachers in the sample colleges apparently felt the need to explain, even to apologize, for remaining in a Black college. They often felt called upon to prove that they could have transferred to white colleges if they had chosen to do so by showing the interviewer written offers from administrators of white colleges or explaining such offers in detail.

Sociologically one's professional pride is highly correlated with the reputation of others who belong to the profession. A teacher would be likely to have more pride in belonging to a distinguished faculty in a prestigious college than he would in belonging to a generally undistinguished faculty in a low prestige college. It follows, then, that the extent to which the sample colleges get the reputation of losing their best scholars is precisely the extent to which pride in belonging to these faculties will be diminished.

The brain drain from private Black colleges, which is now in full swing, did not begin for the sample colleges with the recent white colleges' efforts to recruit Black teachers. It began, in fact, during the 1950s when southern state legislatures made concrete efforts for the first time to improve public Black colleges. They did this in their all-out attempts to circumvent federal court desegregation decisions. Belatedly, most southern state legislatures made efforts to indicate that they intended to achieve the "Separate but Equal" mandate which had been ignored for about 60 years (since the 1896 *Plessy vs. Ferguson* Supreme Court's Decision). They began to improve public Black colleges by appropriating funds to raise faculty salaries. Right away these colleges began a drive to recruit relatively underpaid, yet distinguished, teachers from private Black colleges. Therefore, ever since the 1950s the sample colleges have been constantly losing their most competent teachers to Black state colleges and have not done well at all in competing with them for young Ph.D. recipients. Consequently, despite the much more positive historical academic reputation of some of the sample colleges, the average level of formal training of teachers in Black state colleges is consistently much higher than for the private Black colleges.

Another point: during recent years all Black colleges have been losing actual and potential teachers to non-academic competitors. Teachers have gone in increasing numbers to fill positions in government and industry where salaries and opportunities for promotion are more promising. Many teachers who remain in private Black colleges experience a constant dilemma in having to make choices involving their careers. Practically all of the teachers in the sample have had to re-assess their professional outlook. The dilemma they face is underscored by the fact that most of them are seriously questioning the professional status of their colleagues. While 25 percent rated most of their colleagues as superior professionals, 75 percent rated most of them as average or below. This means that one of the most reliable sources of high morale is absent: pride in belonging to a distinguished faculty.

Student power. There have been some concrete manifestations of significant, unusual student power on each of the campuses studied. All teachers were acutely aware of its reality: it is not a myth! Student power has been effectively directed at the three key areas of decision-making in the college: the policy-making powers of the trustees—including the president; the curricula or academic area, which is the primary domain of the faculty; and the broad personnel area having to do with rules and regulations regarding proper conduct.

At the time of the study no student in the sample had been duly elected to a board of trustees. During the academic year 1970-1971 a few of the colleges had students who were officially appointed to their trustee boards. Their exact status is still unclear, however. Nevertheless, all of the boards had made some provisions whereby the voice of students could be heard. In a few instances, student representatives had been invited to sit with their trustee boards when matters of campus life were to be discussed. All of the boards had appointed certain of their members to meet with student leaders and get their reports and interpretations on all aspects of the campus life.

Most teachers concurred with their board's willingness to consult with students. They generally agreed that this basic level of communication was too long ignored and still not as developed as it should be. An otherwise apparently conservative professor remarked:

> For too many decades trustees made decisions for and about students they never really saw. Most of them thought of students as so many things—not real persons who had inherent rights and individual lives to plan and live after college. I have taught here for more years than I care to remember and until two years ago I never saw a trustee in any kind of honest give-and-take with students. At least now they know that Black youngsters are human beings: mixed up perhaps, but human.

What does disturb just about all of the teachers is the fact that teachers, too, have not been given proper recognition by the trustees. When deemed expedient, a teacher may have been asked to make some report to the trustees and to submit himself to a sort of cross-examination on the report, but very seldom has he been deliberately invited to officially advise or participate with his trustees in the formulation of policy matters. None seemed to have assumed that he was expected to challenge the structure or the distribution of power in the college. Yet this seems to be the exact, primary reason why trustees wanted to hear from representative students, and, according to statements made by trustees, students had no compunction in expressing their blunt criticisms and presenting policy recommendations.

One of the common areas in which students have attempted to influence the decisions of trustees is faculty. Teachers who discussed this with us tended to be quite disturbed about what several of them believed to be students' castigation of faculty. One teacher expressed it this way:

I feel that students should be accorded the right and opportunity to express their opinions about teachers. However, I feel that it is not only fair but necessary for teachers to be able to defend themselves. Our trustees make every effort to get students' opinions of us, but they make no effort to get our side of the story. This is basically undemocratic and causes distrust and fear in this college.

The thing that undermines the morale of some teachers is the feeling that their students have unfair influence over them. In three of the sample colleges several teachers felt intimidated by student activities. A department head in one of the colleges which had been most disturbed by student rebellion confessed:

I'll tell the truth: I don't give failing grades to the militants in my classes. I frankly don't feel they would stand for it. They have the ear of the administration more than I do. Since I'd like to remain here a while longer I bend over backward to go along with the students. Already our students say they want to hire and fire us. They told this to the trustees. I understand that the trustees promised to consider their proposal.

Another teacher said: "Our students want power but are careless about responsibilities. The way they are being catered to today, they can make life hard for any teacher. They have frightened off teachers. Some were Black teachers—as Black as the students."

In most instances, teachers agreed that certain reforms demanded by students were long overdue. There have been always a few teachers in almost all of the colleges who have been plugging for exactly the changes which have come to be the hallmark of student protest. It was not academic reform in their colleges about which so many teachers were primarily disturbed; they felt threatened by the procedures by which students changed policies and practices of long standing. In effect, the teachers contended

that throughout the years individual teachers and faculty committees had worked very hard hammering out what they believed to
be good academic programs and fair rules and regulations. Before
basic changes are made, teachers, along with students, should
have the opportunity of re-thinking these programs and mapping
out ways and means to effect needed changes. Instead, they lamented, revolutionary changes in academic programs and traditional academic procedures have been made in response to student
protest with little or no study or planning.

A division chairman complained:

> When students here want to change something they
> simply get a committee to visit the president. He often
> changes regulations in minutes it took the faculty years
> to formulate and put into practice. We feel that he
> should at least consult the faculty before making such
> decisions. In fact, all decisions regarding the academic
> program and student requirements should be made by
> the faculty—no one else.

For one reason or another, then, 70 percent of the teachers
indicated that students were too aggressive. Most of these teachers
felt that certain basic authority traditionally delegated to teachers
is being rapidly usurped by students. Some of them felt trapped
and powerless. They were convinced that students had too much
control over their (the teachers') destinies. This was indeed a major
reason why there was widespread insecurity and low morale
among teachers on several of the campuses.

The most dramatic show of student power is in the area of
student affairs, rules and regulations pertaining to proper conduct.
During the last three years or so, students have challenged practically all of the traditional rules and regulations governing their
behavior. Most regulations regarding attire, dating, politeness, attendance at assemblies, and the use of campus facilities have
either been abolished altogether, revised, or ignored. Frequently
teachers complained that they had lost control of their campuses.

176

One teacher described student behavior on his campus as "anar-chy." Another, a sociologist, said that his campus was an excellent example of "anomie" (normlessness). He said that "The students are pampered like spoiled children. They do as they please."

Administrative style of the president. Characteristically, teachers in the sample colleges seemed to fear and resent what they regarded as too much power in the hands of the president. We shall subsequently take a close look at the source and nature of this power. It suffices here to point out that the apparent totalitarian power some teachers are convinced their presidents have is a constant source of their insecurity. As a rule, teachers feel that their president makes decisions which should be the perogative of certain individual teachers on the faculty. There is near unanimous agreement among them that their presidents can hire or fire at will with little or no fear of being questioned by trustees or faculty. Several teachers gave examples of this power, such as forced resignations by teachers with tenure, to say nothing about non-tenured teachers whose contracts had been simply allowed to expire.

Most of the mature teachers with long experience seemed resigned to the fact that their professional status and welfare were determined by the president in question. Younger teachers fre-quently expressed deep resentment of the president's personal power over them. In all instances the relative powerlessness ex-perienced by a cross section of teachers was a source of constant irritation which no doubt contributed to low morale.

Powerlessness. As suggested above, a key reason so many teachers in the sample characteristically suffer from low morale is that they all experience some degree of chronic professional frustration caused by their sense of relative powerlessness as a group. A division chairman succinctly expressed a feeling that is widely shared among teachers. He said:

> The board of trustees is well-organized as an authority group. They delegate much power to the president be-cause this relieves them of immediate responsibility. Students are organized in such a way that they are ex-

pected to deal directly with the trustees and administration. We (teachers) are unorganized. We are being crushed in the middle.

The only recognized organization through which teachers are expected to promote their professional welfare is the American Association of University Professors. At the time of the study less than half of the sample colleges had viable AAUP chapters. All of the chapters were small. The number of teachers affiliated with each chapter varied from twelve at one college to thirty at another. In all, just 29 percent of the teachers in the sample colleges had ever been dues-paying members of AAUP. Only 12 percent said that they were active members at the time of the interview.

Lengthy interviews with the president of each AAUP chapter in the sample colleges brought out two main reasons why so few of the teachers were active AAUP participants:

First, some teachers regard the AAUP as anti-administration. This assessment was due largely to the fact that traditionally the AAUP has been primarily concerned with due process regarding condition of employment, promotion in rank, salary level, and the firing of teachers. These are exactly the areas which Black college presidents usually regard as their exclusive domain. Though they may solicit advice from certain teachers, theirs is the final decision in these matters. Therefore, on most campuses few if any of the tenured teachers or those with administrative ambitions were active members of the AAUP. As one AAUP officer observed, "The president of this college and the group of teachers he depends upon to help him run the college think of us (AAUP members) as some kind of subversives."

Second, the great majority of teachers in private Black colleges ignore the AAUP because they do not regard it as an effective organization for countering the established power of the administration. Teachers referred to the AAUP as "powerless, a protest organization;" "usually made up of teachers who think they should have promotions they don't deserve;" "It is a professional organization where professors exchange ideas. It is not a union where teachers support their fellows. It has no effect upon what salary a teacher receives or whether he is fairly treated at contract time." "It has no real power;" or as one teacher crisply phrased it: "It's an organization without teeth."

While it is true that the majority of AAUP members on the campuses of the sample colleges were drawn from among the more unstable, un-tenured segment of the faculty, the actual nature of the membership varied from one campus to another. On one campus the chapter included among its active members a number of the most stable teachers on the faculty. In another college the dean aptly described the chapter on the campus as being "made up of disgruntled teachers. They want to use it as a pressure group." Also, the presidents of all but one of the chapters, and a disproportionate number of members in each chapter, were white, and there were very few younger teachers participating in any of the AAUP chapters studied. When asked to explain this latter fact, an officer in one of the colleges said: The young teachers here are not concerned about anyone's welfare but their own. They couldn't care less about making things better in this college because they don't plan a future here. They are a hit and run group. Another officer said that the younger teachers in his college "scorned the AAUP because it is a talk organization. When they get fed up with conditions here they act on their own. They don't even bother to inform us (AAUP members)."

We may conclude, then, that insofar as the problem of the relative powerlessness of teachers versus the organized power of the trustees and the president is concerned, teachers do not regard the AAUP as even a potentially effective counterbalance. The best any of the teachers seemed to expect from the AAUP was that if they happened to be victims of flagrant violations of due process, the AAUP might be called upon to embarrass the administration by censuring the college. A president, in evaluating his AAUP Chapter, said—"It helps to keep the administration honest." This was the only function he cited, and is perhaps the only real function it serves on the other campuses studied.

179

FACULTY IMPROVEMENT

Private Black colleges will need a greatly improved faculty in order to achieve their traditional avowed goals, to say nothing about their urgent need to revitalize, restructure, and redirect their general programs. Some basic innovations are absolutely essential if they are to become relevant to the demands of our present urban, industrial society and the special needs of Black people. This effort will call for a very definite program of recruitment and development of students with various potentialities, the upgrading of present faculty, and the vigorous recruitment of highly qualified new teachers. The following steps are essential:

1. *"Growing their own."* While 91 percent of the Black teachers in the sample were graduates of Black colleges, and 78 percent were graduates of private Black colleges, those who return to their alma mater as teachers represent a professional accident in that they were simply caught in the recruitment net. There is no official program in any of the colleges whereby prospective college teachers are discovered during their freshman and sophomore years and consciously groomed to become college teachers, in the way that students are enrolled in pre-law and pre-medical curricula. A program is badly needed which would provide selected students with sound academic training and special counselling and academic guidance from teachers in their major fields. This might include special reading assignments, special seminars or honors programs, and the opportunity to do tutorial work under the supervision of experienced teachers. The students who graduate under such programs would be assisted in securing scholarships and fellowships for graduate study.

2. *Special fund for teacher improvement.* As we have seen, at present about 75 percent of the regular, full-time teachers do not have the doctorate. Of course, in many instances a doctorate is not really needed. Some teachers, for example, have had considerable experience in the classroom and have frequently availed themselves of opportunities to attend seminars, in-service programs, and travel, in addition to years of conscientious preparation for the courses they teach. They are often among the most ef-

fective teachers in these colleges, and a doctorate would be an academically unnecessary embellishment. For most of the non-doctorates, however, the degree or additional preparation is necessary. Not only would they be of greater service to their colleges, but they would have more concrete opportunities for professional growth and wider service in the society at large.

A few of the colleges have done well in allowing teachers to take leaves of absence to complete the degree; they have on occasion provided some form of financial assistance. In most instances, such assistance was adequate for regular graduate students, but insufficient for teachers who had accumulated normal economic responsibilities. Private Black colleges need a dependable source of funds for teachers who would continue their study for advanced degrees, for others who could benefit academically from sabbaticals, and for teachers and students who wish to engage in research. It may be that a special foundation needs to be set up to accomplish these goals. Such a foundation would get its funds from a number of other foundations, agencies and corporations interested in the higher education of Black Americans.

3. *Make teachers' salaries competitive*. During the first century of higher education for Blacks, these colleges had only to compete among themselves, as it were, for the most competent Black teachers or for non-Black teachers who sought positions in Black colleges. Thus, despite the perennial shortage of Black college teachers, some of these colleges could boast of having a representative number of excellent teachers.

This near monopoly of Black college teachers has drastically changed. Today, the truly competent Black teacher is sought after by Black colleges, white colleges, government, industry, and various public and private organizations. As one college president put it, "there is a bull market for Black Ph.D.s." Therefore, substantial improvement of the faculties in these Black colleges cannot be made unless they can offer their teachers maximum salaries and opportunities for professional growth. It might be even necessary for these colleges to outbid most other colleges in regard to faculty salaries, because prestigious colleges automatically bestow upon their teachers a highly respected professional status—the status of the institution. Black colleges with much less prestige would have to compensate for this by offering other inducements to teachers.

4. *Planned use of professional resources in the college community*. There are scores of institutions, agencies, and programs in large cities which employ a wide range of highly trained professionals. Most colleges, particularly Black colleges, have made only sporadic, unsystematic use of this rich talent resource. For the most part, the college has remained a sort of island apart from the dynamic, practical, professional know-how in the larger community. One way of making these colleges more relevant to the communities in which they are located would be to have classes taught by those who are active participants in the larger community. It seems desirable for the colleges to establish cooperative programs with industry, professional groups and agencies in order to better tap their rich talent resources.

5. *Research*. As suggested earlier, the concept of research is almost always linked with so-called scholarly publication. This narrow conception discourages the vast majority of teachers in Black colleges from attempting to engage in research. The concept of research must be broadened so that teachers in the sample colleges can make respected contributions. I suggest the following:

(a) There should be research designed to re-examine and reformulate existing theories regarding the Black experience. As it stands now, almost all systematic social research articulates white middle class norms and is so designed that the Black experience *per se* is regarded as pathological. Black-oriented research would test out positive theories which grow out of the Black experience itself.

One example may suffice. Instead of studying the matriarchy as a pathological growth in the Black ghetto emphasizing how the Black family differs from the middle class white family, a different kind of question could be raised. "In what ways has the matriarchy among Blacks contributed to their survival?" Answers to this question would lead to an examination of new patterns of behavior and suggest new approaches and interpretations of the Black experience. Emphasis would be upon inherent strengths, not weaknesses.

182

(b) The Black community (and that part of the larger community impinging upon the Black community) may be used as a social laboratory. Teachers and students would watch the development of incipient social forms as they are related to the human condition. This might mean a systematic study of juvenile gangs, the function of the pool hall, religious manifestations, child rearing, protest, leadership patterns, and so forth. While most reports on these observations may not be original contributions to scholarship, they would provide interesting, needed information, and teachers as well as students could develop new and insightful experiences from an examination of them.

(c) As pointed out before, most of the private Black colleges are located in communities where significant social changes are taking place. Students and teachers could make a worthy contribution toward the understanding of these changes if they were properly geared to study them as they occur. The desegregation of schools and Black political participation are only two viable examples.

(d) Teachers and students in the humanities should make special efforts to understand and interpret the variety of unique experiences and responses characteristic of Black people. Their interpretation could be in the forms of art, music, and literature. So far, this rich resource is virtually untapped by Black colleges.

(e) Special efforts should be made by natural science teachers to develop relationships in their own colleges with other scientists in industry, hospitals, and universities, to provide their students with limited yet basic training in natural science research and the application of scientific knowledge and method.

While the types of research suggested above may not always merit national publication, they would be valuable in the development of the academic competencies of those involved and may be the vital link between objective, often irrelevant research, and the humane focus to which private Black colleges are dedicated. This emphasis might be rewarding when it comes to retaining and recruiting creative teachers.

6. *A program of visiting teachers.* Private Black colleges should attempt to establish programs whereby teachers in other colleges can be made available to their students on a regular,

dependable basis. In this connection, excellent teachers up for sabbaticals in other colleges and universities might be encouraged to spend their leaves in Black colleges; wealthy colleges and universities may be able to lend some of their professional talents to developing Black colleges for some period of time, or industries may be encouraged to pay the salaries of a selected number of established professors in other colleges to serve a limited amount of time in private Black colleges. (Some industries are already supplying these colleges with professors in highly specialized areas. However, there are too few examples.) In all instances, both experienced teachers and young visiting scholars, especially Black scholars in white universities, would be considered.

Such teachers would be paid the same salaries and receive the same recognition as they would have in their own colleges or universities.

7. *The establishment of a Chair in human relations.* The essential need for such a Chair was suggested by Myron F. Wicke in his Annual Report to the Board of Higher Education of The United Methodist Church, (January 28, 1969). He raised two pertinent questions:

> Does a college education have any responsibility beyond the purely intellectual? . . .

and

> Is it enough to bring a man to a full realization of his own potential?

Eventually he answers his own questions:

> It is the essential function of a college related to a church to strain itself to offer the possibility of a complete education, one which struggles with the whole man in the hope of making man and his world more human, more responsible.

184

He perceptively warned that:

> The danger for the college is that it will be so imitative
> of other institutions that it will surrender its great poten-
> tial to be a model among other models.

As we have already noted, teachers and students in church
related or private Black colleges testify that they see no real difference between these colleges and other colleges. They have
drifted into an indistinguishable sameness by slavishly imitating
white models. As such, they have no real, unique basis upon
which they can appeal for special consideration by foundations,
the federal government, or even the religious community. The obvious question is: Why should one sacrifice to support these colleges if students can get the same education in state supported colleges or in more affluent private white colleges?

In order to guarantee the re-affirmation of its college's commitment to the humane values inherent in the Judeo-Christian
tradition, each of the private Black colleges will need to establish
a Chair to be filled by eminent professors with an avowed commitment to its philosophy of humane education. This Chair may be
filled in two ways: first, special effort could be made to recruit
such a tenured professor for each of the colleges; and second,
since such talents must certainly be rare, it may be best to let this
be a distinguished Chair to be filled by a series of eminent scholars
representing various disciplines and experiences. Such professors
may spend a limited time, a semester or a year, in a given college
and move on to another college in a consortium, with a number of
such persons being shared among the several colleges.

8. *The establishment of a central recruitment-placement
bureau.* As it stands now, each of the private Black colleges is
totally responsible for its own faculty recruitment. A study of their
recruitment practices shows that none has what might be termed
an organized program. Their procedures are at best clumsy and
largely ineffectual. None spends anything like the amount of effort
and money necessary to truly build a top flight faculty. In most
instances, the primary aim seems to be simply to fill teaching

vacancies as they come up. All too often these colleges are unable to fill vacancies with the kind of teachers they really need. They generally take what they can get among those more or less easily available.

The central bureau would be modeled after the United Negro College Fund, maybe even an agency under the aegis of that organization. This bureau would discover potential recruits in other colleges who might consider moving; qualified persons in non-teaching positions; retired professionals who might serve as visiting professors for some limited period of time, and established professors in other colleges or universities who might be available on sabbaticals. The central recruiter's main responsibility would be to accumulate what would amount to a potential faculty pool. Participating colleges would be formally advised about available talents and assisted in recruiting the most desirable persons to fill faculty vacancies.

As we look closely, then, at the symbolic "log" of Mark Hopkins as it actually exists in private Black colleges, we find on one end a typical student who comes from an economically poor family, and who graduated from a below-standard, segregated high school. He is characteristically frustrated, angry and disconcertingly aggressive. On the other end of the "log" we find a middle class teacher who is likely to still be struggling to complete requirements for the doctorate, or who is professionally restless and looking for "greener pastures." According to national norms, the teacher is underpaid, relatively powerless, and generally feels insecure. All too often the student and the teacher regard one another as protagonists rather than as closely knit partners in the academic enterprise.

NOTES

1. For a broad discussion of the role of the college teacher, see Charles Anderson and John D. Murray, *The Professors* (Cambridge, Massachusetts: Schenkman Publishing Co., 1971), especially pp. 45-59 and 61-70.

2. Logan Wilson, *The Academic Man* (New York: Oxford University Press, 1942), p. 171.

3. Daniel C. Thompson, "The Problem of Faculty Morale," in *The Journal of Negro Education*, Winter 1960 Issue, pp. 37-46.

4. The average salary in 1972 minus fringe benefits was about $1,000.00 higher. See *From Isolation to Mainstream*, p. 45.

8.

Academic Program

The curriculum characteristic of the sample colleges reflects an almost slavish imitation of prestigious white models. This imitation includes the titles of courses, formal course descriptions, classification of courses, division of the curricula into general education and upper level major requirements, grading, number of credit hours for courses, number of hours required for graduation, and areas in which a major can be completed.

GENERAL CURRICULUM

When a given private Black college does not follow the format of respected white models, there are certain to be extenuating reasons for the deviation. For example, because of limited faculty these colleges can hardly offer the number of courses in a given discipline which might be offered at a more affluent college. This problem is often approached by offering courses in alternate years. That is, a teacher who has 15 hours (5 courses each semester) throughout one year may teach a more or less different set of courses next year. If such courses are offered for juniors and/or seniors, a student will then be able to take a wider variety of courses in his major field than would be possible if the teacher taught the same set of courses year after year. Thus, despite a limited number of teachers, private Black colleges, like their white counterparts, generally offer fifteen or more major areas in which students may concentrate.

In order to compensate for small or one-man departments, most of the sample colleges divide the curriculum into three main academic divisions: Humanities, Social Science and Natural Sciences. A number of specialized majors, or fields of concentration, will be offered in each division. In addition to these main divisions, all of the colleges have at least one other division, education, and often another specialized area which is vocationally-oriented, such as nursing, home economics, or business education.

Usually students in these colleges are literally inundated with course requirements. Majors in some divisions or departments have almost no time to elect a course out of purely personal interest. For instance, it is not unusual for a college to require students to take 30-36 hours in major fields of concentration, from 24-30 hours in the larger division, plus heavy requirements in general education which may include 12 hours of english, at least 6 hours of mathematics, at least 6 hours in the humanities, 12 hours of a foreign language, 12 hours in the natural sciences and 12 hours of history. Needless to say, little or no time is left for elective courses. As a rule, elective courses are simply alternative courses. That is, a student may choose between, let us say, a course in religion or philosophy, education or psychology, sociology or political science. This practice is sometimes referred to as a restrictive elective, because what would be an elective course for students majoring in the natural sciences may be a required course for students majoring in the social sciences. These courses are not designed to be electives in the ordinary sense that they are open to students in various academic disciplines. Most electives in the sample colleges are in fact introductory or survey courses designed as beginning courses for majors in specific fields.

In attempting to follow curriculum patterns characteristic of white liberal arts colleges, private Black colleges manifest a serious, inherent dilemma: from the beginning they have had to concern themselves with the vocational needs of their students. Since the vast majority of their students come from economically insecure homes and will need to enter some occupation immediately upon graduation, these colleges have endeavored, on the one hand, to prepare their students to qualify for some definite occupation so that they might be able to compete successfully for at least limited opportunities in the world of work. On the other hand, founded as they were by northern missionaries who were themselves graduates of liberal arts colleges, the strong liberal arts commitment has been always present. A major dilemma, therefore, has to do with the need to offer a dual academic program consisting of vocational training plus liberal arts. This dilemma is especially pronounced in regard to teacher-training and nursing education. Since a large body of technical or professional knowledge must be mastered for licensing in these fields, the faculty never quite decides definitely what liberal arts courses should be required. In just about all instances, students in these programs will be exempted from some otherwise required liberal arts courses. At one time or place they might be exempted from certain courses in the humanities; at another time or place they might be exempted from courses in the social sciences or the natural sciences. Whatever compromise may be made, most of the faculty with whom we talked felt that vocationally prepared undergraduates are seriously lacking in their exposure to liberal arts courses and experiences.

Another dilemma faced by private Black colleges is the need to give students sufficient depth in their major disciplines to function well in graduate and professional schools or their vocation, while still giving them sufficient breadth in the liberal arts to perform adequately on standardized tests where sound knowledge of general facts is expected. It is difficult for economically poor colleges to take academically retarded students and satisfy both of these extensive needs within a four year period. Consequently, it is not uncommon for graduates of these colleges to make very high scores on those parts of standardized tests dealing with their major disciplines, while failing to measure up on the liberal arts sections. Conversely, there are instances in which graduates make very low scores in specialized areas while performing well in the general or liberal arts sections.

There have been two primary approaches to the dilemma of depth versus breadth insofar as the curriculum is concerned: survey courses and remedial instruction. Both approaches have been based upon a key, perennial academic reality: the vast majority of students enrolled in Black colleges are woefully lacking in background preparation. They come to college reading on a seventh or eighth grade level and are hopelessly deficient in mathematics skills and language arts. In admitting these students, the colleges wittingly or unwittingly commit themselves to survey and remedial courses. Therefore, it might be in order at this point to say some word about the history of the curriculum in the sample colleges.

SURVEY COURSES

As we have noted before, until recently the all-white legislatures, and most others who planned and administered school systems in the South, all but ignored the educational needs of Black children. There was not even a pretense of making Black schools equal to white schools. Without apology, per capita funds provided for the education of white children were usually from three to five times greater than those provided for Black children. In too many instances there were simply no schools at all for Black children in communities where standard schools were provided for white children. Furthermore, even when schools were provided for Black children, little or no care was taken to see to it that these schools met anything near acceptable academic standards. They were often staffed by teachers who were unbelievably unqualified, and little or nothing was done to make physical facilities adequate or conducive to learning. To add insult to blatant discrimination, Black children often lacked adequate textbooks or, at best, were provided with textbooks which were long out of date and discarded by white schools. Of course, no thought at all was given to the special or unique academic needs of the Black students as such. And so the fact that Black children, when compared with white children, were very seriously retarded when they graduated from these schools, simply functioned to validate the theory of racial inferiority apparently unanimously held by whites who determined the educational destinies of Black children. Ironically, the marked academic retardation so characteristic of Black children was used as *prima facie* evidence that they did not deserve good schools, and not that they needed better schools.

In the avowedly racist communities where the sample colleges are located, they have had no choice but to recruit most of their students from notoriously inferior, discriminated-against high schools. Since the Black community had no power to induce state and local decision makers to provide high quality schools for Black children, Black colleges, though pitifully poor, attempted to provide their recruits with at least the minimal amount of information necessary to bridge the gap between an inadequate high school education and college entrance requirements. Accordingly, these colleges organized so-called survey courses generally patterned after survey courses initiated by some large prestigious universities. While such courses were originally intended (in white colleges) to give students in all major fields of concentration a broad, overall knowledge of the liberal arts, Black colleges found it necessary to revise them so that they would serve two additional, practical purposes: to provide remedial information for students who are now popularly referred to as culturally deprived, and to generally prepare their students to take national and/or regional standardized examinations.

In a sense, then, most private Black colleges attempted to give their students the equivalent of two or three years of basic high school knowledge in one easy lesson while they were registered for regular college courses. Admissions officers in these colleges, as well as the rank and file teachers, readily admitted that the high school graduates they admitted did not usually measure up to minimum college standards, and that they had no choice but to adjust their college courses to the scholastic level of the students they admitted. The sample colleges, at one time or another, have offered three or four survey courses and several in-

troductory courses designed to supplement high school deficiencies, while at the same time providing students with as much
bona fide college instruction as possible.

It is important to note that the adjusted academic standards
for admission to and graduation from private Black colleges were
not immorally or dishonestly instituted. They were instituted out
of sheer necessity. Since public education did not meet the
academic needs of Black students, private Black colleges
humanely assumed the responsibility. They knew that it should
not have been their responsibility; teachers and administrators
fretted about it, but eventually accepted it because the Black community desperately needed professionals and leaders. Consequently, it may be that students in Black colleges on the whole
have not been as adequately educated as their white counterparts,
but they were certainly much better prepared than they otherwise
would have been if these colleges had not put forth special efforts
to overcome some of the glaring academic deficiencies of Black
public schools.

White decision makers seemed uninterested in the fact that
Black children were provided very inadequate schooling. After all,
until quite recently the rigid patterns of racial segregation that
existed throughout the South prevented white people from having
to concern themselves directly with inadequately prepared Black
high school students: graduates of Black schools were not admitted to their (white) colleges, and, though graduates of Black colleges frequently did not measure up to the norms set for white graduates, the white community had no immediate fear. Poorly
educated Black graduates who might eventually go into teaching
would not be teaching white children; Black medical students
would not be studying with white students, interning in white
hospitals, or practicing in the white community; Black leaders
would not have white followers or be expected to participate in
decision-making involving the welfare of white people. Very
bluntly, white officials and leaders throughout the decades since
the Civil War have employed a wide variety of legal, extra-legal,
and illegal means to preserve and perpetuate a system of racial
segregation. This racist system continues to be undergirded by the
inferior education of Black children. This has always made it

plausible to advocate a brand of merit democracy while holding on to contradictory racial discrimination in most public and private areas of community and national life.

As a result of deeply ingrained, powerful historical forces, the private Black college has essayed to do for Black youth what public schools have illegally and immorally refused to do: prepare them to perform on an occupational and academic level sufficient to compete as equals in the larger community and to serve the sore needs of the Black community. Fundamentally, even survey courses instituted in Black colleges have sanctioned the basic assumption inherent in their white models—that a college education must encompass a definite minimum body of facts which every student should be required to memorize.

At this point, it is necessary to remember that most of the body of allegedly essential facts covered by standard survey courses tends to reflect the values of the eastern (U.S.) academic elite. Basically, these values assume that college students will be recruited from affluent homes and should have been exposed to culturally-rich informal experiences. Furthermore, it has been generally expected that students would be graduates of superior high schools—even wealthy, exclusive preparatory schools. In both prior situations, prospective college students will have been literally drilled to memorize a large body of facts, often unrelated, but regarded as essential.

Since many "essential" facts college freshmen are expected to know would have been learned in culturally rich environments, southern white colleges, as well as Black colleges, have been forced to admit students who fall far short of eastern academic norms. Indeed, practically all high school graduates from small southern towns and isolated rural communities (white or Black) would have to be classified as culturally-deprived if eastern elite academic standards are rigidly applied. Therefore, even today, no southern white college is regarded as ranking academically among the top Ivy League colleges, and graduates of southern white colleges are not normally expected to score as high on standardized tests as graduates of Ivy League schools. Realistically, too many of the academic facts stressed by the Ivy League elite are simply not relevant to the life styles of southern whites, to say nothing about the everyday survival problems with which the vast majority of Black Americans must struggle.

Private Black colleges have used survey courses as vehicles by which a large array of more or less disconnected facts have been drilled into their students. This has resulted in magnifying two basic, damaging problems:

1. Black students' ineffective oral and written communication. With so many facts to be covered, the generally large number of students in survey courses seldom get an opportunity to study any subject in depth or to discuss major issues. Since practically all of the examinations in these courses are objective, students do not get the exercise in thinking and writing they need so badly.

2. Inadequately prepared teachers. Because most college teachers specialize in one major discipline, survey courses, even in the Ivy League colleges, have had staffing difficulties. Few teachers are so well grounded in the liberal arts that they feel adequate in presenting so vast an array of facts. On large faculties where practically all teachers are highly trained specialists, team-teaching of survey courses has been more or less effectively employed. Team-teaching has never worked well for any sustained period of time in the private Black college because of limited faculty and spotty teacher preparation. There are always units in survey courses which no teacher in the small college is prepared to handle. In any case, even when there are competent teachers in the college, they are most likely to be carrying heavy schedules already and will have no allotted time for team-teaching.

Because private Black colleges have been so anxious to have their students measure up to the academic standards set by the Ivy League, they have tended to clutter up their curricula with year-long survey and introductory courses. An analysis of requirements for graduation in some of these colleges revealed that it is entirely possible for students in some fields to graduate with from a third to more than half of their credits in such general courses.

Instead of offering so many general courses, it might be advisable for private Black colleges to design several short courses as substitutes. These courses would deal in greater depth with selected liberal arts themes and issues, and would be planned to cover periods of from four to eight weeks. Their content and methods of presentation would be determined largely by the peculiar needs of the students involved, rather than by the fiat of elite Ivy League-oriented professors whose heavily endowed chairs in "Ivory Towers" are usually quite far removed from the problems, learning styles, and aspirations of Black ghetto youth.

REMEDIAL INSTRUCTION

The second major attempt Black colleges have made to bridge the gap between inadequate high school preparation and established college entrance standards may be broadly described as remedial instruction. All Black colleges have had to commit a large proportion of their teachers' time and talents to remedial instruction. An academic dean estimated that up to a fourth of the teachers' time in his college is spent in the presentation of information which normally should have been adequately covered by students while in high school.

There are three distinct levels of remedial instruction characteristic of Black colleges:

1. Remedial instruction inherent in regular introductory courses. According to reports of teachers in the sample colleges, practically all of their introductory courses begin at the high school or even the elementary level. Seldom does an experienced teacher in these colleges assume that he can begin his courses on a strictly college level. The amount of pre-college material covered will, of course, vary with the courses taught or the extent of the academic gap to be bridged. Students in such courses as mathematics, statistics, english and the foreign languages must often take from six weeks to a semester or more attempting to catch up to a point at which college level courses are expected to begin. The teacher who does not realize this is likely to have an abnormally high rate of student failures because information in these courses is more or less precisely graded: the mastery of one level becomes the prerequisite of a higher level. Consequently, if the high school

prerequisites have been omitted, they must be supplied before the student can be expected to comprehend college level instruction in these disciplines.

Information included in such courses as history, economics, religion, education, sociology, biology, and literature is not as precisely graded as the courses listed above, yet perceptive teachers in these courses also report that students enrolled in them usually suffer about the same degree of academic deprivation as is readily revealed in english or mathematics. Therefore, the introductory courses taught in Black colleges presuppose that some significant amount of time must be spent in the bridging of academic gaps caused by an inferior high school education.

2. Special remedial courses. Whether or not they are so labelled, all of the private Black colleges offer courses specifically designed to cover pre-college information. During recent years, most of these colleges have also made attempts to extend conventional remedial instruction by setting up so-called reading, language, and mathematics laboratories. These laboratories are almost always organized for students who have the most serious deficiencies in basic academic skills. Here again, it is important to note that the academic skills these courses and laboratories are designed to develop are precisely those which should have been developed on the high school level.

It is not easy to determine the exact proportion of Black colleges' talents and resources which are devoted to the training of students in areas that should have been covered in high school. It might suffice to point out that from half to three-fourths or more of the freshmen students in these colleges require some significant amount of remedial instruction if they are expected to achieve according to national norms. In most instances college administrators admitted that their cut-off points for the admittance of students to remedial courses was determined by the availability of facilities and teachers, rather than by the number of the students who need the courses. They generally concurred with the statement made by one academic dean who said that "at the present time (Fall, 1970) about half of our freshmen students are taking one or two remedial courses, yet I would guess that between 80-85 percent of them should be in these courses. We simply don't have the teachers or the space to teach all of the students who need these courses." He called attention to the fact that the reading laboratory "has only 30 booths, while I'd say most of our 250 or so freshmen should be using the lab regularly, since they are reading far below what is regarded as normal for high school graduates."

3. Remedial programs. As suggested before, teachers of liberal arts disciplines in Black colleges have always recognized that the vast majority of their students come to college with serious deficiences in other basic academic areas besides mathematics and standard english. Special remedial courses in mathematics and english were the first to be set up because deficiencies in these areas can be pinpointed easily. Also, a student who has inadequate preparation in these particular disciplines is likely to do poorly in college, since at least a basic grasp of mathematics and/or standard english is a prerequisite to understanding all other college subjects. Therefore, liberal arts teachers have always insisted that most graduates of segregated Black public schools need what would amount to a full academic year or more of general post-high school education before they are ready for authentic college instruction.

A primary goal of the civil rights movement during the last twenty years has been that of achieving educational equality for Black youth. One of the inevitable consequences of this focus has been the systematic comparison of the scholastic achievements of Black and white students. Extensive data gathered by independent researchers, research teams sponsored by private agencies, public school systems, and by an indefinite number of local, state, and federal commissions have underscored the fact that most Black children have been victimized by tragically inadequate, criminally inferior education—from kindergarten through high school. What has been even more alarming is conclusive evidence that the students' academic deprivation is compounded year after year.[1] Black students in inferior schools usually fall farther and farther behind their white counterparts as they progress through the elementary and high school grades. And so the massive academic deprivation characteristic of most graduates of Black high schools, which has been long-recognized by Black college teachers, has finally been made public. Some foundations, Black and white educators, and men of good will from all walks of life were dismayed and shocked when they came to realize the extent to which academic injustices have been historically meted out to Black children. This realization eventually led to some positive responses on the part of foundations and the federal government. Several of the colleges have received grants to develop extensive remedial programs instead of the narrow courses which they have traditionally offered.

A private Black college, Dillard University, was, in a sense, the fountainhead of such remedial programs. During the late 1950s, a special faculty committee at that college made a careful analysis of the academic handicaps of the typical Dillard freshman. It made several recommendations about how these handicaps might be dealt with in a realistic way. On the basis of the committee's recommendations, Dillard received a grant from the Taconic Foundation in the spring of 1959 to initiate an experimental pre-freshman program designed to bridge the gap between the education its freshmen would have *actually received* in high school and the very minimum of what they *should* have received in order to do acceptable freshman work. That foundation provided sufficient funds for Dillard to invite forty-four high school graduates who had already been admitted to the university's 1959-1960 freshman class as an experimental group. They were expected to spend eight weeks in an especially designed, new pre-freshman program. All participants were required to live on campus and all of their expenses were paid. Students selected were, as far as possible, representatives of all levels of achievement characteristic of the incoming freshman class: Students who had "C" or better averages in their high school classes. (A similar program was initiated at Morehouse College but the students were selected from among the *top* students of the incoming freshman class. Thus, it was not essentially *remedial*, but *enrichment*.) A consultant to the Dillard program made this summary observation: "These students were . . . poorly prepared to engage in college level work. By any objective measure they could not read very well, and the group as a whole was generally insecure in the use of language."[2]

200

Teachers and students in the pre-freshman program at Dillard reported some convincing successes. After three experimental years the pre-freshman program was made an established part of the Dillard offerings, and it is now open to any incoming freshman who applies.

Since the beginning of the experimental pre-freshman programs at Dillard and Morehouse in the summer of 1959, pre-college, or what should appropriately be labelled post-high school programs, have become a fact of life in Black colleges. All of the colleges included in this study have had one or more types of such programs. Some continue to focus on math and reading while others have been much broader, attempting to bridge the so-called cultural gap, as well as the very real academic gap of most Black high school graduates.

The two most ambitious, well-financed and formally structured of the combined remedial-enrichment programs are the Upward Bound and the Thirteen Colleges Curriculum. These two federally financed programs were projected on a much sounder basis than other enrichment programs in that they do not attempt to bridge the wide academic gap between an inadequate high school education and college prerequisites in a short six or eight week summer session. Instead, students may receive special instruction in the Upward Bound program for two years before entering college and the Thirteen Colleges program enrolls an experimental group of students for a total academic program throughout the freshman year.

According to reliable reports, the pre-college enrichment-remedial programs established by and for Black colleges have had some significant successes. However, actual college achievement records indicate that there is still much to be desired. The roots of the cultural and academic deprivations suffered by the vast majority of graduates of inferior, segregated Black schools are far too deeply embedded to be removed during a short summer session or a single academic year, while the students are engaged in other full time high school studies. Neither can we logically expect college freshmen who have come up through the grades in inferior schools and been socialized in poverty to be able to overcome these accumulated handicaps in addition to carrying on formally established college studies during the freshman year. This would be quite unlikely, no matter how carefully the instructional program had been planned or how motivated individual students may be.

Up until now, graduates of Black schools and colleges have been victims of a cruel game of academic buck passing. High schools blame elementary schools for sending them inadequately-educated pupils; colleges blame high schools for the poor preparation of their incoming freshmen, and the world of high education blames Black colleges for graduating incomplete products. In the meantime Black youth suffer. Whether it is just or not, the "buck" must stop with the Black colleges. Since the federal government has permitted a dual racial system of blatantly unequal education to persist for over 100 years, in direct violation of federal laws and the essential spirit of democracy, it must share the blame. The federal government must assume a joint responsibility with Black colleges in a concerted attempt to correct a century of academic wrongs suffered by Black students.

Educators, and hopefully the public, must insist upon two interrelated sets of federal action if this nation is to preserve the otherwise wasted talents of a large majority of Black youth. First, they must insist that Black youth be given the very best public education each of the states provides. Inferior Black schools must be abolished. Second, because millions of Black youth have been already victimized by inferior schools, only the federal government can guarantee that these youth are given a truly equal opportunity to overcome their deep academic and social deprivations. One role of the Black colleges' would be to devise promising programs for the academic rehabilitation of Black students, with adequate support from the federal government. This might mean that federal grants would be made to Black colleges for pre-freshman and certain special remedial programs, including special summer programs and various forms of apprentice experiences, in which selected students could participate throughout their regular college years.

It is now quite firmly demonstrated that the more deprived the student is on one end of "the log," the more he will need a highly qualified teacher on the other end. According to information provided by students, teachers, and administrators in Black colleges, all too often the less experienced, less formally prepared, professionally insecure teachers are assigned to teach in remedial programs. As a rule, these programs attract far less than their fair share of the more mature, most highly qualified teachers. This pattern must be reversed if such programs are to achieve needed success. Teachers in remedial-enrichment programs should be drawn from among the elite in their special academic disciplines, and each major area of a given program would be coordinated by a highly trained, full-time specialist. Specialists in such areas as speech, reading, audio-visuals, the psychology of learning, writing, the teaching of mathematics, and so forth would be among the highest salaried teachers and given every challenge to pursue creative scholarship.

In addition to this select group of enrichment specialists, other mature, highly trained teachers would be expected to give a limited amount of their professional time to the enrichment programs in their college. This means that a given top professor would perform one or more of the following functions: teach a course or two; give a series of special lectures; conduct workshops or seminars; direct certain students in individual study or research projects; and/or participate in program planning meetings. In all instances, the remedial-enrichment programs would be so staffed that the best qualified creative teachers could find new dimensions of academic and professional growth by participating in them. The way such programs are generally handled now, teachers soon begin to feel trapped, professionally frustrated, and looked down upon by their colleagues who adhere strictly to teaching in their specialized disciplines. This situation, perhaps more than anything else, has tended to undermine the effectiveness of remedial courses and programs in Black colleges.

SPECIAL PROGRAMS

In addition to the various types of compensatory programs engaged in by the sample colleges, at one time or another all have instituted special programs designed to extend the education of their better students. For the most part, however, such programs are not nearly so well planned and supported as the compensatory programs. After extensive observations, a research assistant for this study concluded that "there are few if any viable programs in the sample colleges which are specifically designed for above average students." When such programs do exist they are usually the brainchild of individual teachers who assume primary responsibility for them, and they are generally under-supported by students, faculty, and the administration. Practically all of them are short-lived or exist on a more or less unstructured, ill-defined, sporadic basis.

Honors programs. All of the colleges studied list at least one honors course in their catalogues. Some of these courses were designed for students in a cross-section of academic disciplines while others are strictly divisional or departmental.

Interviews with academic deans and division chairmen revealed that seldom does an honors program fulfill needed expectations in the college. Some teachers complained that it was necessary to teach such courses in the same general manner and on about the same academic level as other courses in the college. Others pointed out the difficulty of having a distinctive, recognized honors program on campuses where the prevailing mood is non-intellectual. In such an atmosphere students make few sustained efforts to be singled out from their peers for academic achievements. Some faculty sponsors reported that it was difficult to get already qualified students to pay dues or participate in established honors societies or even to attend campus meetings of honor students.

Another reason why some competent students seem to be reluctant to participate in honors programs is that such programs are always sponsored by faculty persons who are interested in high-level scholarship. As a rule, it is the faculty who extends honors and recognition to students. Enthusiastic participation in honors programs, then, tends to establish close relationships between students and teachers. This could function to alienate such students from their peers, since today student norms expect a sharp division between students and teachers. In other words, there are students on private Black college campuses who would not strive openly to qualify for and join distinctly elite groups because this action may tend to alienate them from the predominantly mass-oriented student culture.

Finally, a faculty advisor to an honors society summarized still another reason for the lack of strong student interest in honors programs. She said that "Students feel that honors programs and societies are 'irrelevant,' 'passé,' 'middle class-oriented' and 'gone with the wind.' They are simply unimportant in most students' system of values. They regard them as part of the 'establishment'."

Although honors programs on these campuses are not as highly valued as they once were, they still have a very definite function. On each of the campuses visited there were students who did value their membership in honors societies and were proud to qualify for participation in honors courses and seminars. A group of honor students with whom we talked did object to being singled out from among their fellows as having succeeded according to established rules in the traditional academic community. This poses a dilemma because, as we noted earlier, those who make the best grades and receive the most desirable fellowships to do graduate study are generally those students who conform to middle class standards and have closer relationships with teachers than do other students. Membership in honors programs is a sure way of facilitating this relationship. Honor students know this, and so the other horn of their dilemma is this: a large proportion of them want to become recognized as campus leaders or at least a part of the gang, but close association with teachers and obvious social conformity seldom help in this regard.

For one reason or another, then, a disproportionate amount of faculty energy and resources in private Black colleges are focused upon compensatory or enrichment programs in which average and below average students are expected to enroll. Teachers frequently complained that relatively little systematic attention or organized assistance is given to the above average performers.

Innovative programs. In attempting to provide the highest standard of education possible for all students, Black colleges have engaged in various experimental programs. Before mentioning some of them it might be instructive to point out that a truly worthy experiment must be given every opportunity to succeed. This has seldom, if ever, been the case in Black colleges where even their most highly touted programs (Pre-college and Thirteen Colleges Curriculum Programs) have never had the best chances of success. All too often such programs suffer from fuzzy definitions of concrete goals, inadequate integration into the general college program, shortage of qualified teachers, rapid turnover of teachers, and/or insufficient, uncertain financial support.

Despite all of the problems and handicaps involved, private Black colleges as a group have been much more inventive than is usually recognized. It is surprising how many experiments they have initiated, expanded and revised in their attempts to provide academically and socially handicapped Black youth with a high quality college education. Even during the decades when a college education was ordinarily regarded as a privilege for youth from the most affluent, fortunate families, private Black colleges were experimenting with open enrollment, certain non-grade courses, team teaching, student tutors, various types of enrichment efforts, mathematics, speech and writing laboratories; Black Studies, and so forth.

Unfortunately, Black colleges and their professors have never had the respectful attention foundations, prominent educators, the news media, and publishers accord Ivy League colleges and their professors. Some of the most promising and inventive programs and practices devised by Black colleges have been given little or no recognition in the world of higher education. Furthermore, certain of their insightful, much-needed, and promising innovations have had to be seriously modified and weakened because they lacked sufficient funds and qualified personnel. Some of their most challenging innovations never really got beyond the drawing board stage. Indeed, it would be revealing to look on the shelves of foundations, state boards of education, and certain federal agencies, where promising innovative proposals in higher education drawn up by Black college administrators and teachers have been put away and forgotten, simply because they came from Black colleges. Even some alleged friends of certain Black colleges, particularly churches related to them, have not taken their innovative potential very seriously. Somehow they too seem convinced that no good thing can come out of Black colleges. Here again, this too often becomes a self-fulfilling prophecy. According to information provided by administrators and teachers, rich funding sources have often shelved proposals submitted by Black colleges which, if they had been properly supported, might have been significant in initiating much-needed innovations in higher education. There is convincing evidence that influential educators and prominent funding agencies—especially foundations and large sponsoring church bodies—have been too slow in recognizing the private Black college as a promising laboratory in which to carry on badly needed experiments in higher education. Their historical commitment to the education of youth representing all social classes and backgrounds, their emphasis upon humanitarian over rigid academic principles, their freedom from conservative alumni control, and their relatively simple organization, make some private Black colleges ideal institutions through which this nation could lead the way in discovering and developing new approaches and methods of providing quality education. This would be true not only for the millions of academically and socially handicapped Black and white American youth, but for countless millions of academically handicapped youth in under-developed nations who want desperately to latch onto and become recognized participants in this fast-moving, nuclear age.

So far, Black colleges have been imitative of prominent white colleges largely because their efforts to change and innovate have been discouraged or actually opposed by accrediting agencies, state boards of education, and by certain other organizations, agencies, and universities which place an almost sacred credence upon standardized tests. These tests presuppose that all college graduates will have been taught pretty much the same body of facts. Any significant deviation from established, standard curricula on the part of Black colleges is likely, therefore, to be reflected in the poor performance of their graduates on these tests. However, there is mounting evidence that the rigid, monolithic, academically-sacred college curricula pre-supposed by standardized tests are not adequate to prepare students for the complex industrial world society now emerging. It may just be that the time has come for certain Black colleges to lead the way toward the development of a new conception of higher education better suited for this frighteningly new nuclear age. On this point Vincent Harding insists that Black educators must, "Leave the ideals and standards of the dying Euro-American world behind and dare to risk the creation of new institutions and new modes of thought on behalf of a new humanity . . ."[3]

If private Black colleges are to lead the way to a new, more relevant, higher education, they must make revolutionary changes. Past experiences indicate that a slow, uncertain, piece-meal course by course approach is bound to fail: too many competing conservative forces within and without the college are automatically activated by the winds of change. These conservative forces quickly conspire to neutralize slow changes before they can become significant.

An excellent example of this is the efforts one of the sample colleges is making to renew itself. This college made a bold and exciting effort to create a new college as a substitute for the old. The idea of a complete self-study was conceived in 1961, and in October of that year the idea received trustee approval. Subsequently, a committee was appointed to plan the self-study. The study was slow getting underway and it was not until five years later (1966) that a committee composed of faculty, administrators, students and trustees finally developed the idea of a "New College." Some of the more progressive members of this committee succeeded in convincing others that the self-study should not aim simply to discover minor errors in a traditional college model, but should aim at designing a new philosophy of education, new administration, new curriculum, and new teaching methods and techniques. In order to achieve this much larger goal, an elaborate "Study for the Future" organization was set up. Just about every teacher, administrator and student at the college was given a definite assignment on one or more of the twelve task forces. A cadre of consultants was also engaged to give constant advice and guidance in the planning of this new college concept.

Throughout the study, analysis and planning for the new college were expected to follow just three basic guidelines:

1. It is to remain for the present an undergraduate college with approximately 1,200-1,500 students.

2. It will continue to accept students varying greatly in terms of their high school records.

3. Its idealistic objectives as stated in the catalogue will remain essentially unchanged, although there may be minor revisions.[4]

These limited, quite liberal guidelines left the participants in the study of the future program relatively free to draw up bold, creative proposals for the new college. As a result, all of the twelve main task forces and the five sub-task forces developed an innumerable variety of well-researched, innovative recommendations. They recommended drastic changes in the total curricula, teaching methods, recruitment of students, grading system, extracurricular experiences, community relations, administration, relations with other colleges, and so forth. In all instances, the recommendations were evaluated in terms of their potential for making the college more relevant to the needs of the students and the dynamic society in which they would live and work.

After the work of the task forces was deemed completed, the all-college Study for the Future organization agreed to implement the findings and recommendations as quickly as possible. Consequently, throughout the summer of 1968 a committee composed of eleven members (students, teachers, and a special consultant) was charged with the responsibility of developing a freshman program designed to implement certain major recommendations. The committee met in long daily sessions in which primary goals were defined and basic academic procedures and methods were discussed. Eventually the committee pooled its talents and energy in the development of a Core Program for Freshmen. The main goals of the proposed freshman program were summarized in one of the several statements of purpose:

Its purpose is to break down outmoded and irrelevant faculty patterns of teaching as a necessary step to change student-learning patterns. Without this openness to change the program will be in dire danger of falling back upon the traditional teacher-directed lecture class.[5]

The committee of eleven developed what it hoped would be a completely new freshman curriculum based upon this general purpose. This program is basically interdisciplinary and deliberately eschews courses as traditionally conceived. It was intended to be a unified approach to the study of man. A syllabus was prepared by the committee of eleven to be used in this freshman core program.

It was expected that this program would constitute what is normally regarded as a full time student load. Immediately a compromise was made whereby students would be allowed to take one course in addition to the unified freshman core. This compromise was forced by divisional and departmental contentions that students must take a traditional course (6 hours) in the freshman year in order to get necessary background to begin major requirements in the sophomore year.

The syllabus to be used in the program throughout the year was divided into five major units and an Inter-term period of four weeks:

Unit I: The Black Man Then and Now - This unit was broken down into four subheads: African Backgrounds; The System of Slavery; Racism; and Black Protest.

Unit II: The Origins of Life - This unit had three main divisions: As Depicted in the Arts; In its Simplest Form—Cell Theory; As Explained by Science—Evolution.

Interim Four-Weeks Period - During this interim each student was to be engaged in a special project in individual study or enroll in an elective offered for freshmen. In many instances, the special project might grow out of a topic studied during the first twelve weeks of the program. However, each student would have the opportunity to discuss with his core teacher possible projects from which he could elect one for study.

Unit III: Social Behavior - This unit had two major divisions: Aggressor and Predator Prey Relationships (psychological

210

readings) and Man and His Various Cultures and His Use of Communication.

Unit IV: Social Change - Study for this unit was under four major divisions: Ideologies that Change the Universe; Social Effects of Technology; Social Movements and Resistance to Social Change; The Arts in Social Protest.

Unit V: Probability - This unit had three approaches: Science; Evidence; and Existentialism.

The academic year for the freshman program is divided into two twelve-week semesters, with a four week Inter-term period between semesters during which students, under careful faculty direction, are expected to engage in independent study and research.

After two years of operation, the freshman program at this college was carefully evaluated by a leading authority in the field of educational innovation. Working very closely with students, teachers, and other knowledgeable persons, he found several strengths and weaknesses in it. It is not the purpose here to discuss in detail the strengths and weaknesses he cited. Instead it might be sufficient to point out what he and other observers suggest may have been the main reasons why the creative approach to the new college has had much less success than its designers anticipated. (I focus upon this program because the same or similar forces which operated to retard or maybe abort this particular new college have been—and will continue to be—inimical to the creation of the new private Black college needed to spearhead a truly innovative, relevant higher education in our present complex society. Only if these forces are recognized and understood can these colleges prepare effective counters to them).

Among the most persistent forces militating against the emergence of the truly innovative, relevant private Black college are the following:

1. *Lack of sufficient funds*. None of the colleges presently has the funds necessary for the additional physical facilities and academic technology required to initiate and develop extensive, creative changes. For example, though the experimental program just mentioned presupposed extensive teacher-counseling, the of-

fice space for teachers was limited, small, and crowded. There was hardly any place in the teachers' offices where individual students could relax, to say nothing of accommodating student groups. Again, while a major purpose of the program was to get away from traditional classroom lectures, little effort was made to develop comparable classroom situations that would facilitate effective departures. Thus, while audio-visuals had a central place in the program, no convenient, attractive facility was regularly available where movies and documentaries could be shown. Neither was there a special library set aside and managed to compliment the goals of the program.

Another problem related to funding must be considered if an innovative program is to have the maximum chance of success: the stresses and strains students experience in order to meet their economic obligations. There were no special funds for scholarships provided for freshmen at the experimental college. Though the core program was structured to present a maximum amount of information to students, many had to accept employment in order to continue in school, and practically all had difficult financial problems. Some of the freshmen reportedly held jobs which required 30-40 hours a week. They did not have enough time to do the reading, research, and analysis built into the program. Therefore, no matter how well structured and feasible such a program might be, it must realistically take into consideration the fact that the vast majority of students in Black colleges will need substantial financial support if they are to give innovative programs a sufficient amount of time and energy.

2. *Inability to recruit and maintain top flight faculty.* Closely related to the lack of sufficient funds is the problem of faculty quality. Though the new college program planners had intended to reduce the central importance of the teacher, the program was unwittingly structured to give the teacher an even more central role. It presupposed a personally involved superior faculty which would include highly trained specialists in speech, writing, and the psychology of learning. But the salaries offered teachers in the freshman program were far too low to attract such teachers in sufficient numbers, and for the most part, teachers in this highly in-

novative program were not as experienced or well trained as teachers of the traditional courses.

Another reason why this freshman program has not attracted a sufficient number of qualified teachers is that it tends to alienate the teacher from his academic specialty, and ultimately from his major professional interests. In this new college venture, teaching in the core program is theoretically regarded as a full-time schedule. That is, teachers are not formally expected to teach upper level courses, although at first a few volunteered to do so in order to maintain relationships with their academic departments. They soon began to complain of too heavy a teaching load and those who continued to teach outside of the freshman program did so under protest. Increasingly teachers expressed the desire to transfer from the freshman program to teaching in their divisions or departments. Some still remain in the program simply because there is no other assignment in their academic departments for them. A few have become what one teacher described as "professional freshman teachers."

In any case and for whatever reason, so far the freshman core program at the sample college has not been able to attract and hold the number of top flight teachers necessary to make the experiment as successful as it might be. There are already an increasing number of teachers in the college who are recommending that the new program should be scrapped and that the college reinstate its old, traditional freshman schedule of courses.

3. *Lack of integration into the total college program.* It must be remembered that the freshman program at the experimental college, as conceived in the summer of 1968, was intended to be only a first step toward a completely new college. It was expected that in 1969-1970 the philosophy and methods of the freshman program would be extended to include the sophomore year. By the fourth year, 1972-1973, the total curriculum was expected to articulate the new academic thrust. This, of course, has not been the case. After four years, the freshman program is still appended onto the traditional college offerings. Though general academic requirements have been reduced, upper level courses are carried on as usual. What was intended to be a total curriculum innovation

has been confined to the first academic year. This means that students coming out of the freshman year must go through another period of orientation and adjustment to the upper college program.

Another phase of integration so essential to the success of an innovative program is that of overall administration. Before a truly innovative college program can have desired success, administrative attitudes and practices in regard to that program must be changed in a complementary fashion. If administrative policies and practices regarding innovative programs are the same as toward traditional programs, there will be a strong tendency for the new programs to resemble the old. I am thinking here specifically of such things as the initiation of budget proposals, the recruitment of faculty, the securing of library resources, dormitory accommodations, extra-curricular activities and any number of other areas where administrative decisions may determine the nature of a new program. We can hardly expect a program to be authentically innovative so long as the particular college is governed by old rules and forced to adjust to traditional, rigid administrative patterns. Incidentally, this is one important reason why significant innovations always stimulate resistance: they tend to interfere with what is normally regarded as *order* by a conventional administration. In order for them to succeed, a new set of norms must be adopted for the total institution.

4. *The pressure to routinize standards.* A major handicap to significant academic innovations undertaken by private Black colleges stems from outside pressure in which their students are inevitably compared with other colleges' products. This is true not only in regard to standardized tests but more specifically to the transfer of credits and credentials. For example, a major problem the planners of the freshman program encountered at the sample college was this: if a student desires to transfer to another college after the freshman year, how will the receiving college evaluate credits accorded in the innovative program? What would be regarded as equivalent course credits in the receiving college? These and other hard questions made it necessary to equate the experimental freshman program in terms of standard semester hours (24), despite the fact that the program was not originally

214

designed on a credit hours basis. Furthermore, since other institutions of higher education evaluate transfer of graduate students' credentials according to their ranking in a competitive grade system, the experimental college found it necessary to rank student performance as "pass" "fail" and "honors." This was another key compromise, as the planners of the program deliberately recommended that grading be eliminated.

5. *The need for routinization.* There is still another basic reason for modifications in certain innovative programs: Almost all colleges, state boards of education, and licensing bodies require certain specific courses to be taken by students. Such courses as mathematics, english, history, psychology and so forth are standard requirements. Ordinarily, a student is expected to take several of these courses during the freshman year. In a program where courses as such are not recognized, the student is likely to face the problem of satisfying these designated course requirements. Somehow an equivalent must be decided upon in the transference of credits and credentials where such courses have not been taken. Therefore, either the core program at the college in question had to be arbitrarily defined in terms of acceptable courses, or the receiving institution or agency would have to voluntarily acknowledge the validity of the total core program. As it stands now, a number of indefinite compromises are being considered.

Not only is routinization a problem in regard to the transference of credits and credentials, but it constitutes an internal college problem as well. Two examples may suffice. First, the experimental college, like most colleges, awards academic honors in terms of grade points. Since there are no traditional grades given students in this freshman program, honors can not be awarded as long as the traditional basis for honors remains. Second, some division chairmen and department heads still contend that as long as the freshman program is independent of the standard curriculum there is no way of knowing whether the students are properly prepared in terms of prerequisites expected for certain upper level courses.

We may conclude then that no truly innovative program can achieve desired success while simply appended onto a larger traditional program. Either the traditional program must give way to principles inherent in the innovative program or the innovative program will eventually lose itself in the larger traditional one.

6. *"Old Wine in New Bottles:" The Concept of a New College*. Ultimately, innovative programs in private Black colleges are seriously compromised by the fact that the concept of the college is generally static and traditional. Since the prevailing concept of the college is that of an institution in which students are to master a rigid, prescribed body of knowledge, innovative programs are naturally evaluated in terms of their contributions to this end.[6] In such a case significant innovations must be restricted to structure and methods—quite superficial since the heart of the college, the curriculum, would have to remain virtually unchanged.

Ironically, even in the evaluation of the erstwhile revolutionary freshman program just described, the teachers, students and consultants involved generally used standardized tests and traditional expectations. There was a tacit assumption underlying the entire evaluation: it was still assumed that Ivy League colleges constitute the desirable academic model. Therefore, the extent to which the freshmen deviated from what might be termed Ivy League norms was the precise extent to which they were regarded as academically retarded. Unwittingly, and very inappropriately, the innovative core program was expected to bring the freshman's performance closer to the ideal Ivy League model. The extent to which this was achieved was the extent to which the program was viewed as successful.

There is no intention to argue here with the validity of the long-established Ivy League model. The main point is that so far all innovative programs in private Black colleges are meant to help students measure up to the traditional, more or less static, concept of the college. They are seldom if ever conceived in terms of a new concept of higher education. Explicitly or tacitly, academic norms in American education have been influenced, even determined, by the nation's orientation toward *production*. Production standards have been influenced, often determined, by market competition. With greatly advanced technology, fewer and fewer people will be needed for the production of goods, so the conception of the college should be seriously examined with the view of arriving at a new concept influenced by an emerging international society where people and human relations will be of supreme value. Students would be educated to live in this larger world where cooperation rather than competition would be regarded as the cardinal principle in human affairs.

To employ an ancient simile, innovations in higher education so far have been largely attempts to put "new wine in old bottles." To carry this simile one step further, when the wines of change undergo normal fermentation, the old bottles burst asunder because their moribund structures are rigid and unable to contain the germinated forces. This is exactly what is happening to traditional colleges today, where the need for broad revolutionary changes is being proposed in order to bring higher education more in line with the demands and opportunities of this very threatening, challenging emerging world society.[7] The new, relevant liberal arts college will need to be one in which old concepts such as nationalism, imperialism, race, social class, war, culture, economic systems, urbanism, democracy, religion, science, morality, all forms of government, and citizenship will be re-examined and re-evaluated in terms of their role in human history and their meaning for humanity in a nuclear era where some effective form of world government and world society is not only desired but possible and increasingly essential.

As noted earlier, the traditional concept of the college is elitist in that the original purpose was to educate a very select minority of youth for one or more of the liberal professions, especially religion, law and medicine. After a careful study of higher education in the principal living societies of the world, Arnold Toynbee concluded:

> It will be seen that the original purpose of universities in all the three societies in question was not to provide a general higher education for the population as a whole or, short of that, even for a majority. The purpose was to pick out a small elite of individuals whose personal temperament and ability qualified them for being educated to practice certain particular professions which require special gifts and a special training and

which, in a society at any stage of social and cultural development, will be staffed by only a small minority of the total population.[8]

The preponderance of expressed thinking by educators and informed laymen relative to the subject indicates that the key or central crisis in higher education today (and in education on all levels) is due largely to a dilemma in its social orientation concerning *who* shall be educated. On the one hand, there are strong, persistent, logical forces which would have colleges remain loyal to their traditional elitist exclusionism in regard to the selection of students, curricula and values. Any apparent deviation from this conservatism is cause for deep concern—even alarm. On the other hand, there are increasingly strong forces demanding drastic, revolutionary changes which would make education, even in the most prestigious colleges, equally available to all youth, regardless of socio-economic origin and circumstances. This different, essentially democratic education would naturally presuppose a series of changes in all other areas of the traditional academic culture including the central purposes of a college education, the curricula, student evaluation, methods of teaching, requirements for graduation and even the nature of social life on the college campus.

Most college administrators today are willing to acknowledge the need for very significant changes. President William McGill of Columbia University, for instance, is quoted as saying that he expects this to be a decade of educational innovations "unlike anything seen in the last 50 years," and that "our survival depends on it. Our problems are monumental and the time available to solve them is growing short."[9]

All leading colleges have manifested a steadfast resistance to such significant changes. For the most part, they do not venture beyond superficial, limited innovations and there has been very little change in their traditional policies and practices. Any innovations made have had to fit into conservative, traditional structures. When students are admitted from substandard high schools or from poor families and Black ghettos, they are patronizingly classified as high risk students and challenged to com-

218

pete with students from superior high schools and affluent, culturally rich families. They are judged by standards created exclusively for the fortunate, affluent students who were deliberately trained to compete in these colleges. The concept of the college and the purpose of higher education remain about the same, and the new type of enrollees must indeed be regarded as high risk because the college itself is not expected to change enough to include them as bona fide students. Instead, their status is that of sociological "strangers," regarded as outsiders until they have clearly demonstrated that they belong and are capable of competing as equals with bona fide enrollees according to rules designed especially for these traditional students by the traditional college. Gilbert Moore insists that "the typical white American institution of higher learning is fundamentally unprepared (and in many cases *unwilling* to be prepared) to meet (their) his needs. From this black standpoint then, it is the institution which should more properly be labeled 'high risk.' "[10]

It is generally agreed that some fundamental changes must be made in the goals and nature of higher education if it is to serve the best interests of this nuclear, industrial society. Since certain strong conservative forces militate against what amounts to revolutionary changes on the part of affluent white colleges, it can be argued that certain private Black colleges offer the best hope of leading the way toward the development of a new, creative conception of higher education. After all, unlike traditional white colleges that were founded to serve and perpetuate the socioeconomic elite, the tradition of private Black colleges is just the reverse: they were founded to serve the poor, disesteemed Black masses who had been severely crippled by over 200 years of dehumanizing slavery and chronic poverty. Throughout their entire history, the main goal of private Black colleges has been to elevate disadvantaged youth to creative citizenship. These colleges, then, have had to grapple with the same knotty problems which, at long last, the traditional colleges are now beginning to recognize as legitimate. It would seem both logical and just that certain private Black colleges, with accumulated wisdom in the education of the masses, should be the institutions selected, supported and recognized as leaders in the development of this new concept of higher education. Instead of classifying these colleges as developing institutions, in the sense that they are struggling to be like traditional colleges as implied by the federal government's definition, they could become developing institutions in a creative, pioneering sense. As such, they could be worthy, valuable participants in the movement to free the minds of disadvantaged youth throughout the world and particularly in our Black ghettos.

NOTES

1. Kenneth B. Clark, *Dark Ghetto* (New York: Harper and Row, 1965). See especially pp. 120-125.

2. Frank G. Jennings, "For Such a Tide is Moving. . . ," *Saturday Review*, May 16, 1964, pp. 74-75, 87-88.

3. Vincent Harding, "Toward a Black University," *Ebony Magazine*, Vol. 25, No. 10, August 1970, p. 157.

4. Lou La Brant and Violet Richards, *A Study for the Future* (New Orleans: Dillard University, 1969), pp. 23-24.

5. *A Study for the Future*, p. 110.

6. See W. John Minter and Patricia O. Snyder, Editors, *Value Change and Power Conflict in Higher Education* (Berkeley, University of California, 1969), selected topics, especially p. 37.

7. See the series of papers on this subject in Alvin C. Eurich, *Campus 1980* (New York: A Delta Book, 1968).

8. Alvin C. Eurich, *Campus 1980*, p. XX.

9. *U. S. News and World Report*, Vol. 72, No. 3, January 17, 1972, p. 21.

10. *Change Magazine*, Vol. 4, No. 3, p. 35.

9.

Governance

Black colleges have traditionally placed much higher value upon administrative roles than they have upon teaching and creative scholarship. The underlying reasons for this proclivity are complex and difficult to isolate. Upon analysis, however, there is convincing evidence that this pattern of valuation has its roots in the ethos of American society where business executives have always enjoyed high prestige and great social power. The peculiar historical conditions experienced by Black colleges have conspired to exaggerate their administrative roles in such a way that they have become considerably more central, even overshadowing, than they are in white colleges. This proposition is basic to the following attempt to describe and interpret the structure and nature of governance characteristic of the colleges in this study.

TRUSTEES

A definitive study of the trustees of 536 American colleges and universities revealed that nearly 50 percent of the trustees of

221

the private institutions are business executives. In most instances, they are regarded as the most authentic symbols of "success, in the usual American sense of that word."[1] Even when the proportion of business executives among the trustees is much smaller (35 percent in public colleges), they still tend to exert significant influence on the colleges since the corporation or big business model serves as a norm for governance. This means that such values as order, discipline, loyalty, respectability, industry, economy, responsibility and so forth constitute the very heart of the culture of academic governance in the United States.

Trustee boards in private Black colleges differ markedly in their composition from those in white colleges in that there are relatively few top business executives among their trustees. This is one of the complaints most frequently voiced by these college presidents; they want more business executives. Yet despite their small number on private Black college boards, there is an overwhelming acceptance of the corporation model as the most effective governance structure. This is suggested by the self-criticisms volunteered by trustees and administrators in these colleges, which generally sanctioned the big business model of governance. Just as private Black colleges tend to imitate the academic programs in prestigious white colleges, they also manifest a strong tendency to imitate their governance structure and philosophy as well.

The boards of trustees in private Black colleges, though differing somewhat from one another, have some basic common characteristics. The following is a brief profile:

Composition. The trustee boards in private Black colleges vary in size from 9-99. The variation in the sample colleges is from 19-50. Since there is no definite, established norm regarding the optimum size of a trustee board, one cannot conclude objectively whether a given board is too small or too large. Ideally, one would expect that each trustee of a particular college would represent some area of expertise or have influence with some specific, relevant public with which the college is, or desires to be, involved. A given trustee board would have a number of members corresponding to the specialized goals and perspectives to be attained and the significant publics to which it is meaningfully related. If this were so, a large number of trustees would indicate that the college is pursuing several clearly-defined goals and related to a large number of sustaining publics. Following this line of reasoning, the larger the trustee board, the stronger and more widely relevant would be the college. Actually, this is not the case at all. There is hardly any correlation between the size of the student body, the nature of the academic program, the viability of the college and the number of trustees on its board: some of the smaller, weaker colleges have more trustees than do the larger more prestigious ones.

The main reason why the size of the trustee boards, as such, indicates little or nothing about the essential nature and relationships of the sample colleges is that in too many instances trustee selections are due more to happenstance than sound logic. This does not mean that the presidents of these colleges who nominate certain trustees, and members of the boards who are ultimately responsible for their own composition, are not logical administrators. As a rule, they are eminently logical people. Rather, the imprecise, poorly defined current goals of certain private Black colleges militate against a truly logical selection of trustees. What may have been wise trustee selections in the past, according to a given tenuous set of national and racial circumstances, may prove to be unproductive, even unwise, when these colleges' basic goals are more clearly defined and more realistically focused in terms of revolutionary changes throughout the world and the rapidly changing status of Black Americans.

The great majority of trustees of private Black colleges seem to have been chosen to implement to some important degree the antiquated, unrealistic, discredited doctrine of Separate but Equal in regard to Black institutions. When asked to express an opinion about the future of Black colleges, the more optimistic trustees usually made statements to the effect that they would become more and more like certain existing white models. Those who may be classified as pessimistic often lamented the fact that these colleges did not have the necessary resources to bring them up to established, traditional norms epitomized by prestigious white colleges. In both instances the traditional white model was accepted as the legitimate norm. Seldom did a trustee suggest that Black colleges might develop into distinct entities with creative programs and imaginative academic standards and procedures specifically designed to achieve a set of non-traditional goals, as well as selected traditional academic goals. Few trustees predicted that their particular college would eventually become truly integrated or in any way become a model for other colleges to follow.

Whatever the underlying reasons, private Black colleges are either unwilling or unable to achieve an effective balance on their boards. The following imbalances are the most obvious:

Age. Only a few trustees are under 40 years of age; a significant number are 70 or over, with the majority being about 60. If there is a real generation gap in American society it is nowhere more real than that existing between the average trustees and students in private Black colleges. All of the trustees have achieved some notable measure of success according to established norms of a pre-nuclear age. When they were in college, and later as they climbed the ladder of success, such concepts as patriotism, wealth, nationalism, respectability, freedom, race, and success itself, had somewhat different meanings than they have in the space age to which the students must adjust and prepare to live in.

Primarily because the basic values of this society have, during the past two or three decades, undergone serious testings which have wrought more depth changes than the previous generation might care to admit, trustees on the whole seem to find it quite difficult to communicate with the more progressive teachers and student representatives. Extensive interviews with representatives of all segments of the colleges suggest that there is a virtual "tyranny of words," so that while trustees, teachers, and students may use the same term they are likely to be talking about quite a different reality.

Sex. Despite the fact that a large majority (from 60-65%) of the students in the private coeducational Black colleges are female, there are very few female trustees. Some of these colleges have no female trustees at all. Ironically, Bethune-Cookman College, which was founded by a great Black female educator and leader—Dr. Mary McLeod Bethune—did not have a single female trustee at the time this study was made (1969). This sex bias is quite evident in all of the sample colleges except an all-female college, where slightly more than half (15 of 28) of the trustees are female. In all, only about 8 percent of the trustees of the sample colleges are female, and this is more than the 5 or 6 percent of female trustees in all private Black colleges.

Race. Private Black colleges differ widely insofar as the racial composition of their trustee boards is concerned. Those colleges related to all-Black denominations have few, if any, white trustees. This is significantly different from colleges sponsored by predominantly white churches, where whites are predominant. About 55 percent of the trustees of all private Black colleges are white. The actual proportion of white trustees on the boards of the sample colleges varies from 3 out of 19 at one college to 20 out of 28 at another.

As a rule, private Black colleges in rural-type communities have a smaller proportion of white trustees than those located in large urban centers. In some communities where old patterns of racial segregation are still doggedly preserved, local white men of influence customarily refuse to serve as trustees of Black colleges. Whites on such boards are usually representatives of related church denominations. When compared with the majority of white people in the communities where Black colleges are located, just about all white trustees may be classified as liberal regarding race relations. The mere act of associating their names with a Black institution is usually enough to set prominent white persons apart from racially prejudiced white men of power who scrupulously avoid contacts with Black people on the basis of equality.

As might be expected, white trustees expressed a wide range of attitudes about the Black colleges they serve. A few expressed enthusiastic identification, and optimism about their future. Others were very pessimistic about the future of these colleges. Most were cautious about expressing any definite opinion about the future role these colleges might play in higher education.

Perhaps a majority of the white trustees seem to be motivated by a strong feeling of paternalism or a sort of neo-missionary spirit. Some apparently think of these colleges as perpetually second-rate and needed primarily for culturally and economically disadvantaged Black youth who are not expected to compete in the mainstream of American life. Therefore, certain of these colleges provide successful, humanitarian white citizens with an excellent opportunity to express *noblesse oblige*. The condescending attitude of certain white trustees was succinctly expressed by a president of one of the colleges. He said: Some of my white trustees feel that they honor the college with their names. To them this college is simply another charity they consider their duty to support.

It seems that a significant number of white trustees think of Black colleges as serving a rather narrow racial role. The vast majority apparently still expect these colleges to prepare Black youth to continue to live and work in segregated Black communities—not as equal competitors in the society at large. This was dramatically revealed by an impromptu question by a white trustee who is a wealthy, strong supporter of one of the colleges. When introduced to a student who had won a national scholarship and several science awards, this obviously surprised trustee retorted—"Why is he here and not at X College?" (a local white institution).

Black trustees in the sample colleges were not exempted from criticism by the colleges' presidents and even by fellow trustees. They were often described as conservative and unimaginative and accused of being quite willing to leave fund-raising and other difficult problems to others. This criticism was particularly leveled at Black clergymen who were assigned to the boards by their churches. All of the presidents said that they would like to have a larger number of young, successful, imaginative Blacks on their trustee boards to replace some of the white and Black trustees they now have.

Occupation. In terms of occupational representation, at first blush trustees in private Black colleges seem quite similar to those in private white colleges. Nevertheless, a close examination reveals that the proportion representing certain occupations differs greatly. As mentioned before, whereas a near majority of trustees in private white colleges are top corporation and business executives, there are very few such top executives on the boards of Black colleges. While there are just a token number of clergymen and lay representatives on the boards of private white colleges, a much larger proportion serves on the boards of private Black colleges, constituting from one-half to three-fourths of trustees of church-related Black colleges.

It is interesting to note that despite the fact that a very small proportion of the trustees in private Black colleges are top business and corporation executives, they evidently exert a dominant influence. They seem to set the business stance of the colleges and greatly influence their overall governance. Even though some of the colleges are now unimaginatively managed, almost all of them accept the corporation model as the most desirable governance structure. In this respect they are characteristically conservative.

An important indication of the prevailing conservatism of trustee boards in the sample colleges is the fact that they have made very little effort to respond positively to the intense civil rights movement or the Black revolution of the 1960s. Seldom are leaders of major civil rights organizations or Black activists elected to board membership, despite the fact that some of the "New Blacks" are eminently successful business and professional men. According to all available evidence, boards of trustees in Black colleges have begun the 1970s with about the same composition, occupationally and ideologically, that they had a generation ago. They are apparently willing to make some concessions to the Black thrust for freedom and power when pressured to do so, but they are patently unwilling to assume the initiative in the organization and guidance of this thrust insofar as the college's governance and social role are concerned. This conservative stance was expressed by a trustee who was asked about his board's position on changes demanded by students. He said, "We do what we have to."

The College Constituency. Until quite recently, persons intimately related to private Black colleges were generally excluded as representatives on their trustee boards. About the only regular representative of the college as such has been the president. Some boards include the president as a bona fide member with voting privileges, while his functions on other boards are restricted to that of observer and as a resource person. Despite the fact that some have limited formal functions, presidents in these colleges have great influence in policy making.

Insofar as governance is concerned, the most overlooked segment of the college community has been the faculty. Only a few private Black colleges, and none of the sample colleges, have faculty representatives on their boards. Occasionally teachers and sub-administrators are called upon to report on programs, serve on *ad hoc* faculty-trustee committees or otherwise provide specific information, but they are not usually expected to engage in policy deliberations or to participate in decision making. This relative powerlessness on the part of college teachers is an important cause of the low morale mentioned earlier. Most teachers doubt that trustees understand the essential nature and problems related to the academic programs of their colleges. Even those with tenure fear that trustees may deal with them in an arbitrary manner if they ever desire to do so.

Where students are concerned, there is still no significant bona fide representation on the boards of colleges included in the sample. Until a few years ago, Black students seemed more or less unconcerned about representation on trustee boards: they certainly did not make an issue of it. Neither was there any serious suggestion from trustees that students should be accorded representation. However, during the last four or five years, as student power has constantly built up, there have been demands by students that they should be represented among their colleges' trustees. Some boards are beginning to give serious consideration to this demand. Students have been allowed to meet with representatives of most trustee boards and encouraged to present their points of view. A few of the boards have extended limited membership to them. But so far students' actual influence in policy making is not significant. Those who sit with trustees are far too unsophisticated and their appointments too tenuous for them to influence top level decision making. One college president summarized a common attitude. "They sit with us, but the trustees treat them more like spoiled children than responsible governors. Let's face it, students simply don't know enough to be taken seriously in the formulation of general policy. They are concerned with having their own way, not with the welfare of the college generally."

Private Black colleges include a few alumni among their

trustees, but they usually represent the trustees, not the alumni. In only a few instances do the alumni select their own representatives to trustee boards, for the most part, trustee boards themselves select alumni to fill occasional vacancies. Alumni-trustees are generally selected to implement the values and goals of the board, which may or may not be the goals or points of view of the alumni. They are selected primarily not because they are alumni, but because they allegedly represent certain values of the trustees and might help the college to attain already established goals.

Generally speaking, boards of trustees in private Black colleges tend to be conservative and limited in representation, and their philosophies of governance are hardly conducive to the kind of bold, creative innovations most of these colleges will have to make if they are to be vital forces in higher education, properly educating Black students to compete as equals in the larger, desegregating American society.

Three criteria have been suggested for the evaluation of college trustees: the extent to which they contribute "wealth," "wisdom" and "work."[2] This is indeed a perceptive approach and functions as a realistic framework by which trustees can be compared and their services evaluated. All individuals asked to evaluate trustees for this study tended to emphasize one or more of these three criteria in the statements they made. The following is a summary of statements from presidents of the sample colleges, other administrative officers, teachers, students, and trustees themselves about the contributions of trustees to these colleges.

Wealth. Church related colleges usually have a relatively large representation from the sponsoring denomination(s). Most of these are clergymen who have little wealth, and the proportion of control they exert over these colleges far outweighs their financial support. As noted before, only a few of the colleges have more than a token number of wealthy laymen-trustees. An analysis of all trustee-givings shows that, with some notable exceptions, they do not usually make substantial gifts to their colleges. Perhaps the greatest disappointment of all is the fact that most trustees of influence and wealth do not use their contacts to provide private Black colleges with entrees into the world of money. Even those who make substantial personal gifts seldom influence others to do the same. A key reason for this may have been given by a wealthy trustee who was asked to explain why he had not influenced other wealthy individuals, corporations and foundations to contribute to the Black college on whose board he served. He responded:

> I have been in the business of selling for more than forty years. I've sold many different products and ideas, but I can't find a handle to sell X college except to say that it is a good place to educate poor Negro youth to get good, worthwhile jobs. There are so many counter sales pitches to this argument that people with really big money simply won't buy it. It may be that they give their money to the college from which they, their relatives, friends and employees graduated. All I know is, they don't respond to me when I want money for X college.

On the whole, then, trustees contribute, or cause to be contributed, very little money to these colleges. The comprehensive study of trustees in Black colleges by Samuel Nabrit, cited previously, concluded that the pattern of giving on a personal basis indicates that the trustees only average between $50 and $150 annually and that only about 6 percent give an average of $1,000 or more. Furthermore, only 25 percent of them had raised $1,000 or more for their colleges during a given year (1968). It is significant that despite their limited giving and unimpressive record of soliciting funds for their colleges, board members regard fiscal management as their major role. According to information received through interviews, trustees in these colleges tend to view their role as more or less exclusively of fiscal planners and managers.

Wisdom. Undoubtedly there are some wise members on the trustee boards in each of the sample colleges. Perhaps there is no more convincing attestation of this wisdom than the fact that, with woefully inadequate support and many complex social and academic handicaps, these colleges, as a group, have survived and are now entering their second century. The serious problem is that apparently there is a narrow range of wisdom on these boards; all of the boards could benefit from the wisdom that would come from a more balanced occupational recruitment. Most, if not all, of the presidents are very much aware of this. Presidents frequently expressed the desire to have more trustees who have accumulated wisdom in such fields as educational innovation, the independent professions, administration, government, community organization, labor, and business. They also agreed that private Black colleges ·badly need more influential Black and white local leaders on their boards.

There is an increasing awareness that trustee boards need the added wisdom of faculty members. So far this is mostly an untapped resource insofar as policy-making is concerned. Despite a great deal of discussion about it, students' wisdom has also been largely overlooked or wasted by trustee boards; only a very few serve and they are usually expected to champion the narrow student cause—not to bring wisdom to overall areas of decision making.

According to information we were able to secure, even when specialized wisdom from several walks of life is represented on the trustee boards, it is too often poorly organized and consequently dissipated. This usually results from either unclear, poorly defined goals to be attained, as reflected in the statement of the wealthy trustee previously quoted, or to the trustees' limited knowledge about the programs, problems and potentialities of the college. In the first instance, a clarification of goals is a prerequisite to a wiser selection of trustees. In the second, some more dependable mechanism is needed to acquaint trustees with all significant areas of their colleges and higher education generally. Most of them apparently also need to know how they may be more effective in helping their colleges to survive and prosper.

Some college presidents have proposed the establishment of trustee seminars designed to coordinate and increase the wisdom of the trustees. A seminar or workshop approach is needed because, as all studies show, trustees are very busy people who seldom find time to do extensive study of the nature, problems and challenges of higher education in general or of Black colleges in particular. Since most of them identify with what students liked to call "the establishment," they find too little time to develop and participate in meaningful communication with a cross section of youth and teachers representing the college culture in our society. It is likely that most trustees of Black colleges need to participate periodically in seminars or workshops in which there would be honest dialogue about problems facing their colleges and on how they may best work with teachers, students and the larger community in the solution of these problems.

It is generally acknowledged that the overall wisdom of trustee boards would be enhanced if more of their members actually represented the alumni. What is badly needed is a significant number of bona fide alumni-trustees who truly represent the Black community in which they live and work. Such persons, if democratically nominated by the alumni themselves, could be valuable in bridging the communications gap now existing between trustees, students, and leaders of non-academic groups with which the college must deal. They could also render valuable service to the college in the enhancement of its public image, the recruitment of students, and the raising of funds.

Work. Boards of trustees are usually organized into standing committees which vary in size but average about seven members. Ideally the work of the board is parcelled out to the various committees. Although trustee committees generally endeavor to accomplish the work assigned them, there were at least two recurring major criticisms of their work.

1. Because many trustees have very limited knowledge of their colleges and lack the time to better acquaint themselves, their committees seem to do little more than listen to reports dealing with specific areas of concern, then recommend that matters be handled by applying existing policies. From what we could learn, such trustees are not often prepared to recommend and push for creative innovations.

2. Most trustees limit their work to participation in one or two annual board meetings and seldom work for the college during the interim. As a rule, only members of the executive committee perform any function during interim periods, and even they usually serve only when there is some emergency. All of those with whom we talked, however, expressed a willingness to do more work for their colleges during the months between board

meetings. This was true even of those who indicated that they were extremely busy.

If trustees would like to do more work for their colleges, then why don't they? The key answer to this question was suggested in the context of their own statements. Essentially, they agreed that the primary reason is that the goals of the college (including the always urgent need to raise money) are so unclear and indefinite that a given trustee finds it difficult to assume responsibility for a specific unit of work, or to cooperate with other trustees during interim periods. Small wonder, then, that most trustees seem to be uncertain about the nature of their role and that some are actually confused about what is expected of them even during formal meetings of the board.

Before the rank-and-file trustees can begin to make worthy contributions to their colleges, basic goals must be clearly delineated and the several units of trustee work defined and coordinated. If this were done, even the busiest trustees would be able to do some important, if limited, amount of work the year around. The situation at present is so generally unstructured that only a few trustees of these colleges are meaningfully involved in the performance of the various tasks essential to their viability. The many complex tasks associated with top level governance are usually assigned to the presidents, who complain that they get far too little help from their trustees.

THE PRESIDENT

As is true universally, Black college presidents are chosen by their trustee boards and all trustees agreed that choosing the president when that vacancy occurs is their prime responsibility. The selection of a president is directly or indirectly determined by a relatively small number of key trustees who constitute the appropriately named Find Committee. Where private Black colleges are concerned, this committee has just three or four policy limitations:

1. *The president should be Black.* This is a radical departure

from the original policy whereby white presidents were usually preferred for Black colleges. It was once assumed that these colleges needed white presidents as mediators with the always suspicious, often hostile local white communities in which the colleges were located. Some of these colleges once preferred white presidents because they were believed to be more acceptable to influential white supporters of higher education for Blacks.

Today, trustees of these colleges openly admit that they restrict their search for new presidents to Black prospects. While a few trustees expressed some skepticism about this policy (one said that it is a kind of "racism in reverse"), the vast majority indicated that they felt that it was necessary to make this concession to the Black militants' strong thrust for Black control of their own institutions.

2. *The president should be male.* The policy regarding the sex of the president is generally tacit yet quite rigid. Most trustees insisted they would accept a female president if she were the best qualified candidate, yet none of the trustees interviewed had ever recommended a female candidate for the sample colleges. At present, all of the presidents of the better known Black colleges (even the two women's colleges) are male.

3. *The president should be active in denominational programs.* Until recently, practically all presidents of private church related colleges were clergymen or laymen of high standing. At present there seems to be a trend away from this policy. Half or more of the Black denominational colleges have lay presidents who were not particularly outstanding in church activities.

4. *The president should be a representative of traditional middle class values.* The style of life of prospective candidates is expected to conform to what might be regarded as upper middle class in white society. This includes his formal education, family life, career pattern, ideology or social philosophy, and his reputation in established middle class circles.

After extensive screening the Find Committee settles upon two or three of what they regard as the most promising candidates. These are brought before other trustees for in-depth interviews. Until recently, the faculty and students were largely ignored in the selection and subsequent tenure of the president. Today, more and more, trustees are beginning to involve all segments of the academic community in the process of selecting the president. When the final decision is made, however, the trustee board may be expected to accept the recommendation of the Find Committee, which may or may not reflect the opinions or evaluations of teachers, students, alumni, or even other trustees.

Despite some modifications such as those just noted, the ritual of selecting the president is about the same as it has always been: trustees listen to many points of view and end up selecting the candidate who most nearly measures up to the prevailing version of the ideal corporation executive, or the one who ranks highest on the more or less subjective scale labelled administrative ability.

As pointed out earlier, none of the trustee boards has as many top corporation executives as desired. Nevertheless, partly because these boards accept the business model as *the* norm of governance, and partly because the relatively few top executives on the boards are so highly respected by fellow members, the ethos of governance in private Black colleges usually articulates well-established bureaucratic values and procedures, and is essentially conservative.

Colleges are non-profit rather than profit corporations. The quality of their finished products—the students and alumni—is not as easily measured and evaluated as material products. Because of this, the production procedures, so to speak, can hardly be as objective and routine as those in industry or other profit corporations. Therefore, the sample colleges have adopted a modified business-like model of bureaucracy. In the true bureaucracy there are definite institutional restraints, such as specifically prescribed duties and clearly defined rules which protect the subordinate from the arbitrary actions of his superior. But in the modified bureaucracy adopted by most private Black colleges, teachers and subordinate administrative officers are virtually unprotected from the capricious actions of their college presidents. A generation ago Myrdal noted that

The organization of life in Negro colleges seems to be definitely less democratic than in white colleges in

America, even, and not least, when the staff of teachers is mainly Negro. The president in his relation with professors, and they in relation with the students, act more dictatorially and more arbitrarily.[3]

Obviously the role of the Black college president has changed considerably since Myrdal made his observations. Strong countervailing forces from the civil rights movement of the 1960s have greatly compromised the erstwhile dictatorial role once superbly played by some Black presidents. It is important to point out, however, that any modifications in the customary presidential role, *per se*, have been due to the need to adjust to pressures which these colleges still regard as illegitimate. The colleges on the whole, and particularly the presidents, have had to respond to pressures such as those generated by persistent student protest, Black militants, and the reality of the brain drain. Yet so far the governance structure of these colleges has not changed significantly; it is still inherently designed to be conducive to the authoritarian role of the presidents.

The management styles of Black college presidents (their characteristic manner of exercising authority) vary considerably from one college to another. At one extreme stands a president who (at the time of the study) was accustomed to making arbitrary decisions, ranging from the employment of teachers to listings on the cafeteria menu, without consulting with subordinates in charge. At the other extreme is a president who usually consulted with a number of faculty members and students who were directly concerned before announcing any major decision. Of course, most presidents may be classified somewhere between these extremes. Most of them will usually personally select a few teachers and students to advise them on certain alternative courses of action which might involve campus order or morale, and then proceed to make their own decisions which may or may not reflect the judgement of their campus advisors. Very seldom do presidents bother to consult with those in their colleges about really top level decisions such as the selection of a person to the trustee board, fund-raising policy, or the problem of general development.

There are, of course, several rather complex reasons why

presidents of Black colleges have characteristically wielded such broad, and occasionally arbitrary, power. The following are three of the most salient:

1. *Absentee control by trustees.* Historically, the center of governance of private Black colleges has formally or informally been in the North, where the headquarters of sponsoring denominations, foundations, and reliable philanthropists are located. Consequently, key supporters are too far from these colleges to become meaningfully involved in the many detailed matters which constitute the orderly functioning of their day to day programs. Since local white (southern) top executives and men of influence often refuse to serve as trustees, a majority of the key trustees are likely to be northerners who constitute a sort of absentee-ownership class. It is only logical in such situations that a strong man is needed to maintain control in their absence.

For the most part, trustee boards in Black colleges are only directly concerned with top level policy regarding the maintenance and expansion of the physical plant, the raising of funds, and the overall operating budget. The administration of policy and the general program of the college are left to the president. Fundamentally, then, the structure and function of trustee boards in these colleges really militate against close, democratic give and take communication and interaction of trustees with teachers, students and subordinate administrative officers. At best, trustees get to know only a few teachers. As a result, when it comes to the actual distribution of salaries, promotions, and privileges on the one hand, and demotions and firings on the other, trustees have little or no definitive choice but to accept the recommendations of the president. This is a particularly threatening practice because trustee boards in most Black colleges tend to operate oblivious to the established principles of faculty rights set forth by the AAUP and The Southern Association of Colleges and Schools.[4] This situation, wittingly or unwittingly, functions to render teachers and other administrative officers uncomfortably dependent upon the considered judgment, or maybe even whims, of the president.

2. *Modified bureaucracy.* As noted earlier, private Black colleges tend to accept the governance structure and values adopted by top business corporations. However, the actual governance of

these colleges usually deviates markedly from the traditional bureaucratic model characteristic of successful corporations. A primary example is that in the ideal bureaucratic structure all offices are clearly defined so that each incumbent knows his exact duties, responsibilities, and authority. This is not so in private Black colleges, notwithstanding the Faculty Handbook and the Student Handbook in which the incumbent roles of all deans, the business manager, developmental officer, registrar, division chairmen, department heads, directors of established programs, and even teachers without formal administrative responsibilities should be prescribed in detail. In these colleges, the functions and authority of all officials may be personally prescribed and interpreted by the president. The office of academic dean in one college, for example, may be quite different from that in other colleges. Even the role of the incumbent dean in a given college may be very different from his predecessor or his successor. This is basically due to the fact that, by design or default, trustee boards entrust nearly all administrative authority to the president. The president in turn is privileged to delegate certain degrees of this authority to other administrative officers. An administrative officer may be delegated more or less authority at one time than another, depending upon the total circumstances and vicissitudes of the situation, and the president's interpretation of it.

Since the roles of administrative officers are often undefined and their authority is unstable, their functional unity in a given college must also be indefinite and changeable. Again, this is a deviation from the ideal type bureaucracy, where chains of command or strata of decision making are clearly understood. It is not uncommon for subordinate administrators in these colleges to be in a quandary about some pressing decision that should be made in the absence of the president. On the one hand, the question about *who* makes certain key decisions could become a major issue that may lead to temporary administrative paralysis. On the other, the officer who ventures to make a key decision in such an unstructured situation may unintentionally usurp the authority of some other officer, or behave contrary to the will of the president. This need to make decisions may bring out damaging power struggles among administrative officers which might otherwise remain *sub rosa*. Such struggles often lead to low morale and undermine administrative efficiency.

3. *The inefficiency of subordinate administrators*. When asked to justify their more or less authoritarian styles *vis-à-vis* their avowed commitment to the democratic process, presidents tended to point to three main administrative weaknesses characteristic of their faculty and subordinate officers.

(a) They said that some of their most able teachers don't want to assume responsibility for administrative details; they only want to teach and pursue goals directly associated with their academic careers. As one president put it, "I have teachers who even resent having to keep record of their class attendance. I have learned not to depend upon them to administer programs and projects."

(b) Presidents often criticized teachers for their apathy. They contended that the faculty, as a group, frequently refuses to exert the degree and kinds of authority which they traditionally possess. Any number of examples were cited to illustrate this point. Among the things they mentioned is the fact that some teachers always *ask* the president for his opinion about some needed action rather than getting his reaction to their proposal. Regarding this, a president said: "They want me to *tell* them what to do, not advise them."

According to the presidents, there are also teachers who refuse to initiate faculty action in situations where it is expected. There were instances cited where basic institutional practices needed to be changed, and the faculty had the authority to do so, yet made no move to handle such situations. Instead, the president was forced to make necessary decisions which often rescinded previous faculty action.

(c) The most pointed reason some presidents gave for exercising near autocratic control in their colleges was the inefficiency of subordinate administrative officers. This criticism was put bluntly by one who, in effect, summarized statements made by all. He said: "If I don't do it, it won't be done properly." This particular president was referring to certain administrative responsibilities he had assumed which should have been done by the business manager in one instance and the dean of students in another.

There was not a single college president interviewed who did not complain about the inefficiency of one or more of his key administrative officers. Academic deans and business managers were especially singled out for criticism. In many instances they were regarded as "weak and unimaginative," as one president brusquely put it.

Though seldom mentioned by the presidents, there are some obvious reasons why most subordinate administrative officers in these colleges do not perform as adequately as might be desired:

First, and perhaps most important, is the fact that the wide, undefined power trustees characteristically grant the president functions to make other administrative officers totally dependent upon him. A normal response to their condition of insecurity and powerlessness would be over-identification with the president. Instead of presenting new proposals and making decisions based upon their own judgement, too many administrators evidently attempt to anticipate the desires of the president, or try to do what they think he wants done. When asked to define and interpret his role as dean of a college one such incumbent retorted "I am the president's flunky."

Logically, then, private Black colleges will continue to have ineffective, or at best mediocre, subordinate administrators as long as all administrative power is entrusted to the president to delegate to other administrators as he personally chooses. The complex responsibilities inherent in the main administrative offices of the college require that the incumbents be delegated prime authority by the trustees, not according to the judgement or the whims of the president.

Second, the president may exercise such wide powers and prerogatives because salaries for administrative personnel and teachers are ordinarily too low to attract top flight people. He might frequently find it necessary to make decisions for subordinate officers who are not qualified to make decisions for themselves. All the presidents complained that at one time or another they had been forced to appoint relatively inexperienced persons to key administrative positions and then found it necessary to train the incumbents to do their jobs. In too many instances, they reported, after the inexperienced administrators eventually learned their job, they were immediately recruited by some other college or firm that offered them larger salaries than the colleges could afford.[5] The process of finding replacements starts all over again as the president seeks to fill vacancies resulting from the brain drain.

It is only realistic, then, that as long as private Black colleges must employ mostly inexperienced and/or second rate subordinate administrators, the presidents have no choice but to supervise the offices of such incumbents and to make certain key decisions which should be inherent in these subordinate offices. While such close supervision may be necessary, it tends to undermine the morale of incumbents. This was precisely the reason deans and other subordinate administrators gave for their generally low morale. One dean summarized the situation. He agonized—

> The president plays his cards close to his chest. He never trusts anyone (meaning administrative officers) with any basic information such as the allocation of budget, negotiations with foundations or government agencies,—or simply what might be on his mind regarding sensitive areas of the college. I don't even know how much money is budgeted for teachers' travel. It is constantly embarrassing for me to O.K. some request by a teacher only to have the president tell me that there is no money for that category of expense. In the same way those of us who are supposedly in positions to make certain commitments to others usually find our commitments rescinded. I'll soon get sense enough to let the president make all important decisions originally. Then I will be spared the embarrassment of being treated like an irresponsible child.

By and large, private Black colleges do not take advantage of in-service and academic programs designed to train administrative personnel which are available in several universities. When asked why they did not have some of their administrative officers enroll in these programs, presidents gave a variety of answers: "I can't find necessary replacements for our key people. . . ," "The training would prepare him (a business manager) to fit into a large operation where his would be specialized work. We'd still have to train him for our place. . . ," or "If he goes away to study he'd never return to us."

For whatever reason, a large proportion of administrative officers in these colleges seem to be performing their duties in a more or less perfunctory manner. Most of them were classified as weak by certain trustees and several presidents. Since there is no great push to secure top flight administrative people, or to train those now employed, there is reason to believe that some presidents don't want the challenge of dealing with strong, creative subordinate administrators. A foundation representative, for example, confided that it was his considered opinion that "most Black presidents do not want to compete with truly capable deans, business managers, and developmental officers. They prefer to surround themselves with 'yes men' who will do their bidding without question."

The statement just quoted is an oversimplification because Black college presidents are, on the whole, extremely capable people who would rank very high on any scale of administrative ability, and should have no need to be afraid of subordinate administrators. It may be more fruitful to look for the original source of powerful, even autocratic presidents, and the generally weak, often apathetic subordinate administrators and teachers. A careful look suggests that this original source is the trustee boards. Until trustees are more representative of Black people, the various viable interests to which Blacks must relate, and the many dynamic social forces impinging upon today's and tomorrow's students of all races and abilities, the governance of private Black colleges will continue to be basically unimaginative and largely unproductive. The choice is clear: trustees, presidents, and other administrative officers must be more thoughtfully selected. They must be capable, and willing to develop relevant, creative innovations, definite goals and logical priorities for Black colleges, as well as having the freedom, conviction, dedication, and courage to see that these programs are launched and goals attained. This must begin to take place soon; otherwise all evidence points to the rapid decline, and in many instances the demise, of private Black colleges.

NOTES

1. Carlos E. Kruytbosch and Sheldon L. Messinger, Editors, *The State of the University* (Beverly Hills, California: Sage Publications, Inc., 1970), p. 48.

2. See Henry M. Wriston, *Academic Procession* (New York: Columbia University Press, 1959).

3. Myrdal, *An American Dilemma*, pp. 732-733.

4. Samuel Nabrit and Julius Scott, Jr., *Inventory of Academic Leadership* (Atlanta: The Southern Fellowship Fund, 1970), p. 16.

5. See also Earl J. McGrath, *The Predominantly Negro College and Universities in Transition*, p. 115.

10.
Economic Status

The annual budget for the sample colleges ranges from
$1,240,722 at one college to $3,399,359 at another. The critical
nature of the poverty experienced by these colleges, however, is
not their small budgets but rather that seven of ten of them have
been operating with substantial deficits for at least two years.
Even for the academic year 1968-1969, the size of these deficits
ranged from $11,834 at one college to $466,906 at another. Their
deficits are even larger today. This is characteristic of private
Black colleges generally, as indicated by William J. Trent, Jr.,
who observed that: "31 of these colleges had deficits totaling
seven and a half million dollars."[1] Ernest Holsendolph also
noted in 1971 that 27 of the 37 colleges of the United Negro College Fund reported serious deficits; nine of them either broke even
or had very small surpluses.[2] The three colleges in the sample
which did not have audited deficits were dangerously marginal.
Their incomes exceeded expenditures by only $572 in one,
$19,212 in another, and $39,823 in the third. The total deficit for
the seven colleges in 1968-1969 was $1,341,894; the total excess

for the three colleges was just $59,607. All but one of the sample colleges are now (1971) operating with deficits. This means that with little or no endowment these colleges are actually operating in the red. This is the main critical difference between these colleges and the more affluent colleges, where deficits can be covered from endowment funds. For instance:

> All thirty-six of the private colleges in the United Negro College Fund together have endowments totaling (only) $76,250,000.00. But the situation is even worse. Five of the colleges hold 62 percent of these funds. The income is of minor importance to most of the colleges, and practically no new endowment funds are being made available.[3]

There are several basic reasons why the sample colleges are experiencing such unusual, dire financial difficulties. Among them are the following:

Economic Discrimination. Throughout their histories these colleges have had to operate on the proverbial "shoestring." They have been forced to provide higher education for Black youth who were recruited, for the most part, from the poorest communities, the most economically disadvantaged families, and the most wretched high schools in the nation. All attempts to provide high quality education for seriously disadvantaged youth—such as the federally sponsored Head Start and Upward Bound, and a variety of such compensatory programs sponsored by public school systems, colleges and private agencies—have all proven that the essential educational cost per disadvantaged student must be considerably higher than the normal cost per average or advantaged student if comparable achievements are to be attained. Yet, despite the overwhelming evidence supporting this conclusion, private Black colleges have had to operate with only token support from major foundations, the federal government, private philanthropy, and the church. In a sense, educational reality has been reversed: Black colleges, with the most difficult educational burden, always receive the most meager support, while colleges whose students are the most advantaged and advanced receive the lion's share of available educational funds.

As an example of the degree to which private Black colleges are discriminated against, we need only note how the ten sample colleges fared as to grants made to higher education by business and foundations. At least one characteristic is clear: the major foundations and corporations in this nation tend to contribute to academic strengths (affluence) rather than to weaknesses (poverty). According to reliable estimates, only 2 to 3 percent of the support those major agencies gave to aid higher education during the 1960s went to Black colleges. When foundation and corporation support are combined, we find that the largest amount received in 1968-1969 by any of the sample colleges was just $164,621. The next largest amount was $128,000. Two of the sample colleges received no such funds at all to support current operations, while six received very small grants ranging from a mere $15,916 to a modest $58,575. The total amount of foundation and corporation grants reported by the sample colleges for current fiscal operations was only $483,589. This was slightly more than two percent of their annual 1968-1969 budgets, which totalled $21,751,576, and less than one (0.7) percent of the $320,900,000 foundations alone contributed to higher education in this country during that year. [4]

The federal government, too, has blatantly discriminated against Black colleges. According to all available pertinent information the financial support government agencies have provided Black colleges is a relative pittance compared with what has been extended to white colleges. The federal government tends to deemphasize the role of Black colleges in its concern to promote the general welfare of this nation. Despite the fact that practically all of their students suffer from major socio-economic disadvantages, Black colleges are somehow expected to miraculously transform them into creative citizens. They have attempted to do this with much less support, very inadequate physical facilities, and a considerably lower level of professional expertise than is expected of private white colleges, which recruit practically all of their students from the more affluent, advantaged segments of the nation's population. When a given government-sponsored program is evaluated and shows that students have had less success according to national (white college) norms than expected, that program is likely to lose the limited funds that had been provided. In too many instances, Black colleges do not receive much-needed available funds because some phase of their program or organization does not measure up to certain national norms. Therefore, just about all private Black colleges are caught up in an impossible vicious cycle: they can't get essential help because they do not measure up—and they can't measure up without essential help.

On October 9, 1969, following a July conference of 111 Black college presidents in Mobile, Alabama, the presidents announced the formation of a new association to seek more substantial financial support from federal and private agencies. On May 20, 1970, a committee of 15 Black college presidents, representing the new association, was invited to the White House. At that time they expressed to President Nixon their "anger, outrage, and frustration about the insufficient support of . . . schools and colleges attended largely by Blacks." They commented on an earlier resolution which stated:

> We are faced with crises in increased demands for relevance and enrichment of our educational programs for greater numbers of Black students. Yet, the national programs amounting to tens of millions of dollars are conceived and operated in a way that does not result in our benefiting from them commensurate with our enrollment of over one half of all Black undergraduates in college in America . . . Despite our historic and our future commitments to and involvement in the education of the disadvantaged, our institutions have been notoriously bypassed in the allocations of funds for the education of the disadvantaged. The larger portion of money for such programs, by far, continues to be diverted to white institutions that have no history of significant enrollment and hence no deep understanding of and appreciation for the problems of the disadvantaged minority student.[5]

The intense feeling expressed by the Black college presidents to President Nixon was indeed well-founded. A study of federal grants to institutions of higher education for the fiscal year 1969 shows that Black colleges received only three percent of the total. In most instances such matching funds had to be diverted from top priority programs of the college and put into programs which came under federal guidelines. This has meant that the programs of the colleges were too drastically influenced by government agencies. A few colleges with a large number of federal programs have had to curtail some of their established programs in order to get government funds.

The total amount of federal funds received by the ten sample colleges was only $3,030,406; the actual amount received by individual colleges varied from $145,803 to $621,251. So far, the federal government has provided no badly needed funds to improve the general level of the colleges' programs *per se*.

Extensive research and sustained communication with knowledgeable representatives of all major elements of the private Black colleges validate a basic conclusion: the overwhelming majority of persons concerned in any way with these colleges want to see the churches continue their support to Black higher education. Most concur with the position expressed by Dr. James P. Brawley, President Emeritus of Clark College. In a statement prepared for this study he wrote:

> The potential value of the Black college is great for the involvement of the church, program-wise in some of the most critical issues of our times . . . The problems of race and human relations are still with us, but have grown in magnitude and complexity. The Black colleges are now valuable instrumentalities available within the church with which to work at these problems in a different, and hopefully, a more fruitful way.

Historically the church's affiliation with Black colleges has been three-dimensional: doctrinal, administrative, and financial.[6] The church's doctrinal influence has been waning for decades. Most of the doctrinal ties these colleges have with the church today are formal and have little influence on the ideological stance of students and faculty. Practically no one thinks of these colleges as instruments to perpetuate religious doctrines. They are certainly not proselyting institutions; neither are they expected to prepare young people for Christian vocations.

While the doctrinal influence in these colleges has tended to decline steadily, the administrative control has held firm. As noted earlier, the churches, through trustee boards, wield important to complete control over the administration of some church-related colleges. Their presidents complain bitterly about the disproportionate control the church exerts.

The proportion of financial support the church gives to Black colleges has declined to about the same point as its doctrinal influence. Denominations today give little more than token financial support to their Black colleges. Insofar as educational and general income is concerned, in 1968-1969, one denomination contributed a high of 12.7 percent to one of its colleges, 10.9 percent to another, just 4.4 percent to still another, to a low of 2.1 percent to one of its more affluent Black colleges. In all only 6.4 percent of these colleges' current budgets was assumed by church bodies. This pattern of giving is apparently more generous than is true of other church-related colleges, some of which reported that they received no financial support at all from their denominations.

It is not within the scope of this study to determine whether denominations are able to contribute more funds to the support of their colleges. Top churchmen themselves differ on this point. At one extreme, Black Methodist churchmen insist that their church is able to raise its contributions to Black colleges "to $20 million dollars for each of the next five years."[7] At the other extreme are churchmen who insist that giving is dropping off in churches and it may be necessary for the church to curtail rather than expand its educational appropriations. Whatever the merits of either position might be, one fact is glaring: the present support churches are giving to their Black colleges hardly justifies their degree of control over the colleges' administration. The meager contribution the church is now making to Black higher education might be expected even if it had no corporate relationship to the colleges.

250

The third and most constructive point of view is that religious bodies should assume a primary responsibility for the support of their Black colleges. They should exert every effort to make these colleges truly viable institutions. Whatever might be regarded as the central mission of the church, contributing to the higher education of disadvantaged Black people would certainly be ideologically relevant. Even now there is some evidence that churches can do better. For example, on the basis of confidential information provided by one prominent denomination, we were able to compare its pattern of giving according to the racial identity of its colleges of comparable size and in the same states. For the academic year 1968-1969 this denomination gave its white colleges 10.5 percent of their current income, and its Black colleges only 6.4 percent of their income.

There must be several complex reasons why related churches provide substantially greater support to their white colleges than they do to their Black colleges. Again, the specific reasons are not the direct concern of this study. Nevertheless, if this particular denomination had supported its Black colleges even on an equal basis with its white colleges, it would have given them $1,529,464 instead of $930,241 for current operation. Certainly the need of the Black colleges was equally as great, and no doubt much greater, than the need of the white colleges.

The Vast Majority of Students in the Sample Colleges are Poor. Another primary reason why the sample colleges are poor is that practically none of their students can afford to pay for their education. Despite the increasing number of middle class Black families, from 80-95 percent of all students enrolled in the sample colleges may be classified as poor or nearly poor. They must depend upon the college to provide a substantial portion, if not all, of the funds needed to pay for their education. *This means that the sample colleges are not getting their share of students from the 25-30 percent of Black middle class families.*[8] Evidently the great majority of affluent Black students are choosing white colleges. This, of course, puts Black colleges at a distinct economic disadvantage: white colleges are getting most of the affluent white students, plus an increasing proportion of affluent Black students.

Not only will these colleges' continual loss of Black middle class students damage their economic stability, but it is certain to damage their academic image as well. Once the negative image of poverty comes to reinforce the traditionally negative image of Negro, it might become extremely difficult for these colleges to continue their renowned historical role—providing higher education for potential Black leadership. They will cease to attract the most talented students and teachers.

Even now, the sample colleges are having to find funds to pay some major portion, from 80-95 percent, of their students' educational cost. Including extensive student aid packages, students in the sample colleges pay an average of only 44.6 percent of their educational and general costs. The average for the sample colleges varies from 38.6 percent at one college to 57.2 percent at another. The ideal, of course, would be 100 percent. An expected minimum would be about 60 percent.

Instable Income. The securing of funds for the operation of any private college today is a constant, ever-present problem. This is especially true of private Black colleges. Black colleges have relatively few wealthy alumni and powerful friends to stabilize them.

The instable economic position of the sample colleges is underscored by their lack of substantial endowments. In 1968-1969 the average income from endowment in all of the sample colleges amounted to only 4.7 percent of their total budget. The percent for individual colleges ranged from a high of 10.9 percent to a low of 0.08 percent. Not only are the endowments small but they are usually narrowly limited to a few areas of conservative, low-risk investments.

Since income from gifts and grants is tenuous, these colleges can do very little concrete academic planning. They simply do not have enough assured income to project costly, long-range innovative academic programs, sustained national student recruitment campaigns, substantial faculty salary raises, and to institute realistic programs of faculty improvement. While such projects are essential to the viability of these colleges, all of them are multi-year commitments. The annual fluctuation of gifts and grants makes such long-range commitments economically dangerous.

Small Number of Students. As has been mentioned elsewhere in this report, experts in college financing generally agree that 700-800 students, which is the average in the sample colleges, is too small a student body to be a sound financial venture.[9] An acceptable liberal arts academic program presupposes a certain number of academic specialists among the faculty. When enrollment is small a college, unless it is quite affluent, can hardly afford to employ enough specialists.

Because so many of their students have serious academic and social handicaps, personnel deans concur that there are far too few specialists on the faculties of Black colleges. A larger enrollment would provide a sound financial justification for adding more teachers, particularly badly-needed specialists.

A second observation is that according to auditors' reports the teacher-student ratio in the sample colleges ranges from 1:9 at one college to 1:19 at another. The average for all of the sample colleges is between 1:14 and 1:15. There is, of course, no unanimously accepted norm as to what constitutes an optimum teacher-student ratio. Economically, some colleges have set the ratio as high as 1:20. However, colleges that strive for excellence in terms of education and image usually adjust the teacher-student ratio at about 1:15. The latter ratio seems to work well for prestigious colleges, since practically all of their students have the advantages of affluent homes and superior high schools.

It is not easy to determine the optimum teacher-student ratio for Black colleges because student needs are greater and require infinitely more teacher time than is likely to be necessary in the most affluent colleges. According to all that we have learned about the problem of educating the disadvantaged, it would seem that a teacher-student ratio of 1:14 plus in the sample colleges is the most practical academically. It does imply, of course, that the colleges must face the fact that it costs more to provide quality education for the disadvantaged than it does for the advantaged. This is perhaps the key to understanding the economic plight of Black colleges.

Finally, the poverty of private Black colleges is so great that making ends meet consumes practically all of the professional energy, imagination, and skills of the trustees and the presidents.

So distressing is this problem that purely academic needs are too often overlooked. In other words, the imminent need for money looms so large and is so central to the very survival of these colleges that those who must plan their future too often overemphasize the need to raise funds and underemphasize the necessity to make major academic innovations. It seems absolutely necessary that, as these colleges reach the decisive crossroads of their development, each should establish a comprehensive planning committee charged with the responsibility of developing much-needed innovative academic programs and realistic estimates of what these and improved traditional programs will cost. When this is done, specific segments of the planned new college should be discreetly submitted to the federal government, foundations, industry, and private philanthropy for their consideration and probable funding. Unless such comprehensive planning is done expertly and expeditiously, there is grave danger that private Black colleges as a group will cease to be a significant aspect of higher education in the United States.

NOTES

1. William J. Trent, Jr., "The Negro College and its Financing," *Daedalus*, Vol. 100, No. 3, Summer 1971, p. 649.

2. Ernest Holsendolph, "Black Colleges are Worth Saving," *Fortune*, Vol. 84, No. 4, October 1971, p. 106.

3. Trent, "Negro College and its Financing," p. 656.

4. See *Higher Education and National Affairs* (Washington, D.C.: American Council on Education, August 3, 1969), Vol. XVIII, No. 27, p. 6.

5. An unpublished manuscript, circulated by individual members of the Committee of black college presidents.

6. For an extensive study of this, see Richard N. Bender, Ed., *The Church Related College Today: Anachronism or Opportunity* (Nashville, Tennessee: The General Board of Education, The United Methodist Church, 1971).

7. "Black Methodists for Church Renewal," Task Force on Higher Education, *Position Paper*, July 25, 1969.

8. "The Spread of Affluence: Black Progress," *U. S. News and World Report*, Vol. 68, No. 22, June 1, 1970, pp. 19-21.

9. The average in all private Black colleges in 1968 was 809. See the Carnegie Commission on Higher Education, *From Isolation to Mainstream*, p. 35.

11.

Beyond the Crossroads: Social Dynamics

Social institutions are the most complex forms of human behavior. Their structure, function, and viability are determined at all times by a variety of internal and external forces. It is difficult to know the exact nature and strength of an institution at any given time, and even more difficult to predict its future. The serious danger in predicting the future of an institution is that the prediction could result in a "self-fulfilling prophecy." When those who strongly influence the direction of an institution predict what kind of future it has, they may wittingly or unwittingly begin to steer the institution in the direction they predicted it would eventually go. This is best demonstrated by the fact that the founders of private Black colleges hardly intended for them to be anything but traditional colleges—yet they predicted that only Blacks would attend, and even now they are still nearly all Black in terms of their enrollment.

As a sociologist, it is fortunately not mine to direct Black colleges toward a definite goal, so the predictions I shall make here are very unlikely to be deterministic. At best they will present a set of possibilities and suggest how these possibilities might come to fruition. I would like to begin with sociological theory and then apply this theory in an interpretation of available data regarding what seems to be the future of private Black colleges.

THEORETICAL ORIENTATION

Over fifty years ago Charles Horton Cooley did a study of social institutions.[1] According to him, social institutions manifest four stages of development: *Incipient Organization, Efficiency, Formalism* and *Crisis.* He predicted a fifth stage which would be either *Progressive Disorganization* or *Reorganization.*

Incipient Organization. This stage is characterized by the problem of defining the essential purpose and designing the effective structure of the institution. It is the stage in which the founders of the institution are responding to a felt need and the institution itself is a more or less trial and error approach intended to meet this need.

The early history of Black colleges demonstrated this stage. In the beginning they were established to assist Black ex-slaves in attaining some measure of dignity, independent employment, and recognized citizenship. At that time approximately 98 percent of all ex-slaves were functionally illiterate.[2] Southern state legislators and other southerners of influence traditionally discouraged the education of Blacks precisely because they did not want them to develop personal dignity and security, and to aspire for citizenship rights. Therefore, as we have seen, in most communities white citizens either attempted to prevent the education of Blacks or ignored their education altogether.

The most important thing to remember about this initial stage in the development of private Black colleges is that it was essentially a missionary venture. The real business of educating Blacks became by default the business of idealistic, northern missionaries. It was fortunate for Black education that these missionaries were idealistic, because only the most unmitigating idealist could have believed that these ex-slaves were educable, since they had had little or no opportunity to validate that belief. The reverse was too often the case, since slaves had been deliberately assigned roles that made them appear childlike in nature and mentally incompetent. The institutions founded by these missionaries reflected at least two important things: their idealism, and their hopes. They did not simply call these institutes schools or colleges, but often universities. Their action also underscored a principle posited by Cooley, who held that a major characteristic of the incipient stage is the mapping out of programs and charting the direction for the institution.

These very inadequately equipped, economically instable schools realistically instituted programs intended to provide exslaves with what they regarded as the elementary or basic knowledge necessary to live as free men in a competitive society. Their students were taught such trades as farming, homemaking and carpentry, along with such basic subjects as arithmetic and grammar. Teachers in these first schools found a very eager group of students and parents. A pioneer southern sociologist observed that "The eagerness of Coloured people for a chance to send their children to school is something astonishing and pathetic. They will submit to all sorts of inconveniences in order that their children may get an education."[3]

Because of the ex-slaves' tremendous enthusiasm for an education, and the teachers' religious dedication and faith, the early Black colleges literally wrought miracles. Not only did they train a large number of students who did, in fact, develop pride, qualify for good jobs and become worthy citizens, but these colleges began to assume almost total responsibility for the systematic reduction of illiteracy among Blacks. They attempted to accomplish this in a sort of multiplier effect pattern by training teachers and preachers who in turn dedicated themselves to the training of other such professionals.

In addition to their purely academic accomplishments, the early private Black colleges were able to train students who went on to become physicians, dentists, and leaders, and who rendered many essential services to the advancement of Black people and the nation. Perhaps more than anything else, the long-oppressed ex-slaves came to believe in themselves as human beings and received the knowledge and spirit to continue to struggle for equal citizenship against great odds.

Eventually, however, Blacks came to reject the missionary philosophy of education because it was inherently designed for second-class citizens. It emphasized adjustment rather than true independence and equality. The most obvious manifestation of their rejection is the fact that they began to demand that these colleges employ Black presidents and predominantly Black teachers.

2. *Efficiency Stage.* Insofar as Black colleges are concerned, this stage differs markedly from the first stage in two main respects: goals and programs were well-established and were administered by Blacks. Though it is often overlooked by those who traditionally criticize Black institutions, most private Black colleges became very efficient in the training of students for professional and leadership positions. Almost single-handedly, these colleges were responsible for reducing illiteracy from 90-98 percent to 10 or 15 percent of the adult Black population.[4] They have trained practically all of the Black medical men until now, and have supplied a disproportionate number of Black leaders wherever Black people are found. When the role of private Black colleges is evaluated in terms of the advancement of Black people during the last century, it is doubtlessly true that no other group of colleges ever accomplished so much with so little in so short a time.

Some of these colleges, of course, entered the stage of efficiency earlier than others. Some are still struggling to achieve accreditation, while a few have demonstrated efficiency according to any traditional criteria applied by accrediting agencies. It should also be remembered that these colleges have achieved exceedingly more in the uplifting of Black Americans than their founders could logically have hoped. Even the poorest and most disadvantaged of them have wrought well in the sense that their graduates continue to make outstanding contributions to racial and national progress. For decades they assumed the primary task of training Black Americans to compete in a white dominated society, and they have met this challenge with surprising success against great odds. Therefore, there are valid reasons why alumni and supporters of these colleges should be proud of their accomplishments.

Another point: between 1935 and 1955 some of the most renowned teachers and effective administrators in this nation were in private Black colleges. Though the colleges themselves were terribly poor and disadvantaged, because of their great teachers and astute administrators, they were able to prepare students who went on to take advanced degrees from almost every major university open to them. This point was made in a most dramatic fashion by President Emeritus Benjamin E. Mays in describing his struggle to make Morehouse College into a better college. He said:

> It wasn't affluence that created and sustained the special Morehouse spirit and appeal. It was a few able, dedicated teachers who made the Morehouse man believe that he was 'somebody'. There were men like John Hope, Samuel Howard Archer, Benjamin Brawley, John B. Watson, C. D. Hubert, and others who widened the Negro's horizon and made him believe that he could do big and worthwhile things . . . It was good for Morehouse that it had such inspiring black men on the faculty in the beginning of the twentieth century. Salaries were miserably low, but devotion was correspondingly high.[5]

When given the opportunity, their graduates did extremely well in some of the most challenging occupations and on all levels of community and national leadership available to Blacks. Perhaps their most significant and far-reaching contribution has been that they achieved great success in refuting the long-cherished racist theory of Black inferiority. Largely because of their great teachers, in December 1957 the Southern Accrediting Association began to rate private Black colleges according to regional norms rather than on a racial basis as had been done before.[6] Some of them are acknowledged to be among the good colleges in their regions and have been so recognized by national honor societies and by some of this nation's most influential universities.

3. *Formal Stage*. Essentially, formalism is the stage in which the institution becomes primarily concerned with its own image and purposes rather than the rendering of needed services to its clientele. All institutions in this stage attempt to both protect their own favorable image and render needed services at the same time. Insofar as prestigious colleges are concerned, this means that they tend to take great care to enroll only those students that have clearly established that they have the background and ability to graduate from any traditional college. Colleges in this stage also attempt to select only those teachers who are willing and technically able to provide students with what the colleges assume to be the best education. Such exclusive colleges may be compared to physicians who only take low-risk patients: their rate of failure is predictably minimized and their record of success is thereby maximized.

Private Black colleges have never had the opportunity or the dubious luxury of selecting students and faculty as finely as have some of the more prestigious white colleges. Most of their students have always been high risk according to standardized achievement tests. Their formalism, however, has been definitely indicated by their deliberate, unquestioned acceptance of traditional middle class norms and their eagerness to accept white colleges as ideal models. Some private Black colleges even attempted to select and judge their students and faculties by the academic norms developed by and for prestigious white colleges and, as far as possible, they have conscientiously attempted to emulate their programs and philosophies. There was a general feeling among the students in the sample that their colleges often ignored the special needs and unique history of Black people in their avowed acceptance of white middle class social norms and academic standards. In the past, some of the private Black colleges were so anxious to be prototypes of certain white colleges that they began to label themselves the "Yale," the "Harvard" or the "X" of the South. Small wonder, then, that many Black students have accused their colleges of attempting to make them carbon copies of white middle class students. This they strongly resented. Student leaders often accused several of the highest ranking private Black colleges of manifesting symptoms of formalism in the sense that they are no longer as relevant to the specific needs and aspirations of Black people as they once were, or as is necessary if the majority of their teachers and students are to be creative participants in this rapidly changing urban society.[7] This is a major reason why all private Black colleges are experiencing some dangerous degree of crisis in regard to their identity.

4. *Crisis Stage.* A crisis exists when a problem urgently needs to be solved and there is no reliable solution available. For more than a decade now, education in this country has been caught up in a social revolution. Practically all school systems and colleges have felt the need to pause and take a long, hard look at themselves and try to find a new relevance. This is particularly important for private Black colleges, because Black students and Black leaders have been in the very center of the social revolution this nation is experiencing. Black youth have been the revolution's most reliable participants and constant victims. Therefore, they insist that it is shortsighted and unwise for Black colleges to assume that they can long continue to do business as usual. They are demanding that their colleges become relevant to the peculiar needs of the present nuclear age, and become more concerned about the very special plight of Black Americans.

Throughout their history private Black colleges have manifested an unusual, surprising ability to survive by adjusting to major changes and crises. Since their beginning as unique institutions over a hundred years ago, this nation has witnessed revolutionary changes in science and technology and in political, economic and social structures, and has evolved from a relatively weak, divided nation into the most powerful nation in the world. Even more *apropos* with regard to their present identity crisis is that during the last 100 years this nation has witnessed at least five kinds of "New Negro" to which Black colleges have had to relate:[8]

(a) The first distinctly "New Negro" appeared during the Reconstruction period and most whites were shocked when certain ex-slaves suddenly began to conduct themselves with new dignity based upon a sense of freedom and pride. Since most Americans, regardless of race, had little or no formal education, Blacks generally wanted only enough education to communicate well and protect their own rights. Many Blacks were lynched because some whites interpreted their attempt to get a functional education as dangerously arrogant. Nevertheless, private Black colleges insisted upon teaching race pride along with training in mathematics, grammar, speech and moral uplift.[9] Blacks who behaved like educated people were customarily referred to as "biggity niggers," and stimulated a strong, dangerous white backlash. Therefore, before the end of the 19th century, the vast majority of Blacks were quickly reduced to a peasantry almost as cruel as slavery. Their schools were kept extremely poor and inadequate. Private Black colleges valiantly attempted to relate to this New Negro and his needs despite their woefully inadequate funds, almost non-existent physical plants, and little or no recognition in the world of higher education.

(b) The second "New Negro" appeared after World War I.[10] Many Black soldiers returned to civilian life and demanded that white society treat them like the men they had proven themselves to be in war. Also, an increasing number of Blacks began to aspire to careers in the professions and business. The white backlash stiffened again, and was expressed in new Black Codes and complex, punitive social restrictions. Lynching was the most drastic means of preventing this growing awareness of a new positive self-concept on the part of Black people. Black colleges, like Black individuals, were expected to be "good niggers," and a system of discriminatory laws, traditions, and circumstances kept these colleges almost totally segregated from the mainstream of higher education in this nation. They set about preparing their students to live in a segregated world. Though Black educators protested these restrictions, Black colleges had no other logical choice but to prepare their students to become professionals and leaders who developed their own segregated institutions and uplift organizations that kept Blacks organized and moving toward self-fulfillment in a rigidly segregated, racist society.

(c) The third "New Negro" appeared during the decade after World War II. This type was characterized by a strong feeling that Blacks *deserved* equal opportunities. While the fundamental contention was for equal education, every legal effort was made to break down the most obvious forms of discrimination in all areas of public life. Though he seldom fought for integration as such, he did demand that his *separate* schools should be, in fact, equal in every way to white schools in the same communities.

As a result of this New Negro's efforts, another powerful white backlash responded by actually increasing the areas of segregation. Segregated institutions and activities were reinforced by scores of new Black Codes, countless ordinances, and various kinds of informal social rules contrived to extend and preserve white supremacy in every aspect of Black-white relations. All of these were designed, directly or indirectly, to prevent this New Negro from acquiring the dignity and economic rights he seemed bent upon achieving through top quality education.[11]

Yet, despite the powerful well-organized white backlash, some left-handed educational gains were made. White legislators began to appropriate more funds for Black state colleges in a calculated attempt to circumvent federal court demands for equal educational opportunities. Ironically, it was these newly enriched Black state colleges that began the brain drain from private Black colleges by recruiting talented students once destined for them, and by paying faculty salaries these colleges could not match. In fact, this was the beginning of the present crisis for private Black colleges.

Private Black colleges responded to this unexpected challenge by streamlining their curricula to eliminate all but definitely essential courses, thus employing a minimum number of teachers; curtailing expensive intercollegiate sports; deliberately recruiting white and foreign born teachers, and binding themselves more closely together in a united effort to raise funds. With these necessary adjustments, they still managed to serve this New Negro's generation as they had served the previous types of New Negro: they continued to educate the great majority of this nation's Black professionals and leaders, whom Frazier referred to as the "Black Bourgeoise." However, in addition to the negative qualities Frazier chose to emphasize, this Black college-oriented middle class founded new institutions, stabilized old ones and mounted a Black protest movement on several significant racial fronts, especially against segregation and discrimination in education.[12]

Commenting on this point, Patricia Harris writes—

Although it has been fashionable in the last quarter century to decry all bourgeois elements as decadent, the reality is that the changes wrought in the status of American blacks were due almost entirely to the efforts of the black middle class. The middle-class product of Negro colleges . . . Largely independent of the white community . . . could serve the cause of Civil rights in relative safety. [13]

(d) The fourth "New Negro" resulted from the Martin Luther King, Jr., movement. This New Negro was not as concerned with legal means as were his predecessors; his chief strategy was civil disobedience. Since it had traditionally been assumed that a violation of a civil law was *ipso facto* a violation of college regulations, Black colleges were immediately put on the spot by their activist students who became involved in the civil rights movement.

From the very beginning, this New Negro's non-violent resistance was met with the most cruel punishment. As in the past, the brutality meted out against non-violent Black activists was designed to frustrate their growing sense of racial pride and personal dignity. Unfortunately, some Black colleges also sanctioned this punishment by disciplining and even expelling students who were arrested as civil rights activists. This identified certain Black colleges as a party to efforts made by white racists to maintain white supremacy against this New Negro thrust.

Although it was slow in coming, private Black colleges eventually responded positively to the civil rights thrust of the New Negro. They painfully made one unprecedented concession after another to his demands. Students were extended broad social privileges and given just about complete freedom to participate in activist civil rights movements and demonstrations. They were accorded a strong, even decisive, voice on erstwhile faculty-administration committees, and won official college recognition of certain civil rights organizations whose avowed policies were to upset the racial status quo. Surprisingly, a few of the private Black colleges openly supported student activists in their bold attempts to "fill up the jails" if necessary as a means of destroying *de jure* racial segregation.

Though some important gains were made by the non-violent New Negro, very soon he ceased to be a significant force in the larger society. Opposition persisted and progress was too slow and painful. Black youth lost patience and generally deflected from the non-violent approach. Out of the ranks of civil rights activists there arose another distinct type of New Negro.

(e) The fifth version of the "New Negro," or "Black Militant," is one who shouts about Black power, self-determinism and "Black is beautiful." There are, of course, different degrees of Black militancy. At one extreme are leaders of urban riots who have apparently ruled out every means of solving the problem of Black-white relations except violence, and others who advocate a rigid pattern of racial separatism, a kind of apartheid American style. At the other extreme are some prominent Black educators who still rely upon education, and leaders of traditional civil rights organizations who still maintain faith that legal means plus constant social pressure are the best combination to improve the lot of Black Americans.

It remains to be seen how effective Black Militants will be in their attempts to improve the lot of Black Americans. Like the other New Negroes who preceded them they too are encountering organized, brutal resistance. Most have gone underground or, like the Black Panthers, have shifted their emphasis to community relief and uplift programs. There is mounting evidence that this nation is becoming even more divided racially than ever before: "Two societies, one Black and the other white."[14] Not unexpectedly, increasing numbers of Black youth are demanding that their colleges become actively involved in the militants' cause. Some are even demanding that the names of Black colleges be changed to honor *Black*, not white, heroes, and that they deliberately ally themselves with the Black revolution.[15]

There is also mounting evidence that the violent Black separatists have already reached the nadir of their popularity and another type of New Negro is beginning to emerge, best exemplified by college students. This New Negro can afford to be less concerned about racial barriers and discrimination than were his predecessors who daringly opened up a wide variety of opportunities not yet fully explored. The emerging New Negro has much more racial pride, self-confidence, and hope for the future than any previous generation of Black college youth. Underneath the bitter, often violent, rhetoric of today's Black college students can be detected a distinct note of optimism about their own future. They talk confidently about entering top graduate and professional schools, careers in government, industry, and the independent professions, and apparently assume that during their lifetime race will cease to be a barrier to success.

This emerging New Negro expects considerably more of his Black college than it has had to deliver in the past. He expects it to prepare him for successful competition on an equal basis with graduates from even the most affluent colleges. This expectation on the part of their students may be the greatest challenge ever faced by Black colleges. In order to meet this unprecedented challenge, they will certainly need a higher level of financial and professional support than they have ever had before.

In summary then, in response to the dynamics in American society generally, and in race relations specifically, Black colleges have changed and must continue to do so. While the first Black colleges were spawned by racial segregation, and provided the only opportunity for Black youth to get higher education, today's Black youth may realistically plan to enter practically any college in the United States for which they qualify academically and financially. Already some of the most prestigious white colleges, North and South, are actively, even vigorously, recruiting Black students, particularly those with the greatest obvious academic promise.

Also almost every major white college in the nation now admits what they call high risk students. These are mostly Black students with manifestly high academic potential but low standardized academic performance records. In the past, the strongest private Black colleges recruited a large proportion, perhaps a majority, of their students from this group. If white colleges continue to siphon off the most promising Black high school graduates, within the next two college generations (four to eight years) it will be quite difficult for private Black colleges to recruit the number of qualified Black high school graduates needed for a truly viable, first-rate program.

Fundamental to all of the problems faced by private Black colleges is the fact that as a group they are poor. This is so well-known and thoroughly documented that it is not necessary to spell it out in this conclusion. As we have seen, it is the basic reason why college presidents have organized in a form of mutual aid and support. They have clearly documented the fact that churches, foundations, individual philanthropists, business corporations and government on all levels have blatantly discriminated against Black colleges. According to all available data the financial support these agencies provide to Black colleges generally, and especially to private Black colleges, is negligible compared to what is provided white colleges. Despite very limited funds, these colleges are evidently expected to turn out graduates equipped to compete as equals with graduates from infinitely more affluent colleges. When they fail to do this, their very failure is the rationale for not providing them with the support they need. This circular reasoning is the supreme irony faced by private Black colleges in a racist society.

Because private Black colleges are desperately poor, they are not able to erect the kinds of physical plants, recruit the level of faculty, and provide the amount of scholarships they must have if they are to attract the number of qualified students they need. They are now upon the critical crossroads of their existence and the imperative is inescapably clear: *They must be truly equal in order to survive.*

NOTES

1. Charles H. Cooley, *Social Organization* (New York: Scribner's Sons, 1909), Part V.

2. For a comprehensive discussion of the development of Black colleges, see St. Clair Drake, "The Black University in the American Social Order," *Daedalus*, Vol. 100, No. 3, Summer 1971, pp. 833-892. See also John Hope Franklin, *From Slavery to Freedom* (New York: Vintage Books, 1969), p. 203.

3. Ray Stannard Baker, *Following the Color Line* (New York: Doubleday, Page & Co., 1908), p. 53.

4. For a systematic discussion of this, see W. A. Low, "The Education of Negroes Viewed Historically," in Virgil A. Clift et al., *Negro Education in America: Its Adequacy, Problems and Needs* (New York: Harper and Row, 1962), pp. 57-58. See also Franklin, *From Slavery to Freedom*, pp. 549-550.

5. Benjamin E. Mays, *Born to Rebel: An Autobiography* (New York: Charles Scribner's Sons, 1971), p. 173. See especially Chapter 8.

6. The Commission on Colleges, *Black Colleges in the South* (Atlanta: Southern Association of Colleges and Schools, 1971), p. 6. See also Christopher Jencks and David Riesman, *The Academic Revolution* (New York: Doubleday & Co., 1968), p. 433.

7. See also The Commission on Colleges, *Black Colleges in the South: From Tragedy to Promise* (Atlanta: Southern Association of Colleges and Schools, 1971), pp. 24-25.

8. See the several articles in Mathew Ahmann, Editor, *The New Negro* (Notre Dame, Indiana: Fides Publishers, 1961), and also Rayford W. Logan, *The Negro in the United States: A Brief History* (New York: D. Van Nostrand, 1957), pp. 28-38, and August Meier, *Negro Thought in America* (Ann Arbor: The University of Michigan Press, 1963), especially Chapters 2 and 3.

9. For an excellent discussion of the moral uplift role of private Black colleges, see C. Eric Lincoln, "The Negro Colleges and Cultural Change," in *Daedalus*, Spring 1971, pp. 610-614.

10. For a comprehensive summary of the attitudes and moods of the "New Negro," the Harlem Renaissance of the 1920s, see Arna Bontemps, *American Negro Poetry* (New York: Hill and Wang, 1968). See also Franklin, *From Slavery to Freedom*, especially Chapter 26.

11. Daniel C. Thompson, *The Case For Integration* (Atlanta: Southern Regional Council, 1961), p. 10.

12. Frazier, *Black Bourgeoisie*, especially Chapter 3.

13. Patricia R. Harris, "The Negro College and Its Community." *Daedalus*, Vol. 100, No. 3, Summer 1971, p. 724.

14. This is the central fact underscored by the National Advisory Commission on Civil Disorders, *U.S. Riot Commission Report* (New York: New York Times Company, 1963).

15. Mack H. Jones, "The Responsibility of the Black College to the Black Community: Then and Now," *Daedalus*, Vol. 100, No. 3, Summer 1971, pp. 732-742.

12.

Beyond the Crossroads: The Future

According to Cooley's formulation presented in Chapter 11, private Black colleges are challenged to institute revolutionary reorganization or face progressive disorganization. Most of these colleges, which have performed so nobly in the past, are now threatened by extinction (progressive disorganization) unless they seriously examine themselves, find the constant support needed, and bravely make the program and structural changes necessary in order to be truly relevant in the world of higher education (revolutionary reorganization). There is no way of escaping their central, essential responsibility: their graduates must be prepared to compete as equals in this very complex industrial society.

When it comes to the question of what the future of private Black colleges *should* be there are several well thought-out, logical answers. Among the most persistent are the following:

First, some educators, who are essentially defenders of the status quo, contend that these colleges will continue to be needed in more or less their present form for the next few decades. They would like to see these colleges receive the level of financial support necessary to make them truly sound institutions. They hold that instead of providing higher education for Blacks who are systematically excluded from white colleges, as was the case until a decade ago, these colleges should now provide educational opportunities for Black students who lack academic and financial qualifications for admission to white colleges. They would have private Black colleges specialize in the education of the so-called culturally disadvantaged, assuming the educational role now primarily associated with the experimental community colleges which are cropping up in certain urban Black ghettos, particularly outside the South. While agreeing that disadvantaged Black ghetto youth should have an equal opportunity to acquire a college education, it must not be forgotten that it is the public educational system which has illegally shortchanged most Black youth. White legislators have never provided Black public schools with the facilities nor the quality of teachers and rich programs Black students needed to prepare them to compete for entrance into, and adequate performance in, high standard colleges. Educating those deliberately disadvantaged by this nation's neglect is logically the problem of the nation at large and should not be the exclusive domain of Black colleges. Certainly the problem itself is too complex and the solution far too expensive to be assumed primarily by private Black colleges.

Second, some apparently well-informed individuals and organizations accuse these colleges of perpetuating *de facto* racial segregation since they enroll only a very small, token number of non-Blacks, and most have no non-Black students at all. The critics thus conclude that these colleges should be phased out or become truly integrated.

While Black educators agree that colleges, especially Black colleges, should be truly integrated, they also realize that this cannot be accomplished by fiat. It seems that a prior mandate is in order: certain private Black colleges must be given the kind of support needed to make them first-rate colleges in every respect. Their academic programs and image must be made so attractive that highly qualified students and teachers of all races would want to study and teach in them. When necessary innovations are established it should then be expected—even required—that these colleges, like all others, admit students and employ faculty without regard to race or creed.

Third, some top educators and interested laymen would have private Black colleges become "Islands of Excellence."[1] Applying this concept to private Black colleges would mean:

1. Certain private Black colleges should seriously consider specializing in one or a few interdisciplinary academic areas instead of attempting to offer fifteen or more bona fide majors as is now the case. For example, a given college might specialize in the fine arts, business administration or some other discipline while offering the strong general education program needed to undergird such a major. Other colleges might offer well-planned comprehensive interdisciplinary majors in the social sciences, natural sciences, humanities or Black Studies.

In a modified sense, certain private Black colleges might become preparatory colleges in that their recruitment of students and total academic program would be deliberately designed to prepare students to qualify for graduate and professional schools or for definite occupational careers. This is a central issue because it is a well-established fact that up until now—

> In the United States, the organizations most clearly dominated by the WASP (White Anglo-Saxon, Protestant) upper class are large, nationally-organized business corporations, and the largest law firms (and) schools which produce the most elite graduates will be most closely linked to elite occupations; schools whose products are less well socialized into elite culture are selected for jobs correspondingly less close to elite organizational levels . . . From the point of view of the culture of WASP employers, Catholic schools (and all-black schools) are less acceptable . . . In general, the evidence shows that graduates of black colleges have attained lower occupational positions in business than graduates of white Protestant schools.[2]

It would seem logical, and even essential, that the reorganization of private Black colleges would have the eventual placement of

Black students in large national business and professional firms as one of its primary goals. This cannot be accomplished by accident; it must be deliberately planned and engineered and the *raison d'être* of all innovations instituted by private Black colleges.

2. Every attempt should be made to attract a larger proportion of students with superior academic potential, maybe even the "talented tenth."[3] Du Bois' original concept emphasized the importance of being "well-bred and well-born;" here it refers essentially to talents which may be found on all socio-economic levels of society, talents that have hitherto remained dormant because they were rejected by established white colleges and underdeveloped or neglected by traditional Black colleges. This does not mean that ability will be measured by the traditional standardized tests now widely used. Instead, Black scholars are challenged to find more valid tests of academic ability.

Systematic recruitment programs would need to be mounted to attract students from all socio-economic levels of society, with special efforts made to discover and recruit talented students from Black ghettos in large cities. As it stands now, from 90-95 percent of the students in private Black colleges in the South are from southern states, despite the fact that almost half (48%) the Black population lives outside the South. A great reservoir of potential students are virtually overlooked by Black colleges. Black students constitute only 6 percent (less than a half million) of the nation's 8 million college students, though they constitute about 14 percent of college age youth. Some experts estimate that over half a million potential Black college students are not in college.[4] Vigorous recruitment programs aimed at this out-of-college population would certainly attract enough able students to bring the enrollment of the private Black colleges up to the minimum of 1,200, or the optimum of 1,500, that seems necessary for academically and economically sound institutions of higher education.

3. The curricula in these colleges must be relevant to the peculiar needs of the Black community as well as the purely academic demands of graduate schools. They must also provide a broad but sound basis for students who may wish to enter a career upon graduation. Curricula must not be burdened down with

272

courses of dubious quality and relevance, as is too often the case today. Every course should be logically included in the curriculum based on sound aesthetic, academic and service needs, and the length of such courses should be determined by relevant content not tradition. Then private Black colleges could cease to be simply imitators and help lead the way in long-overdue, truly modernized curriculum reforms.

Ample provision should be made for students who need special training in reading, writing, speaking and mathematics skills. A flexible yet creative honors program for students with superior academic background and exceptional learning abilities should also constitute an integral part of the curricula. As we have already noted, such students are largely ignored in the present structure of the Black colleges' curricula. The honors curriculum should include opportunities for wide field experiences so that students would not only learn theory but also have occasions for supervised participation in the world. This latter goal is particularly important for Black college students, because practically all of them have been systematically excluded from · the mainstream of business and industrial life and have had only limited contacts with adults who participate in decision making.

4. These colleges must vigorously recruit the very best teachers available, and it should be fully understood that the missionary incentive is no longer adequate. Three very basic and more realistic incentives must be built into faculty recruitment. First, in order to attract the quality of teachers needed, they must offer salaries comparable to those in the most affluent colleges. Second, teachers must be assured opportunities to continue their academic and professional growth. Third, teachers must be confident that they are rendering worthy and highly respected professional services. If these conditions are met, teaching in these colleges would be seen as an opportunity to create and serve in a unique professional category. The status of the teacher would be enhanced by the colleges' creative, scholarly image, as is true now of teachers who serve on the faculties of the most prestigious white colleges.

5. Fluid channels of communication must be established between private Black colleges and other top colleges and universi-

ties, and the world of business and government. Various kinds of cooperative efforts must be devised and built into all phases of the programs for mutual benefit. Teacher-exchange and teacher-lending programs are badly needed.

Ways must be found to reverse what is now a one-way brain drain from Black colleges. There are several promising approaches to this problem, including the following:

(a) Established professors in prestigious colleges may be recruited to serve on these faculties for a limited time. These might be highly trained, experienced specialists a small college would hardly require on a permanent basis, and outstanding Black professors who are already established in white colleges.

(b) Special efforts may be made to recruit promising young scholars just out of graduate school. Private Black colleges, with the full cooperation of certain top universities, would recruit young scholars with the assurance that their services in private Black colleges would be accorded the same professional recognition as if they taught in a top university.

(c) Definite programs may be planned to make full use of non-academic professionals in the community who have acceptable academic credentials. Such persons may be associated with business, industry, government, community agencies or independent professionals. They could serve these colleges as visiting lecturers, resource leaders, and seminar speakers.

More specifically, how can these colleges become "islands of excellence"? There are at least the following basic prerequisites:

First, they must be located in culturally-rich communities.

Second, they must provide top quality education for their students.

Third, they must secure both compensatory and innovative funding.

MERGERS

Several Black colleges are located in relatively isolated, culturally poor communities. These colleges could better serve the ends of higher education and the needs of Black people if they relocated in culturally rich cities with a large Black youth population; a large number of annual high school graduates; strong supportive institutions, agencies, and voluntary groups; considerable wealth, and varied cultural life. In such settings, students, teachers, administrative officers, and the colleges themselves would have a variety of valuable opportunities to participate in and cooperate with vital programs, movements, and leaders which shape the current affairs and destinies of the world in which they will live and contribute.

As it stands now, some of the most potentially strong Black colleges, which have already had considerable success in the educational advancement of Black people, are suffering slow but definite decline. Major population shifts, accompanied by revolutionary economic, political, social, and technological changes, have conspired to leave a number of these colleges relatively isolated geographically and culturally. According to certain dominant trends inherent in twentieth-century urbanization and technology, these colleges and other major institutions in all areas, will need to effectuate systematic mergers, relocation and reorganization.

In a proposal to carry out an evaluation of college mergers, a team of consultants and managers pointed out that

> The need to provide a richer and more complete educational experience and the rich and continuing growth of salary and other operating costs have combined to place many small and medium-sized colleges in an adverse educational and financial condition. An obvious solution which many such colleges have adapted is to merge with another institution . . . a total of approximately 500 such mergers or consortia have taken place in the U. S. over the past ten years.[5]

Although very little definitive information is available on the most promising steps to take in effectuating mergers, there are three types of mergers that private Black colleges should consider:

(a) *Denominational Mergers.* Eighty-six percent of all private Black colleges were founded by religious denominations, and all

275

but two of the forty colleges in the United Negro College Fund were not only founded by denominations but are still denominationally related to some degree.[6] As noted before, religious denominations make relatively small financial contributions to their Black colleges, and none lends the level of support necessary for a first-rate college without major support from non-religious sources. Some of them more or less ignore denominational roots and ties while others are struggling along as small, under-financed institutions clinging onto denominational ties and control. Apparently none has worked out a satisfactory relationship with its founding church body.

If the independence and ideological stance of denominational colleges are truly valuable in higher education, some definite steps should be taken to preserve certain church-oriented colleges. This means that systematic mergers among them must be effectuated as quickly as possible. Perhaps the preferred merger would be among colleges representing the same denominations. Some of the ten struggling and isolated senior Black Methodist colleges, for example, might merge with similar colleges to form a smaller number of stronger Black Methodist colleges. The same would be true of other traditional church-related colleges representing various denominations.

(b) *Inter-denominational Mergers.* Some of the most fruitful mergers might occur between or among colleges representing different denominations. There are already some success stories regarding such mergers of Black institutions: Dillard University is the result of a merger between Straight College, which was founded and operated by the American Missionary Association of the Congregational Church, and New Orleans University, founded by the Freedman's Aid Society of the Methodist Episcopal Church. A similar merger occurred between Samuel Houston College of the Methodist Episcopal Church and Tillotson College, which was related to the Congregational Church. The merger of Gammon Theological Seminary (Methodist) with the School of Religion in Morehouse College (Baptist) and Turner School of Religion in Morris Brown College (AME) is another example of how inter-denominational mergers can result in the enhancement of the academic program of the college, the expansion of recruitment potentialities and a broader base of economic support for the resulting institution.

(c) *Inter-racial Mergers.* Population shifts and economic changes have caused many predominantly private white colleges to be as poorly located as some private Black colleges. They too are struggling for survival against great odds. Since racially integrated education is rapidly becoming a fact of life throughout the nation, certain private Black colleges might consider the feasibility and advantages in merging with similar private white colleges. If such mergers could be democratically worked out, they would constitute a new and promising step toward truly integrated higher education. Each partner in such a merger would bring certain unique dimensions of education and human relations which may result in a viable, creative new college—more relevant to the issues, problems and promises of our newly emerging urban, world society than either of the traditionally segregated colleges might be, even with optimum financial and academic support.

RACIAL SURVIVAL

While all promising patterns of mergers should be carefully investigated and open-mindedly considered, two basic principles or propositions ought to be regarded as key factors in all decisions about the reorganization, relocation and merger of certain Black colleges:

First, in the foreseeable future, as in the past, the progress of Black Americans will continue to be deterministically related to Black institutions. The concept "Black college" is not intended to describe the racial composition of the student body or faculty, as is implied by the much-used concept "predominantly Black college." It means instead that whatever the racial composition of the student bodies or faculties in these colleges, *control will remain with Black trustees and administrators and with selected non-Blacks acting in behalf of Black people and their unique interests.* There is convincing evidence that the very survival of Black Americans as a distinct ethnic group will depend heavily upon the

277

survival and continuous development of such colleges because the unique history of Blacks in America can best be understood and appreciated in the context of their struggle to survive biologically, socially, and ethnically.

> The road from Slavery to Freedom has been long (beginning in 1619) and extremely hazardous. Every generation of Negroes has encountered just about every kind of obstacle imaginable in their attempts to survive. Every effort made to achieve some normal measure of citizenship has been fraught with great danger. Yet with a sort of unique courage (which some now call 'Soul') Black Americans have continued to struggle against powerful destructive social forces such as have destroyed some other ethnic and racial groups in history. They have survived and multiplied rapidly despite the very worst forms of personal, social, economic, political, legal, non-legal, and illegal restrictions and intimidations.

> No other people in history—not even the ancient Jews in Egypt or the modern Jews in Germany—have had to fight for survival on so many fronts, for so long a period as have Black Americans.[7]

Reflecting upon the many movements to eliminate and seriously reduce the number of Black Americans (from colonial movements supported by the federal government to the illegal process of lynching) Myrdal concludes:

> There is no doubt that *the overwhelming majority of white Americans desire that there be as few Negroes as possible in America.* If the Negroes could be eliminated from America or greatly decreased in numbers this would meet the whites approval—*provided that it could be accomplished by means which are also approved.* Correspondingly, an increase in the proportion of

Negroes in the American population is commonly looked upon as undesirable. [8]

A generation or more after Myrdal's statement Black leaders still recognized survival as the most challenging problem facing the race. In a speech made before a meeting of United Negro College Alumni, Herman Long, President of Talladega College, reminded the participants of Blacks' long struggle for survival and the importance of Black colleges in facilitating this survival. He said:

The whites in this country have a subtle wish that somehow the Black man would disappear. They felt that if the Black man will not disappear in his physical reality, he should disappear in some physical way. Integration is often seen, even by the enlightened liberal, as an opportunity to fulfill this deep and lasting wish for disappearance. [9]

President Long's statement has far-reaching interpretive implications regarding the role of Black colleges in the survival and progress of Black people. It is perhaps the most fruitful approach to understanding the movement toward token integration accepted by most white liberals. Insofar as the integration of Black students into white colleges is concerned, the best way to make Black students invisible would be to absorb them on the 2,500 or so white college campuses, where they would constitute from 2-5 percent of the enrollment. Such a proportional distribution meets with Myrdal's observation that Blacks would be eliminated as a significant group by approved, democratic means.

The inherent drive to survive as an identifiable group may also be a basic explanation for the persistent unity Black students on white college campuses maintain through their essentially separatist Black student organizations. Therefore, strong viable independent Black colleges are absolutely essential if Black Americans are to survive as an ethnic group and move rapidly as such into the mainstream of American life. In order to preserve and enhance the Black heritage, and facilitate what would amount to mass social mobility on the part of Blacks, several private Black colleges (perhaps twelve or fifteen), must be truly first-rate in every respect.

Second, since nuclear war looms larger and larger as an imminent threat to civilization itself, the kinds and quality of creative, humane leadership badly needed in this emerging world society must be developed as rapidly as possible. There is a greater need than ever for colleges dedicated to the discovery and preparation of humanistic leaders. This is especially *apropos* to church-related Black colleges, where the search for spiritual verities and the preparation of people-oriented leaders have been their *raison d'être* for existence, and is precisely the area in which private Black colleges with meager resources and dubious recognition have had the treatest success.

INNOVATIVE CURRICULA

Private Black colleges must deliberately prepare their students to qualify for top graduate and professional schools or to acquire satisfying positions in mainstream American life as well as the Black community. Bill Howard calls attention to the Carnegie Commission's study of Black higher education, authored by Frank Bowles and Frank A. De Costa in *Between Two Worlds*. He reemphasizes their conclusion that Black professional men and women are uniquely responsible for the welfare and progress of their race and quotes the following key statement from the study:

> Clergymen, teachers, and lawyers have taken the place of civil servants and elected officials in speaking for the Negroes. For this double burden—both professional and political—the small size of the Negro professional group has been a handicap beyond all measurement. It is this small size which necessarily attenuates the communications between Negro and white society, reduces the internal leadership that professionals can exert within Negro society, deprives Negroes of the services of

professionals . . . and, perhaps most important of all deprives young Negroes of models to follow in shaping their lives.

In the terms that are stated, it seems evident that, among the many crises facing Negro society, the professional deficit must rank as of high, possibly highest, importance.[10]

Commenting upon this point, Howard reviews disturbing statistics on the dangerous shortage of Black professionals. For example, in stressing the need for a radically expanded cadre of Black professionals, he cites the Bureau of Labor Statistics estimate that in 1970 there were 766,000 Black professionals in the United States—only 6.9 percent of the 11,140,000 total professional force in this country. There is an urgent need to expand this Black professional force to the 11.5 percent which Blacks represent in the total population. Unfortunately, the number of Black professionals remained relatively stable during the 1960s, while the number of white professionals soared. Howard quotes Fred Crossland, Director of the Ford Foundation's Doctoral Program, who expressed great pessimism and discouragement about the plight of Blacks entering the professions. Crossland pointed out while 15 percent of the school age population is Black, they constitute only 6 percent of those graduating from high school and only 3 percent of those graduating from college.[11]

If the private Black colleges are to make a significant and badly needed contribution to the development of a professional class of Blacks who will perform competitive service functions as well as being Black power-brokers and leaders, they must develop unique programs. Among other vital innovations, this will call for very special curriculum planning so that Black students will not simply develop into carbon copies of traditional college students. While providing their students with basic knowledge and skills, excellent Black colleges will need to provide this distinct, plus dimension of education for their students. Perhaps the most significant, unique quality these colleges should endeavor to instill in their students may be described as creative skepticism. Such an academic predisposition would result in motivating teachers and students to engage in systematic, objective examination of all contemporary values, beliefs, traditions, institutions, and social systems. These would be criticized and evaluated in terms of their contribution to human dignity and the development of democracy throughout history.

In order to prepare Black students for maximum participation in a society which has always been dominated by white individuals, institutions and values, Black colleges must have the best qualified teachers and the most modern plants and academic technology available. They simply cannot afford to continue to "make do" in these vital areas if they are to modernize their curricula to meet the challenges and opportunities faced by the New Negro during the remainder of this century.

FUNDING

Private Black colleges will need two main types of generous funding to become excellent:

They badly need compensatory funding to enable them to eliminate deficits and bring them up to present national norms of financial stability. This is the area in which the federal government must assume primary responsibility. So far the very opposite is true. A study of federal funds granted to American higher education has shown that in 1969 Black colleges received only three (3) percent of the total.[12] While it may be argued that since Black colleges only enroll about 3 percent of this nation's college students the funds they receive are relatively just, the truth is that students in Black colleges represent the most economically deprived segment of the population and must receive special assistance if they are to get the amount and quality of education needed for competition in this complex urban society.

Another reason private Black colleges must have unusual funding from the federal government is that they have very few wealthy alumni and seldom get substantial financial support from foundations and industry. By giving only nominal support to Black colleges, the federal government has perpetuated the poverty of Black colleges and widened the perennially wide economic gap between them and their white counterparts. It may be that before the federal government can provide necessary compensatory support for Black colleges, Congress will have to design and validate special measures such as those passed to create the Freedmen's Bureau during the Civil War and the Office of Economic Opportunity. The basic justification for such action is that all studies show that Black Americans need such compensatory assistance today just as they did when newly emancipated and as has been extended to the poor and to inhabitants of disaster areas.

This drastic approach to alleviate serious disadvantages experienced by Black Americans was inherent in a much-publicized statement by President Lyndon B. Johnson. He said, "You do not take a person who for years has been hobbled by chains and liberate him, bring him to the starting line of a race and say, 'you're free to compete with others,' and justly believe that you have been completely fair."[13] This is certainly applicable to private Black colleges as well as the vast majority of their students. They will need extensive compensatory support if they are to develop a significantly large professional class necessary to move Black Americans toward the promise of freedom this nation symbolizes.

Commenting on this point Samuel Cook of the Ford Foundation concludes:

> The tragic irony is that instead of the allocation of *more* resources for Black students and institutions, the norm in virtually every case is the allocation of less—and generally embarrassingly less. Prevailing is a strange assumption, beyond the realm of rational intelligibility, that the cost of educating Blacks is infinitely less than that of educating whites. But if reason, justice, and a sense of history are relevant, the assumption should be the reverse.[14]

Private Black colleges will need funds to make necessary innovations. Once they have caught up to national norms, new and creative ways must be found to keep these colleges on an equal footing with the more affluent schools. Among other things they should be truly treated as equals by the church, federal government, foundations, private business enterprises and private philanthropy.

Finally, private Black colleges constitute an indigenous, unique, most challenging aspect of higher education in this society, and as such are still badly needed. College enrollment is expected to continue to increase for at least another generation and Black colleges will be needed to participate in the education of more and more students. Some of this nation's colleges have already become too large and impersonal, according to many students and some knowledgeable educators. Private Black colleges could lead the way toward certain far-reaching revolutionary innovations and the institutional diversity some thoughtful educators have insisted are needed[15] Given the support required, they might develop a "creative minority," as conceptualized by Arnold Toynbee.[16] This creative minority of skilled, humane professionals may lead the race and the nation toward a level of unity badly needed if we are to weather the dangerous crises in race relations and become creative participants in the world-wide revolution in which under-developed nations and peoples are impatient to achieve freedom, dignity and power.

NOTES

1. This concept was presented in an oral statement by Dr. Willa B. Player, Director, Division of College Support, Department of Health, Education and Welfare (also, former president of Bennett College) to a Commission of the Black Colleges of the United Methodist Church, "The Future of Church Related Colleges," (unpublished), January 6, 1971.

2. Randall Collins, "Functional and Conflict Theories of Educational Stratification," *American Sociological Review*, Vol. 36, December 1971, p. 1013.

3. Francis L. Broderick, *W. E. B. DuBois* (Stanford, Calif.: Stanford University Press, 1959), pp. 50-54.

4. See Ernest Holsendolph, "Black Colleges are Worth Saving," *Fortune*, Vol. 84, No. 4, October 1971, p. 118.

5. Robert H. Hayes and Associates, *An Evaluation of the Effectiveness of College Mergers* (Chicago: 1971).

6. *Forty Places to Expand Your Mind* (New York: United Negro College Fund, 55 East 52nd Street, 1971).

7. Daniel C. Thompson, "The History of Black Americans," *Faculty Forum*, Vol. 46, October 1968, pp. 1-6.

8. Myrdal, *An American Dilemma*, p. 167.

9. Herman Long, "The Future of Private Colleges," at the 26th Annual Conference of the National Alumni Council, as quoted by Thomas Hine in *The Philadelphia Inquirer*, February 5, 1972, p. 3.

10. Bill Howard, "Blacks and Professional Schools," *Change Magazine*, Vol. 4, No. 1, February 1972, p. 13. For an extensive discussion of this, see Frank Bowles and Frank A. De Costa, *Between Two Worlds: A Profile of Negro Higher Education* (New York: McGraw-Hill, 1971), pp. 195-209.

11. Howard, "Blacks and Professional Schools," pp. 13-16.

12. The Carnegie Report on Higher Education, *From Isolation to Mainstream* (New York, McGraw-Hill, February 1971), p. 51.

13. Lyndon B. Johnson, *Commencement Address* (Washington, D.C.: Howard University, 1964).

14. Samuel B. Cook, "Position Paper" (Unpublished, Ford Foundation, 1971).

15. See The Honorable John W. Gardner, "Agenda For The College and University" in Alvin C. Eurich, *Campus 1980* (New York: Dell Publishing Company, 1968), p. 3.

16. Arnold J. Toynbee, *A Study of History*, Abridged and Edited by D. C. Somervell (New York: Oxford University Press, 1964).

Selected Bibliography

Ahmann, Mathew, ed. *The New Negro*, Notre Dame, Indiana: Fides Publishing Company, 1961.

Anderson, Charles H. and Murry, John D. *The Professors*, Cambridge, Massachusetts: Schenkman Publishing Company, Inc. 1972.

Astin, Alexander W. "Folklore of Selectivity," *Saturday Review*, Vol. 52, December 20, 1969.

Baker, Ray Stannard. *Following the Color Line*, New York: Doubleday Page and Company, 1908.

Bender, Richard N., ed. *The Church-Related College Today*: *Anachronism or Opportunity*, Nashville, Tennessee: The General Board of Education, The United Methodist Church, 1971.

SELECTED BIBLIOGRAPHY

Bontemps, Arna. *American Negro Poetry*, New York: Hill and Wang, 1968.

Bowles, Frank and Frank A. De Costa. *Between Two Worlds: A Profile of Negro Higher Education*, New York: McGraw-Hill Books, 1971.

Boyer, Alan E. and Robert F. Boruch. *The Black Student in American Colleges*, Washington, D.C.: American Council on Education, March 1969.

Broderick, Francis L. *W. E. B. Du Bois*, Stanford, California: Stanford University Press, 1959.

Bullock, Henry A. *A History of Negro Education in the South*, Cambridge, Massachusetts: Harvard University Press, 1967.

Calitri, Charles J. "The Nature of Values," *Improving English Skills of Culturally Different Youth*, Washington, D.C.: U.S. Department of Health, Education, and Welfare, Office of Education, Government Printing Office, 1964.

Clark, Kenneth B. *Dark Ghetto*, New York: Harper and Row Publishers, 1965.

Coleman, James S. and others. *Equality of Educational Opportunity*, Washington, D.C.: U.S. Department of Health, Education and Welfare, U.S. Office of Education, Government Printing Office, 1966.

Collins, Randall. "Functional and Conflict Theories of Educational Stratification," *American Sociological Review*, Vol. 36, No. 3, December, 1971.

Commission on Civil Disorders, *U.S. Riot Commission Report*, New York: NewYork Times Company, 1963.

Selected Bibliography

Commission on Colleges. *Black Colleges in the South*, Atlanta, Ga.: Southern Association of Colleges and Schools, 1971.

Cooley, Charles H. *Social Organization*, New York: Scribner's Sons, 1909.

Coombs, Philip H. *The World Educational Crisis: A Systems Analysis*, New York: Oxford University Press, 1968.

Cruse, Harold. *The Crisis of the Negro Intellectual*, New York: William Morrow and Company, Inc., 1967.

Drake, St. Clair. "The Black University in the American Social Order," *Daedalus*, Vol. 100, No. 3, Summer 1971.

Du Bois, W. E. B. "Careers Open to College Bred Negroes," *Pamphlet*, Nashville, Tennessee: Fisk University Press, 1898.

———"The Talented Tenth," Booker T. Washington and others. *The Negro Problem*, Chicago: McClurg Publisher, 1903.

———and A. G. Dill. *The College Bred Negro American*, Atlanta: Atlanta University Press, No. 5, 1900.

Eurich, Alvin C. *Campus 1980*, New York: A Delta Book, 1968.

Forty Places to Expand Your Mind, New York: United Negro College Fund, 1972.

Franklin, John Hope. *From Slavery to Freedom*, New York: Vintage Books, 1969.

Frazier, E. Franklin. *Black Bourgeoisie*, New York: Free Press, 1957.

———*The Negro In The United States*, New York: The MacMillan Company, 1957.

Geier, Woodrow, *Campus Unrest and the Church-Related College*, Nashville, Tennessee: Board of Higher Education, The United Methodist Church, 1970.

Haggerty, Melvin E. *The Evaluation of Higher Institutions*, Chicago: University of Chicago Press, 1938.

Harding, Vincent, "Toward a Black University," *Ebony Magazine*, Vol. 25, No. 10, August 1970.

Harris, Patricia R. "The Negro College and its Community," *Daedalus*, Vol. 100, No. 3, Summer 1971.

Havice, Charles W., ed. *Campus Values*, New York: Charles Scribner's Sons, 1968.

Hayes, Robert H. and others. *An Evaluation of the Effectiveness of College Mergers*, Chicago: Hayes Company, 1971.

Healy, Timothy S. "Will Everyman Destroy our University," *Saturday Review*, Vol. 52, December 20, 1969.

Herge, Henry C. *The College Teacher*, New York: The Center for Applied Research in Education, Inc., 1965.

Higher Education and National Affairs, Washington, D.C.: American Council on Education, Vol. 27, No. 8, August 1969.

Holsendolph, Ernest. "Black Colleges are Worth Saving." *Fortune Magazine*, Vol. 84, No. 4, October 1971.

Howard, Bill. "Blacks and Professional Schools," *Change Magazine*, Vol. 4, No. 1, February 1972.

Jencks, Christopher and David Reisman. *The Academic Revolution*, New York: Doubleday and Company, 1968.

Selected Bibliography

————"The American Negro College," *Harvard Review*, Vol. 37, No. 1, 1967.

Jennings, Frank G. "For Such a Tide is Moving," *Saturday Review*, May 16, 1964.

Jones, Mack H. "The Responsiblity of the Black College to the Black Community," *Daedalus*, Vol. 100, No. 3, Summer 1971.

Journal of the Academy of Arts and Sciences. "The Future of Black Colleges," *Daedalus*, Vol. 100, No. 3, Summer 1971.

Kruytbosch, C. E. and S. L. Messinger, eds. *The State of the University*, Beverly Hills, California: Sage Publications, Inc., 1970.

LaBrant, Lou. "The Goals for Culturally Different Youth," *Improving English Skills of Culturally Different Youth*, Washington, D.C.: U.S. Department of Health, Education, and Welfare, Government Printing Office, 1964.

————and Violet K. Richards. *A Study for the Future*, New Orleans: Dillard University Publication, 1969.

Le Melle, Tilden and Wilbert L. Le Melle. *The Black College*, New York: Frederick A. Praeger, Publishers, 1969.

Lincoln, C. Eric. "The Negro College and Cultural Change," *Daedalus*, Vol. 100, No. 3, Summer 1971.

Lipset, Seymour Martin. *Rebellion in the University*, Boston: Little, Brown and Company, 1971.

Logan, Rayford, W. *The Negro in the United States: A Brief History*, New York: D. Van Nostrand Company, 1957.

Long, Herman. "The Future of Private Black Colleges," Philadelphia: *The Enquirer*, February 5, 1972.

Low, W. A. "The Education of Negroes Viewed Historically," Virgil A. Clift and others. *Negro Education in America; Its Adequacy, Problems and Needs*, New York: Harper and Row, 1962.

McGrath, Earl J. *The Predominantly Negro Colleges and Universities in Transition*, New York: Bureau of Publications, Columbia University, 1965.

Martorana, S. V. *College Boards of Trustees*, Washington, D.C.: The Center for Applied Research in Education, Inc., 1963.

Mays, Benjamin E. *Born to Rebel: An Autobiography*, New York: Charles Scribner's Sons, 1971.

————"The American Negro College," *Harvard Educational Review*, Vol. 37, No. 3, Summer 1967.

Meier, August. *Negro Thought in America*, Ann Arbor: The University of Michigan Press, 1963.

Merton, Robert K. *Social Theory and Social Structure*, Glencoe, Illinois: The Free Press, 1949.

Miller, Harry L. *Education for the Disadvantaged*, New York: The Free Press, 1967.

Minter, W. John, ed. *Campus and Capital*, Boulder, Colorado: Western Interstate Commission for Higher Education, November 1966.

————and Patricia O. Snyder, eds. *Value Change and Power Conflict in Higher Education*, Berkeley: University of California Press, 1969.

Mobberley, David G. and Myron F. Wicke. *The Deanship of the Liberal Arts College*, Nashville, Tennessee: Board of Higher Education, The United Methodist Church, 1962.

Moore, Gilbert. "The Dot and the Elephant," *Change Magazine*, Vol. 4, No. 3, April 1972.

Myrdal, Gunnar. *An American Dilemma*, New York: Harper and Brothers Publishers, 1944.

Nabrit, Samuel and Julius Scott, Jr. *Inventory of Academic Leadership*, Atlanta: The Southern Fellowship Fund, 1970.

National Advisory Commission on Civil Disorders, *U. S. Riot Commission Report*, New York: New York Times Company, 1963.

Newcomb, Theodore M. and Everett K. Wilson. *College Peer Groups*, Chicago: Aldine Publishers, 1966.

Pattillo, Manning M., Jr., and Donald M. MacKenzie. *Eight Hundred Colleges Face the Future*, St. Louis, Missouri: The Danforth Foundation, 1965.

Peter, Laurence G. and Raymond Hull. *The Peter Principle*, New York: William Morrow & Company, Inc., 1969.

Pettigrew, Thomas F. *A Profile of the Negro American*, Princeton N.J.: D. Van Nostrand Company, Inc., 1964.

Public Negro Colleges: A Fact Book, Office of Advancement of Public Negro Colleges, Atlanta, Georgia, March 1971.

Rauh, Morton A. *The Trusteeship of Colleges and Universities*, New York: McGraw-Hill Books, 1969.

Report of the U.S. Department of Labor, Bureau of Labor Statistics, U.S. Government Printing Office, Washington, D.C., 1971.

Rudolph, Frederick. *Mark Hopkins and the Log*, New Haven: The Yale University Press, 1956.

Simmel, Georg. *Sociology*, translated and edited by Kurt H. Wolf, Glencoe, Illinois: The Free Press, 1950.

Tannenbaum, Frank, ed. *A Community of Scholars*, New York: Frederick A. Praeger Publishers, 1965.

Task Force on Higher Education. "Black Methodists for Church Renewal," *Position Paper*, July 25, 1969.

Task Force Report. *Special Financial Needs of Traditionally Negro Colleges*, Atlanta: Institute for Higher Educational Opportunity, Southern Regional Education Board, 1968.

The Carnegie Commission on Higher Education. *From Isolation to Mainstream*, New York: McGraw-Hill Book Company, February 1971.

"The Spread of Affluence: Black Progress," *U.S. News and World Report*, Vol. 68, No. 22, June 1, 1970.

The Student Protest Movement: A Recapitulation, Atlanta: The Southern Regional Council, September 29, 1961.

Thompson, Daniel C. "Our Wasted Potential," *The Dillard Bulletin*, Vol. XXIV, No. 4, April 1960.

————"Teachers in Negro Colleges," Ph.D. Dissertation, Columbia University, January 1956.

————"Teaching the Culturally Disadvantaged," in *Speaking About Teaching*, New York: College Entrance Examination Board, 1967.

————*The Case for Integration*, Atlanta: Southern Regional Council 1961.

————"The Civil Rights Movement" in Pat W. Romero, *In Black*

Selected Bibliography

America: 1968 The Year of Awakening, Washington, D.C.: United Publishing Corp., 1969.

————(Rohrer, John and Monro Edmonson, eds.) *The Eighth Generation*, New York: Harper and Brothers, Publishers, 1960.

————"The History of Black Americans," *Faculty Forum*, Feature Article, Vol. 46, October 1968.

————*The Negro Leadership Class*, Englewood Cliffs, N.J.: Prentice Hall, 1963.

————"The Problem of Faculty Morale" in *The Journal of Negro Education*, Winter Issue, 1960.

————"The Socialization of Upward Bound Students," an Unpublished Research Report, 1970.

Toynbee, Arnold J. *A Study of History*, abridged and edited by D.C. Sommervell. New York: Oxford University Press, 1946.

Trent, William J., Jr. "The Negro College and its Financing," *Daedalus*, Vol. 100, No. 3, Summer 1971.

U.S. Department of Commerce, Bureau of the Census. *The Social and Economic Status of Negroes in the United States*, Washington, D.C.: Government Printing Office, Report No. 394, 1971.

U.S. News and World Report, Vol. 72, No. 3, January 17, 1972.

Wicke, Myron F. *Annual Report to the Board of Higher Education*, The United Methodist Church, January 28, 1969.

————*Handbook for Trustees*, Nashville, Tennessee: Division of Higher Education, Board of Education, The Methodist Church, 1962.

Willie, Charles V. "Black Student Life on White Campuses," Unpublished Manuscript, 1971.

Wilson, Logan. *The Academic Man,* New York: Oxford University Press, 1942.

Wriston, Henry M. *Academic Procession,* New York: Columbia University Press, 1959.

Znaniecki, Florian. *The Social Role of the Man of Knowledge,* new introduction by Lewis A. Coser, New York: Harper Torchbooks, 1968.

Index

Index

Index

Index

Student power movement, 98
  teacher and, 173–177
Student recruitment programs, 42
Student responsibility, 99
Student revolt
  Black college presidents and, 20
  Black leadership and, 17
  compromise position in, 21
  of 1960s, 12–21
  segregationists and, 18
Students (Black college)
  admissions standards and, 76–78
  alienation of from teachers, 91
  average annual increase in, 41
  in Black Methodist colleges, 70
  Black militant organizations and, 115
  campus scene and, 75–115
  choice of college by, 68–70
  earnings of, 64
  fraternities and sororities for, 114
  intellectually oriented, 80
  non-Greek lettered, 114
  number of, 39, 41
  orientation of at admission, 80–81
  participation of in student organizations, 114
  pragmatically oriented, 80–81, 102
  pre-Civil War, 3–4
  religious background of, 69
  self-evaluation of, 79
  social characterization of, 46–71
  sub-culture of, 91–103
  violence-oriented, 106
  see also Black colleges; Black students
Student-teacher relationships, 37, 90–91
"Study for the Future" organization, 208–209

Subordinate administrators, inefficiency of, 239
"Super Toms," 14, 108
Supporting equipment and services, adequacy of, 34
Supreme Court, U.S., 100, 107, 172
  1954 segregation decision of, 45
Supremes, The, 40
Survey courses, in academic program, 192–197

Taconic Foundation, 200
Teacher(s)
  AAUP and, 178–179
  academic rejection of, 134–135
  administrative role of, 143
  attitudes of, 148
  Black experience and, 183
  Black pride in, 120–121
  brain drain and, 171–173, 274
  brainwashing of, 126–127
  competitive salaries for, 180
  cultural isolation of, 156–157
  in culturally poor communities, 25   .
  dedicated professional type, 130
  differences among, 141
  discrimination against, 158–159
  education of parents of, 118
  evaluation of, 148–152
  experience and tenure of, 140
  female, 123–125
  function of, 147
  "good," 148
  as graduates of Black colleges, 180
  high-morale type, 148
  human relations and, 184–185
  missionary type, 130–133
  need for, 10
  outwardly mobile, 149
  overwork and, 170–171
  para-academic activities of, 162–165

306

Index

INVENTORY 1983